Creating Family Web Sites For Dummies®

Photoshop Elements Options Ba...

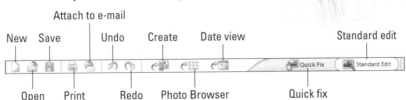

When the type tool is selected, you see these options in the second row:

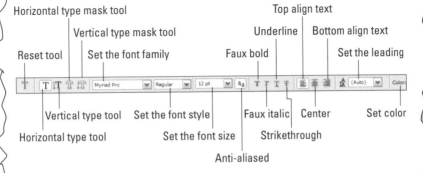

When the brush tool is selected, you see these options in the second row:

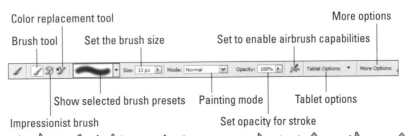

My Favorite Keyboard Shortcuts

Even if you're not in the habit of using keyboard shortcuts, the ones listed below are worth putting into practice. These shortcuts work in every program featured in this book.

Keys	Function	Keys	Function
Ctrl + S	Save	Ctrl + Z	Undo
Ctrl + C	Copy	Ctrl + A	Select All
Ctrl + V	Paste	Ctrl + F	Find
Ctrl + X	Cut	Ctrl + H	Find and replace

Creating Family Web Sites For Dummies®

Cheat Sheet

FrontPage Toolbars

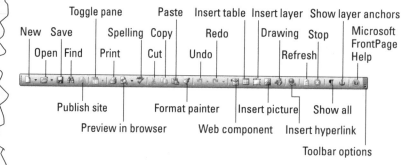

New, Save, Open, Find, Toggle pane, Spelling, Print, Paste, Copy, Cut, Insert table, Redo, Undo, Insert layer, Drawing, Refresh, Show layer anchors, Stop, Microsoft FrontPage Help

Publish site, Preview in browser, Format painter, Web component, Insert picture, Insert hyperlink, Show all, Toolbar options

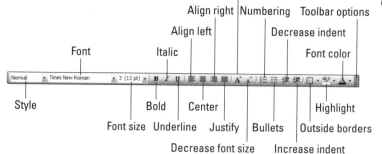

Increase font size, Align right, Align left, Numbering, Toolbar options, Decrease indent, Font, Italic, Font color

Style, Font size, Bold, Underline, Center, Justify, Bullets, Decrease font size, Increase indent, Outside borders, Highlight

Photoshop Elements Tools Palette

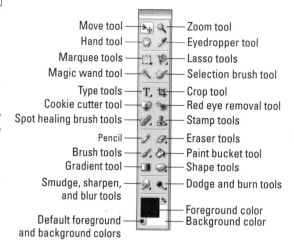

Move tool — Zoom tool
Hand tool — Eyedropper tool
Marquee tools — Lasso tools
Magic wand tool — Selection brush tool
Type tools — Crop tool
Cookie cutter tool — Red eye removal tool
Spot healing brush tools — Stamp tools
Pencil — Eraser tools
Brush tools — Paint bucket tool
Gradient tool — Shape tools
Smudge, sharpen, and blur tools — Dodge and burn tools
— Foreground color
Default foreground and background colors — Background color

For Dummies: Bestselling Book Series for Beginners

Creating Family
Web Sites
FOR
DUMMIES®

Creating Family Web Sites

FOR DUMMIES®

by Janine Warner

WILEY

Wiley Publishing, Inc.

Creating Family Web Sites For Dummies®

Published by
Wiley Publishing, Inc.
111 River Street
Hoboken, NJ 07030-5774

Copyright © 2005 by Wiley Publishing, Inc., Indianapolis, Indiana

Published by Wiley Publishing, Inc., Indianapolis, Indiana

Published simultaneously in Canada

For general information on our other products and services, please contact our Customer Care Department within the U.S. at 800-762-2974, outside the U.S. at 317-572-3993, or fax 317-572-4002.

For technical support, please visit www.wiley.com/techsupport.

Wiley also publishes its books in a variety of electronic formats. Some content that appears in print may not be available in electronic books.

Library of Congress Control Number: 2004116889

ISBN: 0-7645-7938-X

Manufactured in the United States of America

10 9 8 7 6 5 4 3 2

1O/QS/QV/QV/IN

WILEY

About the Author

Janine Warner is a best-selling author, professional speaker, and strategic Internet consultant. Since 1995, she has written ten books about the Internet, including the best-selling *Dreamweaver For Dummies*, a guide to Macromedia's award-winning Web design program, *50 Fast Dreamweaver Techniques*, and *Managing Web Projects For Dummies*.

Janine was inspired to write a book about family Web sites after giving her sister-in-law a digital camera for Christmas and then helping her learn to use her computer to make the most of all those digital pictures. In *Creating Family Web Sites For Dummies*, Janine combines her personal experience using the Internet to communicate with family and friends with more than 10 years of professional experience working on the Internet. She still remembers what it was like when computers were a mystery to her (they still are sometimes), and she draws on her background in journalism to serve as a "techy translator."

Drawing also on her international experience, Janine uses a broad range of examples from many countries in this book. Her expertise in multimedia, technology, and education have taken her on consulting assignments from Miami to Mexico and on speaking engagements from New York to New Delhi. She is fluent in Spanish and travels regularly to Spain and Latin America for consulting projects and speeches.

A recognized Internet expert, Janine has been a featured guest on numerous radio and television shows, including news programs on ZDTV, ABC, and NBC.

Janine is a former member of the faculty at the University of Southern California Annenberg and the University of Miami, and she currently serves as the Multimedia Program Manager for the Western Knight Center, a joint project of USC and Berkeley that provides specialized training for professional journalists.

From 1998 to 2000, Janine worked for *The Miami Herald*, first as their Online Managing Editor and later as Director of New Media. She also served as Director of Latin American Operations for CNET Networks, an international technology media company.

An award-winning reporter, she earned a degree in Journalism and Spanish from the University of Massachusetts, Amherst, and worked for several years in Northern California as a reporter and editor at *Vision Latina Newspaper* and the Pulitzer-Prize-winning *Point Reyes Light*, and as a freelance writer for more than a dozen other publications.

To learn more, visit www.JCWarner.com.

Dedication

To all the families and friends who long to be closer, I offer this guide and encourage you to share your pictures, stories, and dreams. May you always be surrounded by those you love.

Author's Acknowledgments

Let me start by thanking my own family for their love, support, and inspiration to create this book. My sister-in-law Stephanie's optimism and regular cards and photos helped me develop the idea for this book, my brother Kevin has been a solid source of support and guidance over the years, and their three beautiful daughters are a regular source of joy in my life.

Thanks to all four of my fabulous parents, Malinda, Janice, Helen, and Robin. Thanks to my brother Brian, my uncle tom and aunt mindy (whose preference not to use capital letters in their names is just one of their charming quirks), and all of my extended family.

Thanks to David LaFontaine, the man of my dreams who I look forward to creating my own family with, and to his sisters, Linda, Beth, and Sarah, for helping break him in for me. Thanks to his wonderful parents for raising him to be such a caring and thoughtful man, and to his entire clan for making me feel like part of the family. David, your patience, support, and inspired sense of humor are such a gift, especially when I'm up against tough book deadlines.

Special thanks to the wonderful team that made the production and creation of this book possible: my agent Margot Maley, Acquisitions Editor Bob Woerner, and especially Susan Pink, for her extraordinary effort and attention to detail in editing this book.

Thanks to Susie Gardner (www.hopstudios.com) for her contributions to the blogging chapter. I wish you all the best with your own book and highly recommend *Buzz Marketing with Blogs For Dummies*.

Special thanks to some of the talented people who helped create the many photographs, images, and designs featured in this book. Thanks to Photographer Zach Goldberg, his beautiful wife, and their adorable son Max for sharing their amazing images. Zach is available for personal and professional photo assignments in LA and will travel by arrangement throughout the U.S. For more information, visit www.FrozenFoto.com or call 323-662-7751. Thanks also to photographers Jessica Verma (www.jessicaverma.com) and David LaFontaine (www.davidlafontaine.com).

A Spanish *gracias* to Miguel Calderon and everyone at GrupoW (`www.grupow.com`). With more than five years experience creating Web sites, Miguel's company has won more Internet awards than any other multimedia agency in Mexico and has been recognized internationally, especially for its exceptional design work. As the organizers of the premier conference on Macromedia Flash in Mexico (`www.flashformexico.org`), GrupoW specializes in creating animations, interactive games, and other complex Web projects for clients around the world.

Over the years, I've thanked many people in my books — former teachers, mentors, and friends — but I have been graced by so many wonderful people now that no publisher will give me enough pages to thank them all. So let me conclude by just thanking my lucky stars that this book is finally done. Complete. Finished. This is it. (And don't even tell me those aren't complete sentences.)

Publisher's Acknowledgments

We're proud of this book; please send us your comments through our online registration form located at www.dummies.com/register/.

Some of the people who helped bring this book to market include the following:

Acquisitions, Editorial, and Media Development

Project Editor: Susan Pink

Acquisitions Editor: Bob Woerner

Technical Editor: Lee Musick

Editorial Manager: Carol Sheehan

Media Development Specialist: Laura Moss

Media Development Manager: Laura VanWinkle

Media Development Supervisor: Richard Graves

Editorial Assistant: Amanda Foxworth

Cartoons: Rich Tennant (www.the5thwave.com)

Composition

Project Coordinator: Maridee Ennis

Layout and Graphics: Lauren Goddard, Joyce Haughey, Stephanie D. Jumper, Lynsey Osborn, Jacque Roth, Heather Ryan, Julie Trippetti

Proofreaders: Leeann Harney, Jessica Kramer, Charles Spencer, TECHBOOKS Production Services

Indexer: TECHBOOKS Production Services

Special Help

Angie Denny and Bonnie Mikkelson

Publishing and Editorial for Technology Dummies

Richard Swadley, Vice President and Executive Group Publisher

Andy Cummings, Vice President and Publisher

Mary Bednarek, Executive Acquisitions Director

Mary C. Corder, Editorial Director

Publishing for Consumer Dummies

Diane Graves Steele, Vice President and Publisher

Joyce Pepple, Acquisitions Director

Composition Services

Gerry Fahey, Vice President of Production Services

Debbie Stailey, Director of Composition Services

Contents at a Glance

Table of Contents

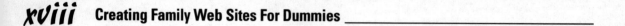

Introduction

∙ ∙

*W*ant to create a Web site for a wedding, a new baby, or a teenager's sporting event? This book is dedicated to helping you build beautifully designed Web pages, as quickly and easily as possible — even if you're new to the Internet. The instructions and ideas you find here will help you harness the power of the Web to share stories, images, and anything else you can imagine — whether your family and friends live down the street or on the other side of the world.

About This Book

If your family is like most of the families I know, you don't have time to wade through a thick book before you start working on your Web site. That's why I wrote *Creating Family Web Sites For Dummies* in a way that makes it easy for you to find the answers you need quickly. You don't have to memorize this book or even read it in order. Each section is designed to stand alone, giving you easy answers to particular questions and step-by-step instructions for specific tasks.

The first part of the book will help you master the basics, from registering a domain name to taking the red out of someone's eyes in a photo to creating a custom Web page. In the second part of the book, project-specific chapters show you how to use predesigned template pages to develop some of the most popular family Web sites: baby sites, wedding sites, travel sites, and hobby sites. The CD that comes with this book has all the templates and graphics, and each corresponding chapter includes step-by-step instructions to help you customize the pages and images. If you're in a rush to get a baby site or a wedding site up and running, go directly to the specific chapter and you should find everything you need.

Don't worry about memorizing the new technical terms you find in this book. I've tried to keep the tech-talk to a minimum, but if you don't understand a word, turn to the glossary in the back. Feel free to dog-ear the pages, too — I promise they won't complain!

Conventions Used in This Book

Keeping things consistent makes them easier to understand. In this book, those consistent elements are *conventions*. Notice how the word *conventions* is in italics? That's a convention I use frequently. I put new terms in italics and then define them so that you know what they mean.

Here's another convention. When I include URLs (Web addresses) or e-mail addresses in text, they look like this: www.janinewarner.com. When I present URLs on their own lines, they look like this:

```
www.janinewarner.com
```

I assume that your Web browser, like most, doesn't require the introductory http:// for Web addresses. If you use an older browser, remember to type http:// before the address.

When I introduce you to a set of features, such as options in a dialog box, I often set the items apart in a bulleted list. When I want you to follow instructions, I use numbered steps to walk you through the process.

What You're Not to Read

You don't have to read this book cover to cover (and I certainly don't expect you to read it on the beach). If you're in a hurry, go right to the information you need most and get to work. If you're new to Web design, skim through the chapters to get an overview and then go back and read in greater detail whatever is most relevant to your project. Whether you're building a simple site for the first time or working to redesign a more complex site, you find what you need in these pages.

Foolish Assumptions

Although *you* may think that you need to be a professional Web designer to create a beautiful Web site for your family, *I* don't. In keeping with the philosophy behind the *For Dummies* series, this book is an easy-to-use guide designed for readers with a wide range of experience.

In Chapter 1 you find an introduction to the wide range of options for creating a Web site, some of which don't require any special software. But if you want to get the most out of this book and create your own custom site, you need a Web design program and an image editor. I use Adobe Photoshop Elements 3 and Microsoft FrontPage 2003 in the exercises in this book.

How This Book Is Organized

I organized *Creating Family Web Sites For Dummies* into parts that walk you through the various steps to creating a Web site — from registering a domain name to publishing your site on the Internet. I also included a variety of alternatives, so you can upload a few pictures to a photo site to get a baby picture online right away or take more time and create a completely customized Web site in a program such as FrontPage.

This section provides a breakdown of what you can find in each part so you can find the information that's most useful to you. Remember, you can always start with a simple solution and build a more complex Web site later (like maybe when your kids are old enough to do it for you.)

Part 1: Introducing Family Web Sites

Part I introduces you to the wild world of Web design and the things you should do to get started creating your own home page on the Internet. In Chapter 1, I take you on a tour of family Web sites that I think are especially well designed and organized, using them as examples to help you come up with ideas for your own Web project. Chapter 1 also features an overview of the many different ways you can build a Web site, from free photo album sites that make it easy to get pictures online fast to comparisons of online design services and software programs you can use to create your own completely customized Web site.

In Chapter 2, it's time to get organized and gather the elements you'll want to include on your Web site, sketch the structure and navigation for your site, and develop a simple project plan to keep you on track. Chapter 3 shows you how to search for and register a domain name, and includes a few tips about what to do if your first choice is already taken. Chapter 4 explains how Web servers work and how to choose the best service provider to host your site. You even find out about a few places where you can host a Web site for free.

Part II: Lookin' Good: Images and Design

The best way to make your Web site shine is to fill it with gorgeous images — and then make sure they don't take too long to download. This part is all about finding great images, making them look their best, and optimizing them for the Internet. In Chapter 5, you discover where to find clip art and royalty-free photographs you can use to add color and a more professional look to your pages. You also find instructions for downloading images from the Web, tips for scanning images and artwork, and information on retrieving photos from a digital camera. In Chapter 6, you get an introduction to Adobe Photoshop Elements, an image editor designed to be easy enough for beginners, yet powerful enough to create great images for the Web. In Chapter 7, you discover the timesaving tools in Photoshop Elements that can help you organize your images and automate the process of creating photo albums and Web galleries.

Part III: Creating Web Pages and Adding Multimedia

In Part III you find out how to build Web pages, work with templates, and bring your site to life with multimedia. Chapter 8 introduces you to Microsoft FrontPage, with instructions for creating and editing pages, setting links, and publishing your site on the Internet. In Chapter 9, you see how templates work and how to use them to simplify page creation and to develop a consistent look for your site. And in Chapter 10, you discover the sites and sounds of multimedia with an overview of the many options for adding audio, video, and animation to your Web pages.

Part IV: Creating Special Project Sites

In Part IV, you find a range of project-specific chapters for creating —right away — some of the most popular family Web sites. Chapters 11 through 14 feature specially designed templates and graphics included on the CD with this book — simply follow the step-by-step instructions in each chapter and you can customize your own sites from these predesigned pages and images. Chapter 11 starts you off with a baby Web site and tips for getting photos of a newborn online fast. Chapter 12 covers the steps for creating a wedding site, from the invitation, to directions to the reception, to a photo album of your best wedding photographs. You even find tips about using online gift registries and including links to your favorite online stores. In Chapter 13, you discover the modern answer to family vacation slide shows: a Web site that showcases your travel pictures. In Chapter 14, you find out to create sites to show off your favorite activities, such as hobbies, clubs, and sports teams. Chapter 15 introduces you to one of the fastest growing trends on the Internet — blogging. Also known as Web logs, *blogs* are sophisticated online journals your entire family can use to post regular messages and stories on your family Web site.

Part V: The Part of Tens

The Part of Tens is a quick reference. In Chapter 16, you discover ten family-oriented Web sites featuring educational and entertaining destinations for the whole clan. Chapter 17 lists ten important rules for designing Web pages, and Chapter 18 completes the book with ten ways to test, update, and promote your Web site.

Part VI: Appendixes

Appendix A features online calendar services you can link to your Web site or use as stand-alone solutions to keep your family organized and on time. You also find great resources for researching your family history, exploring genealogy, and creating a family tree. Appendix B is a glossary of the terms you need to know when working on the Web — and then some!

And finally, Appendix C is a guide to the CD-ROM and the great templates, images, and software that accompany this book.

Icons Used in This Book

This icon points you toward valuable resources on the Web.

When I want to point you toward something on the CD that accompanies this book, I use this icon.

This icon reminds you of an important concept or procedure that you'll want to store away in your memory bank for future use.

This icon signals technical stuff that you may find informative and interesting but that isn't essential for you to know to develop the Web sites described in this book. Feel free to skip these sections if you don't like the techy stuff.

This icon indicates a tip or technique that can save you time and money — and a headache.

This icon warns you of any potential pitfalls — and gives you all-important information on how to avoid them.

Where to Go from Here

Turn to Chapter 1 to get started with an intro to the many ways to create a Web site and a tour of family sites designed to get your creative juices flowing. If you're anxious to start working on a particular type of site — such as a site for a baby due to arrive any day or a wedding that's fast approaching — jump right to the specific chapter in Part IV. And remember that you don't have to build the most elaborate or technically sophisticated pages to create a great family Web site.

You'll find more great Web design tips at www.digitalfamily.com, a site I created to provide additional resources and updates for this book.

Part I
Introducing Family
Web Sites

The 5th Wave   By Rich Tennant

"Good news, honey! No one's registered
our last name as a domain name yet!
Hellooo Haffassoralsurgery.com!"

In this part . . .

This part introduces you to Web design and covers the basics of what you need to get started. Take a tour of the family Web sites featured in Chapter 1 to get your creative juices flowing, and discover the many ways you can create a Web site — from easy-to-use photo album services to the best software programs. Invest some time developing a plan of action and getting organized in Chapter 2, and find out how to search for and register a domain name in Chapter 3. In Chapter 4, you find an overview of how Web servers work and tips for choosing a service provider that fits your project and your budget.

Chapter 1

Touring Family Web Sites

In This Chapter

▶ Appreciating the range of sites you can create

▶ Comparing different types of Web sites

▶ Getting ideas from great examples

▶ Choosing the best tools for the job

As photo albums turn digital and e-mail addresses become commonplace, modern families are building their own Web sites, contributing to an increasingly popular part of the Internet where you can find everything from elaborate wedding invitations to vacation pictures to the first photo of a newborn.

You don't need advanced computer skills anymore to create a family Web site. Today, sharing photos online is as easy as pressing the Enter key to upload images to a photo site. And you can create a wedding or baby site by simply filling out a form. Even if you want to create a customized Web site, the software programs and resources available now make it easier than ever to personalize the way you share family stories and memories over the Internet.

In this chapter, I introduce you to the many ways you can build a Web site so you can better appreciate your options and decide which method is best for you. Then I take you on a tour of family Web sites so you can see what's possible. Finally I compare the most popular Web design and image editing programs so you can find the best tools for your project.

Connecting Families Over the Web

My goal in this book is not just to help families create Web sites but to help people around the world get closer by sharing their stories and photos with loved ones over the Internet. Here are a few ways people like you are using the Internet to keep in touch:

✔ **Baby sites:** Many parents are using Web sites and blogs (online journals) to chronicle every milestone of their child's life, from the first tooth to the first day of school. Chapter 11 features templates and tips for creating a baby Web site, and Chapter 15 covers blogs, which are becoming increasingly popular on the Web.

✔ **Sites for younger kids:** Better than a bumper sticker, Web sites are a great way to showcase your favorite student's work, clubs, after-school activities, hobbies, and more. Chapter 14 features templates and instructions for creating a sports or hobby Web site.

✔ **Sites for older kids:** Tech-savvy high-school kids are showing off with graduation sites, prom sites, and team sites. Creating a Web site is like having your own yearbook, only better. If you want to create your own completely customized site, see the introduction to FrontPage 2003 in Chapter 8.

✔ **Travel sites:** The days of vacation slide shows in the living room are fading fast. Today, families are creating vacation sites with online photo albums to share snapshots from their latest adventures. Chapter 13 provides examples and templates.

✔ **Wedding sites:** Before they say 'I do,' more and more couples are building wedding Web sites that feature invitations, directions, guest registries, and more. Chapter 12 provides templates and instructions for creating a wedding site.

If you're anxious to put up a Web site right away, skip ahead to one of the chapters listed in the preceding list. You find everything you need to get a site up quickly. If you have a little more time to think about your project or you want to create a more general family site, continue reading this chapter to discover more about the range of options for creating a Web site.

Comparing Web Site Options

If you've never created a Web site before, you may not realize how many ways you can publish photos and other information on the Web, or how many software programs and service providers there are to choose from. You've probably seen Web sites in many styles, but you may not know that some of the differences in how those sites look depends on the type of technology used to create them.

Choosing how to create a Web site is an important first step. You can start simply, with an online photo album site or with an online service that does nearly everything for you. Or you can create a site based on templates, like the ones featured on the CD for Chapters 11 through 14, or you can create a completely customized Web site. This section provides a brief review of your options.

Photo album and printing services

If you're looking for an easy way to share photos online, but you still think it's nice to have a physical, tangible photo printed on paper, you may be happy to discover the services listed in this sidebar, which provide both free online photo album services and an easy way for you — or anyone else with access to your photo album — to order prints.

To create a photo album, you just upload your images; they become instantly available on the Web to anyone with your user ID and password. (Passwords are required to ensure privacy so you can restrict who views your personal images.) You don't even have to optimize your images (*optimizing* involves reducing the file size of images so they download faster), so you won't need an image program such as Photoshop. Indeed, sites such as Ofoto and Shutterfly encourage you to upload high-resolution images because the better the resolution, the better the print quality.

The following sites offer online photo album and printing services:

✔ **Ofoto** (www.ofoto.com): Kodak's online photo site makes it easy to upload images for free and share your photo album with

friends and family. Like other photo sites, Ofoto makes money by charging for prints. At 29 cents per print, Ofoto is not the cheapest, but they boast that the archival quality of their pictures means they'll last as long as conventional film prints. The site offers basic image editing and cropping tools and enables you or anyone with access to your site to create and order printed calendars and photo books from your pictures.

✔ **Shutterfly** (www.shutterfly.com): Shutterfly offers simple editing tools, enables you to post and share photos for free, and sells printing services. Shutterfly has an intuitive interface, and their specialized printing options enable you to turn your pictures into greeting cards, bound photo albums, personalized calendars, coffee mugs, T-shirts, or tote bags. Prints at Shutterfly cost 29 cents each.

✔ **Yahoo Photos** (photos.yahoo.com) offers online photo album services similar to Ofoto and Shutterfly, but their digital prints are priced at only 19 cents each.

Different types of sites

Here's a brief list of some of the different kinds of Web sites you can create and the technical options that go with them:

✔ **Online photo album sites:** Even if you plan to create a more complex Web site later, you may want to set up an online photo album site because it's one of the fastest and easiest ways to put photos online. Best of all, these photo sites are free, and they don't bombard your pages with lots of advertising like the free Web site services at Geocities or Tripod. Photo album sites make their money by charging for prints, which they are happy to send to you or your loved ones for about 20 or 30 cents each. The most popular free online photo album sites, including Ofoto.com, shown in Figure 1-1, are featured in the "Photo album and printing services" sidebar.

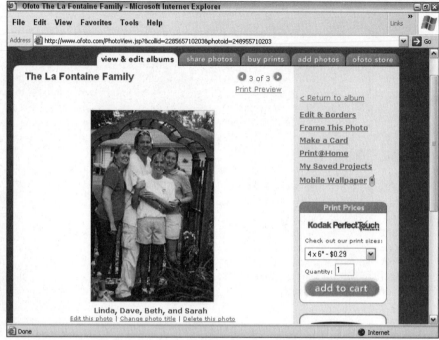

Figure 1-1:
Online photo
album sites
let you
upload and
showcase
photos
for free.

✔ **Free online services:** If price is your biggest concern and you want to create a Web site, you may be pleased to find that several companies will let you publish your site for free. The catch is that these companies then sell advertising on your pages, and you have no control over what ads will run next to your words and pictures. Yahoo! features a free Web site creation tool at `Geocities.com`, and you'll find similar solutions at `Angelfire.com` and `Tripod.com`. All three enable you to create template-based sites or to upload your own pages to their system (although they offer limited space and visits to your site). You find more about these and other Web server options in Chapter 4.

✔ **Specialty Web-based solutions:** The easiest way to create a professional-looking Web site for your family is to use an online service, such as `family.myevent.com`, as shown in Figure 1-2. You'll find similar services at `www.eweddings.com` and `www.babyjellybeans.com`, but I chose to feature `family.myevent.com` because I think it's one of the best in terms of price and ease of use and because you can create a variety of Web sites in one place (for weddings, babies, bar mitzvahs, or any other event). The `family.myevent.com` site offers a complete package of features, including planning tools, maps, and hotel reservation systems. Simply choose the template you want for your design, fill in a few forms, and upload your photos. You can create and publish a complete Web site in a matter of minutes.

Figure 1-2:
An online service like this one makes it easy to create a family-oriented Web site without special software or technical expertise.

✔ **Blogging software:** Millions of people now have blogs, or online journals, on the Internet. Their popularity has spawned a variety of software programs designed to facilitate easy updates, such as `Blogging.com`, as shown in Figure 1-3. A blog may be your best option if you want to make frequent updates to your Web site. One of the more famous family blogs is The Trixie Update, which Trixie's stay-at-home dad updates many times a day to keep her mom informed while she's at work. That site and many other blogging sites are featured in Chapter 15.

✔ **Predesigned templates:** I included with this book a collection of templates to make it easy for you to create a variety of common Web sites, such as a wedding site and a baby site. To use these templates, you need a Web design program, such as Microsoft FrontPage 2003, and an image program, such as Adobe Photoshop Elements 3. Although you have to know the basics of these programs to create a template-based site, the process is still much easier than creating a site from scratch. You also have more design control than you do if you use templates at an online service such as Tripod, where you can change only the content. When you edit templates in a program such as FrontPage 2003, you have the option of altering the design as much or as little as you choose. Many Web design programs include templates you can use, and you can buy or download free templates from a variety of Web sites. To use the templates included on the CD, check out Chapters 11 through 14.

Figure 1-3:
Blogging
has become
a popular
way to
create a
Web site,
especially if
you want to
make
regular
updates or
create an
online
journal.

✔ **Fully customized sites:** If you use a program such as Macromedia Dreamweaver MX 2004 (which is what I used to create my own Web site, featured in Figure 1-4) or Microsoft FrontPage 2003 (featured in this book), you can create a fully customized Web site. You'll need more technical expertise to create a customized Web site than you need to use one of the template options, but you'll have the greatest design control over your pages. Even if you start by using a template to create your site, you can always go back later and further customize your pages in one of these programs. However, just mastering the technical features of a Web design program doesn't make you a great designer. Templates can help you avoid common design mistakes and create a professional-looking site, even if you can't draw a stick figure. (To find out more about design, check out the design tips in Chapter 17.)

✔ **Database-driven sites:** The most sophisticated Web sites on the Internet, such as the online store at Amazon.com or the news site at CNN.com, were created by using complex programming and databases. Combining a database that records information about users with the ability to generate pages automatically is what enables Amazon to greet you by name when you return to their site, track your orders as you buy books, and even make recommendations based on your previous purchases. I definitely don't suggest that you begin with a custom database. You don't need anything this sophisticated anyway, unless you want to sell lots of products or publish dozens of articles and photos to your site every day.

Figure 1-4:
I created my
own Web
site with the
Web design
program
Dream-
weaver.

Recommendations

The type of Web site you create depends on your budget, your expertise, and your time. If cost is your biggest concern and you don't mind sharing your pages with advertisers, try Angelfire.com or Geocities.com, but be aware that you'll have limited design options and no control over the ads that appear on your pages.

If your goal is to get a feature-rich site online as quickly and easily as possible, I recommend family.myevent.com. For a nominal fee, you can choose from a variety of high-quality site designs, add sophisticated features such as an online calendar, and use their simple system to publish your site in a matter of minutes or hours, even if you have no technical expertise. You do the development online, filling out a series of forms with the text you want on your site and then uploading your photos through a system that's similar to attaching a photo to an e-mail message.

If you use a service like family.myevent.com, you don't need any software, unless you want to edit your images before you post them to your site. (You find instructions for resizing, cropping, and editing images in Chapter 6.)

Protecting your privacy

Many parents wonder whether it is safe to put their children's photos on the Web; others simply don't want to share their stories with the world for fear that they may attract unwanted attention. Although there have been some highly publicized cases of children running into trouble because of someone they met online, such incidents are rare. I consider a child's photo appearing on a Web page to be roughly equivalent to his or her image appearing in a school yearbook or in a sports team photo in a local newspaper.

Millions of families have created Web sites and enjoy sharing their photos and stories. Rather than expressing concern about making their stories and photos public on the Web, many families report that they have made new friends and reconnected with old ones thanks to their Web sites.

Here are some other things you can do to protect your personal information:

- ✔ Don't include your home address or phone number on your Web site.

- ✔ Don't include your work address or phone number.

- ✔ Be careful when writing about the times when you won't be at home, such as the dates you'll be on vacation.

If you want more control over your site and no ads, a Web site built with the templates included in this book and hosted on a commercial service provider is a great option. With just a little knowledge of a program such as FrontPage 2003 (covered in Chapters 8 and 9), you can customize predesigned Web page templates. The beauty of creating your own site design with a program like FrontPage is that you can add as much text and as many images as you want, and you can change the design as much or as little as your talent and time allow.

When you use a program such as FrontPage (whether you use templates or not), you create and edit your Web pages on your own computer and then transfer them to the server when you're ready to publish your site to the Web. The transfer process is easy and the benefit of building the site on your computer first is that you can test your work and experiment with different options before you publish your site on the server and make it available on the Internet.

No matter what option you choose, you can register your own domain name and point it to your Web site. This means you can direct people to your own special Web address, such as www.the-smith-family.com, whether you host your site at AngelFire.com, at family.myevent.com, or on your own server. You find out how to register a domain name in Chapter 3 and how to choose the best service provider in Chapter 4.

Best Practices and Models

A great Web site combines beautiful images and well-written text in a design that makes it easy to find your way to the most important information. But if you're staring at a blank computer screen, creating a Web site can seem daunting. To help inspire you, this section presents a few well-designed or innovative Web sites. So sit back, relax, and get your browser ready to go for a ride — after reading the descriptions of these sites, you may want to see them for yourself.

Wedding sites that inspire

When Jonathon and Joanne decided to get married on a Caribbean island, they knew that creating a Web site would make it easier to coordinate the travel arrangements and accommodations for their guests. On the site, shown in Figure 1-5, they posted helpful information, such as the "Things to Bring" section, which includes passports, suntan lotion, and snorkel gear. If you visit the site at `wedding.studio2f.com`, you'll find many wonderful stories about how they met, as well as regular updates for friends and family who couldn't travel to attend the wedding.

Figure 1-5: This site combines a simple, elegant design with valuable information, such as all the special things guests should pack for a wedding on a tropical island.

Jonathon and Joanne's Web site was created using blogging software, which makes it easy to add updates (even from a tropical island). You find more information about blogs in Chapter 15. In Chapter 12, you find instructions for creating a customized wedding site using the templates provided on the CD.

Studying other people's wedding sites is a great way to see what you can do with your own site. You'll find many more wedding sites online at

```
www.topweddingsites.com/
```

Baby sites to make you smile

The `MoriCentral.com` Web site, shown in Figure 1-6, features photos and stories from everyone in the Mori family, but there's no question that the children are the stars of the show. In addition to a photo gallery and guest book, the Moris have included a section called Jared's Anecdotes filled with fun stories about their son. Visit the site to see a great example of a clean, simple design, with lots of great photos and clever stories about the kids.

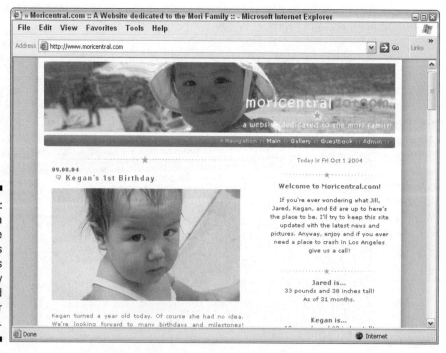

Figure 1-6: This site is a showcase of photos and stories about baby Kegan and her brother Jared.

Family sites for everyone

Martin and Emiko created a Web site (`www.martin-emiko.net`) to help keep their distant families informed about their lives and growing family. He's from Switzerland and she's from Japan, so they are always far away from someone in the family. In addition to a great collection of stories and photos, the use of a long image across the top of each page, shown in Figure 1-7, is a simple but dramatic design trick and an ideal way to showcase the many landscapes they've photographed in their travels.

Here are a few other family Web sites you may want to visit for ideas:

✔ The Demar Family Web site at `members.cox.net/botiff` features an animation on the front page that includes a recording of the voices of some family members. The combination of the mother's voice welcoming you to the site and the kids making snide comments in the background as she talks provides a humorous introduction that draws you into the site and gives you a good idea about what to expect when you get there.

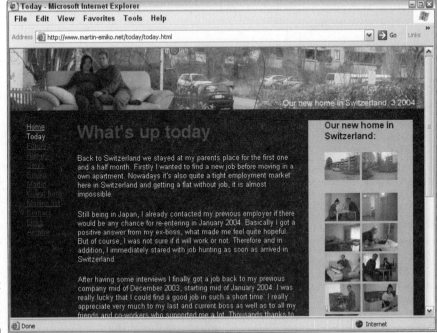

Figure 1-7: Martin and Emiko's web site helps them stay in touch with distant family and friends.

✔ The Miller Family Web site at www.millfam.org boasts several sophisticated features, put together by using a combination of services. Check out the bulletin board for neighborhood and family events, and visit their content-managed site, as they call it, to see a family blog linked to a custom family Web site. (You find out more about blogs in Chapter 15 and more about calendars in Appendix A).

✔ The Bratz family Web site, at webpages.charter.net/bratz, features a fall sports schedule with a full calendar of games and other sporting events of interest to family and friends.

✔ Vicki and Tony's Web site at www.geocities.com/vickips/ is an example of how much you can do with a good sense of humor, even on a free Web site like Geocities.

Travel sites around the world

The Mansz and McKerral family Web site at www.mansz.com, shown in Figure 1-8, is more than just a place to share photos of friends and family. They've created a site that's a showcase of bird photos from their travels and a great resource for other birders. Whatever your hobby or passion, a family Web site can provide a great place so share your expertise and even make new friends.

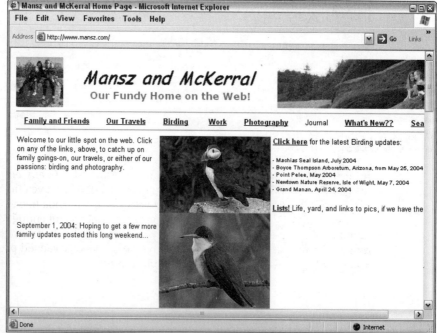

Figure 1-8: This site features photos from bird-watching trips and great tips about birding.

Tribute sites to make you proud

Creating a Web site for friends or family members is a beautiful way to pre-serve their memory and pay tribute to their life. Figure 1-9 features a simple Web page that my Uncle Tom created for my grandmother, Carol McCain. We all have fond memories of grandma's house on the lake, where I learned to water ski and enjoyed sitting on the long deck staring out at the water and waiting for a chance to wave at the Dixie boat.

Figure 1-9: Even a simple Web page, like the one shown here of my grand-mother, provides a loving way to pay tribute and remember someone you love.

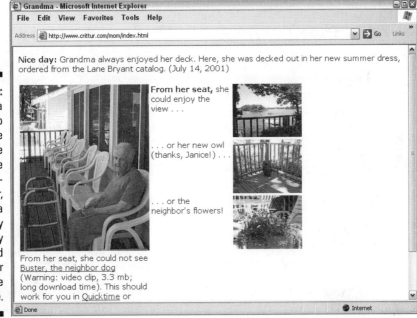

Choosing Tools

All Web pages are simply text pages that can be opened in any editor capable of reading text, such as Microsoft Word or even Notepad. I've chosen to use FrontPage 2003 and Photoshop Elements 3 in this book because they're relatively easy to use and reasonably priced, yet powerful enough to create complex Web sites. I recommend that you start with these programs if you're new to Web design. You can always move on to more advanced programs if you decide you want more features and options.

A note of caution, however. It's easy to get dazzled by all the effects, filters and tools. Don't fall into the trap of using filters and other fancy features just because you can. ("Look Ma, I made my photo look like a watercolor! Now it looks like a Japanese print! Wait, let me try Fresco.") Keep in mind that the most important thing is to make your photos and Web pages look good and download quickly on the Internet.

My goal in this section is to help you understand the strengths and weaknesses of the most popular Web design programs so you can find the program that's best for you now and in the future.

Comparing image editing programs

You'll find many choices in the world of image editing programs, from high-end programs such as Adobe Photoshop (which retails for about $650) to simple programs that you can download for free over the Internet. Here's a quick comparison of some of the most popular image editing programs.

- ✔ **Adobe Photoshop cs:** By far the most popular image editing program in the history of computer design, Photoshop cs is a powerful program that lets you create, edit, and manipulate images. This is a professional tool, with a professional price tag (about $650), so unless you have a huge budget or you're a serious photographer or designer, it's probably not the right choice for you.

- ✔ **Adobe Photoshop Elements 3:** Shown in Figure 1-10, Photoshop Elements 3, which now comes bundled with the creation tools from Photoshop Album, features many of the same powerful tools as Photoshop cs but is easier to use and costs about $100. Elements provides more than enough power for almost anything you'd need to do on a family Web site. That's why I've chosen Photoshop Elements 3 as the image editing tool for this book. You find instructions for how to use Elements in Chapters 5, 6, and 7.

The difference between the two versions of Photoshop boils down to this: The expensive version is used by people like magazine editors and high-fashion photographers to do painstaking, exacting work on their photos, to make a flawless image suitable for viewing by millions and optimized for print. Given enough time, you can use Photoshop to make a mule look like a supermodel. For the rest of us, who just want to edit photos, or maybe make it look like Uncle Ernie's basset hound was driving the lawn-mower, Photoshop Elements 3 should be all you'll ever need.

- ✔ **Macromedia Fireworks MX 2004:** This image design program has many special features that make it easy to create images that download quickly and look good on the Web. A few years ago, Fireworks was the best image program for the Web, but that's no longer true due to enhancements to Photoshop Elements and other programs in this list. Today, the main reason for choosing Fireworks is if you use Dreamweaver as your Web design program, because the two programs are fully integrated.

✔ **Corel Draw Graphics Suite 12:** Although not as popular as Adobe Photoshop, CorelDraw is a professional-grade image program that is rich in features. This suite of programs costs less than Adobe Photoshop but more than Elements.

✔ **Ulead PhotoImpact XL:** This image editing program often comes bundled with the software for digital cameras and scanners. It's easy to use and has a wide range of features, including several automated correction features. The ExpressFix Photo Wizard, for example, helps correct for common photography mistakes such as red eye and lens distortion. You'll also get everything you need to edit and convert images for the Web — and at a lower price than Adobe's or Corel's products.

✔ **Apple iPhoto:** Often bundled with Apple computers as part of the iLife suite, iPhoto is an excellent image editor and by far the best choice for Mac users. (You can't get this program for a PC.) If you have iPhoto, you have everything you need to create images for the Web.

Figure 1-10:
Elements
is a "light"
version of
Photoshop,
ideal for
anyone new
to working
with an
image
editor.

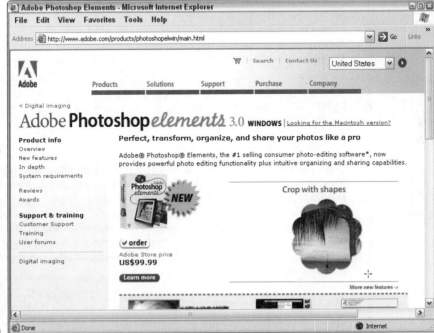

Comparing Web design programs

In the early days of the Web, people were using lots of different visual HTML editors. Today, only a few major ones are left: Microsoft FrontPage, Adobe GoLive, and Macromedia Dreamweaver:

- ✔ **Microsoft FrontPage 2003:** I chose to use FrontPage 2003 in this book because it is less expensive than its competitors and relatively easy to use. It's also the most popular Web design program among consumers (although Dreamweaver wins among professional designers). If you work with other Microsoft Office programs, you should feel comfortable with FrontPage because it's similar to Microsoft Word and is integrated into Microsoft Office. You find a basic guide to FrontPage in Chapter 8 and a special guide to working with templates in FrontPage in Chapter 9. For more about FrontPage, visit `www.frontpage.com`, as shown in Figure 1-11.

- ✔ **Macromedia Dreamweaver MX 2004:** By far the most popular choice among professional Web designers, Dreamweaver has received great reviews and attracted considerable attention because it offers high-end Web design features and lots of control for programmers who like to work in the code behind their Web pages. Dreamweaver features many customizable palettes and floating dialog boxes, which makes it look more like an image editor than a word processor. If you're serious about Web design, this is the tool to use. If you're still new to the Web, you'll save money and probably have an easier time with a program such as FrontPage. For more about Dreamweaver, visit `www.dreamweaver.com`, shown in Figure 1-12, or buy my book, *Dreamweaver MX 2004 For Dummies* (published by Wiley).

  If you want to use the templates provided on the CD, but prefer to use Dreamweaver to do your Web design, visit `www.digitalfamily.com`. You'll find a special bonus for readers of this book — instructions for using Dreamweaver to create the template sites featured in Chapters 11 through 14.

- ✔ **Macromedia Contribute 3.0:** This program is reasonably priced and easy to use, but it's not a stand-alone program. Instead, it works with Dreamweaver. Contribute can be used to edit a Web site created in Dreamweaver, which makes it easy for anyone to update pages, but you'll need a pro to create the site in Dreamweaver first. Contribute is an ideal choice if you're hiring a Web designer to create your site or if one member of the family is an experienced designer who wants to use Dreamweaver.

- ✔ **Adobe GoLive CS:** Similar in features to Dreamweaver MX 2004, GoLive CS is used by many professional Web designers, especially those who are loyal to Adobe and are already using Photoshop CS. GoLive CS is a professional design tool and not generally recommended for beginners or hobbyists.

Figure 1-11: FrontPage was designed to look and work much like Word.

Figure 1-12: Dream-weaver is the most popular choice among profes-sional Web designers.

No matter what software programs you choose for image editing and Web design, the basic concepts are the same. If you're new to Web design, I recommend that you start with FrontPage 2003 and Elements. However, don't forget that you can use whatever image or Web design program you prefer with this book, and you can always move on to more advanced programs later if you decide you want more features and options.

Chapter 2

Getting Organized

*B*efore you dive into building your first Web site, do yourself a favor and save your family some grief by spending a little time thinking through what you want to put on your site, how you plan to build your site, and how you will add new pages, images, and other content in the future. Then spend some time thinking about how you're going to organize the links on your site so visitors can find what they're looking for on your pages. If you don't, you may get an e-mail message from someone like Uncle Alf or Cousin Squeegee when he can't find the pictures of Bobbie Junior's latest Little League game.

One of my favorite sayings is, "Learn from other people's mistakes; you won't live long enough to make them all yourself." My goal in this chapter is to share some of the best tricks and techniques the experts have learned the hard way — so you can spend more time on the fun stuff, such as creating graphics and cool page designs.

Determining What You Want on Your Site

When creating a family Web site, one of the first things you may want to do is hold a brainstorming session with the people who will be working on, and appearing in, your site. The purpose of this initial meeting is to think of the stories, images, and other features you may want to include on the Web site, such as photos (old and new), lists of favorite books, awards and schedules of team events, descriptions of other activities, and favorite family anecdotes.

Writing it down

To tell the best story with your Web site, someone in the family has to do some writing. Many people find this a daunting task, so here are a few tips:

✔ **Write about what interests you.** If you're not interested in what you're writing, why should you assume anyone else will be? Step away from overused introductions and clichés and look for creative verbs, colorful adjectives, and unusual ways to tell a story. Instead of starting a biography with "Jessica was born on July 25," consider writing something like, "It was so hot the day Jessica was born, grandma still remembers the chocolate cigars melting all over the sheets in the guest room."

✔ **Interview family members to get the best stories and details.** Don't trust your memory to get the facts right. Grab a notebook or a tape recorder and interview each family member to collect the best stories and the intimate details that bring a biography to life.

✔ **Write in a conversational tone.** Many people are more formal and serious when writing than they would ever be when talking. The result is often stiff and dull writing. To avoid this trap, try writing your Web site text as if you were writing a letter to a favorite aunt or telling a story to a friend.

✔ **Write one thing at a time.** Trying to write too much at one time is a quick way to discover writer's block. Instead of sitting down to write all the text for your Web site, focus on one section or one family member's biography. Then move on to the next writing assignment.

✔ **Determine who, what, where, when, and how.** These provocative little words provide a powerful tool for making sure you've covered the key points in a story. If you're stuck, ask yourself each of these questions. As you review your writing, make sure you've answered them all.

✔ **Read other Web sites for ideas.** Still not sure what to say on your Web site? Consider reading what other families have said on their sites. Many great family Web sites are featured in Chapters 1 and 16.

✔ **Write a first draft.** Don't expect your writing to be perfect the first time you sit down to put pen to paper or fingers to a keyboard. If you do, you'll probably have a hard time getting anything on the blank page. Most professional writers revise their work over and over again and then have someone else edit and revise it again.

✔ **Less is more.** When revising and editing, cut out unnecessary words. Trying to fill space is a bad habit some of us learned when we *had* to write a ten-page paper in high school. It takes more time to write concisely, but a story that is told well in few words has more effect than one that drags on and on and on.

✔ **Make sure the text is readable on your Web pages.** When you lay out the text, don't use a type size that's too small or distracting background patterns. Make sure the color of the text contrasts well against the background.

✔ **Find an editor.** Every writer needs an editor. Before you let your words go on a live site, ask someone who has a good eye for detail to look over your work. And don't get defensive if the person suggests ways to improve your work. Constructive criticism is not personal; it's about getting the best story on the page.

A good brainstorming session is a nonjudgmental free-for-all — a chance for everyone involved to make suggestions without worrying about whether anyone will like their ideas. If you stifle someone's creativity early in the process, that person may feel less inclined to voice other ideas in the future. And you never know when a seemingly crazy idea will lead to a great one.

You should end the session with a long "wish list." Your next challenge is to pare that list down to what's most important, and create a plan for putting all the items on the list online.

Here's an example of a slimmed-down wish list:

- Photos of each member of the family
- A picture of our house
- A welcome letter for the front page of the site
- A picture from mom and dad's wedding
- Baby pictures of Joanne and Tim
- Excerpts from the baby books
- School pictures of Joanne and Tim
- A picture of Joanne in karate class
- A picture of Tim playing baseball
- Stories from Tim and Joanne about school and sports activities
- A family history page with genealogy information
- Pictures of grandma and grandpa
- Links to favorite Web sites

While you're considering the possibilities for what you want to include in your Web site, you may also want to go through the questions in the planning guide that follows to help decide how you want to build, host, and design your site.

Whether you are working alone or have a team of family members involved, the following guidelines are designed to help you sort through some of the most common questions you'll have to answer as you start working on your site:

- **What do you want to accomplish with your Web site?** It's easy to get distracted by all the things you *could* do with your site. This first question is designed to help you clarify what's most important to you. For example, is your main goal to share photos with distant family members? Or do you want to communicate better within your immediate family? After you define your goals, use them to guide the rest of your decisions and keep you on track.

If you find that you want to accomplish many goals with your site, try to prioritize them so you have a sense of what's most important to you as you start building your site.

✔ **Who will work on your site?** If you will be sharing the project, consider breaking up the Web site development into different tasks, such as building the site, writing the text for each page, and designing the look of the site. Think about the interests and skills of each family member and assign different tasks accordingly.

✔ **What software will you need?** I chose FrontPage 2003 as the primary Web design program covered in this book because it's the most common program used by consumers, but you may prefer a more sophisticated program, such as Macromedia Dreamweaver MX 2004. You find an overview of software options and online services in Chapter 1.

✔ **Do you want to include multimedia files, such as video or audio?** Although editing multimedia files is more complex than creating Web pages, adding digitized video and audio to a Web page is relatively easy. If you want to add clips from your family movies but no one in your family is an expert in video, consider having a local video lab digitize the video for you. Look for video services in the phone book, in a local Internet directory, or by using a search engine such as Google, which features the ability to search for businesses in a local area.

✔ **Do you want interactive features, such as a calendar or gift registry?** Creating your own interactive calendar requires more sophisticated programming skills than creating a simple Web page with text and pictures, unless you use an online service, such as the one at `calendar.yahoo. com`. Gift registries are great features for baby and wedding sites. You find instructions for creating pages that feature gift sites in Chapters 11 and 12.

✔ **Do you want to register a domain name, such as** `www.smithfamily. com`**, for your site?** It's a good idea to register a domain name early because it can take at least a few days for the registration process to be completed. (You'll find information on searching for and registering a domain name in Chapter 3.)

✔ **Do you want to pay for a commercial service provider or use a free hosting service?** Commercial service providers cost as little as $5 a month, making them a more viable option than ever before. If you choose to use a free hosting service, such as the ones at `www.tripod. com` or `www.geocities.com`, you'll save some money but your design options and the size of your site will be limited. (See Chapter 4 for more information on hosting options.)

Site Development Overview

In a nutshell, building a Web site involves creating a *home page* (often called the *front page*) that links to other pages representing different sections of the site. Those pages, in turn, can link to subsections that can then lead to additional subsections.

Two big parts of Web site planning are

- ✔ Determining how to divide your site into sections
- ✔ Determining how pages link to one another

If you're new to Web design, you may think that you don't need to worry about how to manage updates and additions to your Web site. But all good Web sites grow (or they grow stale), and the bigger they get, the harder they are to manage. Planning how you will link new sections of your Web site now can make a tremendous difference later.

It's even more important to create a structure and plan for your site if more than one person is working on the site (perhaps each child in the family is building his or her own section). Without organization and a few conventions for naming files and creating new links, confusion may rule in your virtual world.

Creating a preliminary map of your site can help you plan and manage the site's development. To create a diagram that represents the pages on your site, you can sit down with a piece of paper and a pen, use a program designed for developing flowcharts, such as MacFlo or Visio, or use a word-processing or graphics program. I like to draw boxes to represent pages and use arrows to show how one page will link to another.

Paper sticky notes are also great tool for Web site planning because you can move them around. Each sticky note can represent a page or a section of your site. As you're planning the structure and flow of the site, rearrange the sticky notes to accommodate new ideas. You may want to use string to show how the pages will be linked.

Try grouping pictures and other content that you want on your site into sections. For example, you might create a section about your kids and include their baby pictures as well as more recent photos. Or you might take those same pictures and group them in separate sections to create a Web page for each sibling.

Refer to the Web site wish list described earlier in this chapter to make sure you remember all the things you wanted on the site when you first started planning.

Navigating and linking

As you start planning the organization of the pages and links on your Web site, consider these questions. When site visitors arrive at your home page, where do you want them to go? How will they move around your site? How will they find the information that is important to them?

A good way to help answer these questions is to imagine that you are a typical user of your site. For example, you might say to yourself, "If I were grandma and I came to the site looking for Susan's new school photo, what would make it easy for me to find it?"

In a well-designed Web site, users navigate easily and intuitively from one page to another and can make a beeline to the information most relevant to them, such as the freshly posted photos of a newborn. Figure 2-1 is a sample structure for a family Web site.

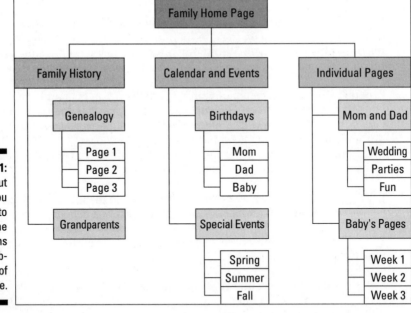

Figure 2-1:
Think about how you want to organize the sections and sub-sections of your site.

As you plan the navigation of your site, make sure that visitors can do the following:

- ✔ **Follow different paths to the same important information.** It may seem repetitive at first, but providing more than one link to the same page makes it easier for visitors to find their way around your site. For example, if you have a family history section, you may want to link to that page from many other pages in your site, such as the page about your daughter's wedding as well as the page about your grandparents.

- ✔ **Move back and forth between pages and sections.** Links that help users move forward and backward through a site can be especially useful. In a slide show or image gallery, navigational arrows that link from one page to the next make viewing a series of photos a breeze.

- ✔ **Return to main pages and subsections in one step.** To make it easy to jump to the main pages and sections of your site, provide a menu of links on every page. Most big Web sites feature this kind of navigational element, often called a menu bar. When links to key pages appear on every page on the site, visitors don't have to retrace their steps back to the home page. Here's an example of a menu bar you might create with a row of links to the main sections of a family site:

```
Home Page ~ Dad ~ Mom ~ Mikayla ~ Savannah ~ Jessica
```

Following the rules for file names

When you're building a Web site, you have to follow stricter rules for naming the Web pages, images, and multimedia files in your site than you do on a Macintosh or PC computer. That's because most Web servers run on the Unix operating system, which can't support the kinds of complex file names you can use on a Mac or PC computer.

When you create HTML pages, images, or other files for your Web site, you can't use any spaces or special characters, such as apostrophes or asterisks, in the file names. You can, however, use hyphens and underscores (the underline character above the hyphen on your keyboard). Web designers routinely use hyphens and underscores in place of spaces. For example, you can't name an image `dumb picture of Sue.jpeg` or `Sue's picture.jpeg`, but you can name it `dumb-picture-of-Sue.jpeg` or `picture_of_Sue.jpeg`.

Being thoughtful about how you name the pages on your site can help you keep track of the content. For example, suppose that your Web site includes a section for your annual New Year's family letter. Simple names such as `family-letter.html` may make sense to you when you first start. But what do you name the file next year and the year after that, when you add more family letters?

Under construction? No hard hats here!

Good Web sites are always under construction. Don't greet your visitors with an "Under Construction" placeholder, which seems to say, "You clicked this link for no good reason. Come back another day, and maybe we'll have something for you to see." Instead, let visitors know that new treats are coming by putting notices on pages that already have content. A message like "Come here next Thursday for a link to something even cooler" is a great idea. Never make users click a link and wait for a page to load, only to find that nothing but a person with a hard hat is waiting for them.

The simple solution is to add dates to the end of file names. For example, a good file name for the yearly letter is `family_letter_date`.htm, where `date` is the four-digit year. The first year's letter might be `family_letter_2005`.htm, and the next year's would be `family_letter_2006`.htm.

Adding dates to image files is even more important because you typically have many photos from the same event or of the same person. Therefore, you may want to be even more specific when naming image files, for example, `Susan-swimming-06-05-2005`. For special events, such as a birthday, you may want to create a separate folder with a name like `susan-birthday-05`, and then save all the images inside that folder so you don't have to add a date to each image file.

If more than one person is working on your Web site, come up with a naming system that makes sense to everyone involved. Doing so will make keeping track of pages and images easier.

Understanding file name extensions

All files in a Web site need to include what's called an *extension*, usually a three- or four-character identifier tacked to the end of the file name and preceded by a period. The extension is used to identify the type of file. For example, a file name followed by `.html` or `.htm` was created by using HTML (HyperText Markup Language), which is the programming language used to create Web pages.

Although most Web servers support both `.htm` and `.html` file extensions in file names, some service provides require that you use the longer `.html` extension, especially for the main page of your site, which should be named `index.html`. This can lead to problems because most Web design programs, such as Microsoft FrontPage, automatically name the main page of your site `index.htm`. If you have trouble viewing the page when you transfer your site to your server, the problem may be that the file needs to be renamed `index`.

html. I've never found a server that doesn't support the longer .html
version, so I've used that naming convention throughout this book.
FrontPage makes it easy to rename your files with the .html extension without risking broken links. (See Chapter 8 for more information about working
with FrontPage.) If you're not sure what is required on your Web server,
check with your service provider.

If you're not used to seeing something like .html, .gif, or .jpeg at the end
of a file name, that's because most Windows computers hide this last part of
a file name to make names appear simpler for users. Macintosh computers
don't require extensions, so you won't see them on a Mac unless you add
them yourself. Table 2-1 provides a list of common file extensions.

Table 2-1	Common Extensions for Web Site Content
Extension	*What it is*
.gif	An image format for the Web best suited for cartoons, logos, and other images that use limited colors
.jpeg or .jpg	An image format ideal for photographs and other images that include millions of colors or gradients
.html or .htm	A Web page document in HyperText Markup Language
.doc	A document created in Microsoft Word (these should be saved as HTML files before they're added to your Web site)
.txt	Plain text files, usually created in a simple text editor such as NotePad or Simpletext
.pdf	A popular option for long documents or pages that have complex formatting on the Web
.rm, .qt, and .wmv	Used for three of the most popular video formats; these and other multimedia extensions are covered in Chapter 10.

Programs such as FrontPage 2003 and Photoshop Elements 3, which I use
in later chapters, take care of putting the proper extensions on your files
for you. If you stick with these programs, you shouldn't have to worry
about extensions. Make sure, however, that you never delete a file name's
extension.

If you're having trouble opening a file, a missing extension may be the problem. This is a common occurrence when someone on a Mac e-mails a file to
someone on a PC (because extensions are not used on the Mac). Because the
PC system requires extensions to identify file types and to determine what
program to use to open the file, you may need to manually add the extension
before you can open the file on a PC. (For details on this task, see the next
section.) For example, if someone on a Mac sends you a digital photo and you

can't open it on your PC, adding `.jpeg` to the end of the file name may solve the problem. If you use a Mac, you can avoid this problem by adding the appropriate extension to your files before you send them to a PC.

Adding a file name extension

To add an extension to a file name, simply select the file name as you would select any file name to rename it, and add a period followed by the appropriate extension to the end of the name. For example, a GIF image called `silly-kitty` should be renamed to `silly-kitty.gif` before it is linked to your Web pages. Make sure you don't add a space between the name and the extension.

The easiest way to rename a file on a Windows computer is to place your cursor directly over the name and right-click. Select Rename from the list that appears, click to place your cursor at the end of the existing file name, and then type a period and the extension.

On a Macintosh computer, click once on the file name to select it, and then click to place your cursor at the end of the existing file name and type the period followed by the extension.

Viewing file extensions under Windows

Many Windows computers come preset not to display file name extensions. That means you won't see extensions, such as `.gif` or `.doc`, at the end of a file name. The extensions may still there; they're just not visible.

If you're creating all the files for your Web site on a Windows computer with programs such as FrontPage and Photoshop, you shouldn't have to worry about extensions and your best option may be to leave them hidden. However, if you receive files from someone who uses a Macintosh or you're having trouble with links that don't work or images or other files that can't be displayed on your computer, missing extensions may be the problem.

Before you can add or change an extension, you have to be able to see it. To make extensions visible on a PC, simply change your folder preferences as follows:

1. **Double-click any folder name to open that folder on your hard drive.**

   The folder opens and the files in the folder become visible.

2. **Choose Tools⇨Folder Options from the top of the folder window.**

   The Folder Options dialog box appears.

3. **Click the View tab.**

4. **Scroll down to the Hidden files and folders section, as shown in Figure 2-2.**

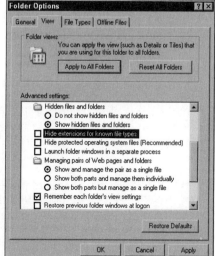

Figure 2-2:
Many
Windows
computers
are set to
hide the
extension at
the end of a
file name.

5. **Make sure that the Hide Extensions for Known File Types option is turned off.**

   If the option has a check mark, click to remove it.

6. **Click the Apply Changes to All Folders button, at the top of the dialog box.**

   If you click OK at the bottom of the dialog box, you apply these changes only to the folder you are viewing. You may consider this option if you want to make the extensions visible in the folder where you have your Web site pages but don't want visible extensions in any other folders on your computer.

If you find that any of your files are missing extensions, see the earlier section titled "Adding a file name extension."

Viewing file extensions on a Mac

Macintosh computers don't use file extensions to identify file types the way Windows computers do. If you use a Mac you may need to add file extensions for your Web pages, images, and any other content you want on your Web site.

Some software programs, such as FrontPage, add file extensions automatically, even when you create files on a Mac. Other programs, such as Photoshop, don't add extensions automatically, so you'll need to add them manually as you name your files. (For a list of common extensions, refer to Table 2-1.) Macs don't hide extensions, so after you add one to the end of a file it should be visible immediately.

Setting Deadlines for Finishing Your Web Site

It's easy to have big ideas and think of all the ways you can create a cool Web site for your family. But when you get down to the task of developing the pages, you may find that accomplishing everything is not as easy as you thought it would be. One problem I've seen with personal projects, such as family Web sites, is that they aren't managed as formally as you might manage a business project and the people working on them are almost never given deadlines

The first challenge is setting realistic deadlines. The second is making everyone involved believe that the deadlines are important. If you want to set deadlines that family members will stick to, plan the launch of your Web site around a special date. For example, plan to get your new family Web site online to show grandma when she comes to visit in August, or to surprise mom on her birthday, or before the first day back to school. Use a date that's special to you or your family and one that will help keep everyone motivated.

The Never-Ending Project

One of the best and worst things about building a Web site is that there is no clear beginning, middle, or end to the task. You can always add more pages, pictures, and links, and you can never do enough testing.

Don't underestimate the importance of checking your Web site regularly to make sure it has no broken links or missing images. If you're building the site by yourself, ask someone else to check over your work and test it, especially after you've published it to the live server. If you have a team of people working on your family Web site, you may want to assign them to check each other's work regularly.

And remember, you don't have to do put everything on your Web site all at once. The best model is to start small and keep it simple until you see how much your family will use your site and what features they consider most important. You can always add old family photos or create a new section for a hobby or a special event later. The best family Web sites are much like the families who build them: They grow and develop and continue for generations to come.

Chapter 3

Registering Your Site's Domain Name

In This Chapter

▶ Searching for names to see whether they're already taken

▶ Registering a domain name

▶ Understanding domain name options

▶ Creating e-mail addresses

*T*he address for your Web site is called its *domain name*. It's what visitors need to know to find your Web site. For example, Walt Disney's Web site has the domain name www.disney.com.

Even before you start building your Web site, I recommend that you register your own domain name. The process is simple, painless, and costs less than $10 per year. (You find detailed information about the best places to register your domain name later in this chapter.)

I registered my own name, www.JanineWarner.com, years ago, but I didn't think of registering a domain name for my entire family until recently. And because we have a common name, I was too late to get www.warner.com. In this chapter, you see how I found a name for my family Web site even though my first choice was already taken. You also find step-by-step instructions for searching for and registering your own domain name.

Finding and Registering a Name

If you don't register a domain name, your Web site's address will be an extension of the domain that your service provider registered and will look something like this:

www.serviceprovider.com/users/yournamehere

If you register a domain name, you can point the name wherever your Web site is hosted, and your address should look more like this:

```
www.yourfamilyname.com
```

(For information about choosing a service provider to host your Web site, see Chapter 4.)

TIP

Your domain name is your calling card — it should be short and sweet, and easy to say and write. If your Web address is too long or complex, it will be hard for family members to remember or type on a keyboard.

Searching for a new name

You can register any domain name that hasn't already been taken by someone else. To check to see whether a domain name is already registered, do a simple search at any domain registration Web site, such as www.godaddy.com, as shown in Figure 3-1.

Figure 3-1: Search for the domain name you want to register at any registration service, such as www.godaddy.com shown here.

Finding out whether a name is already in use is easy — and free. In the early days of the Web, you could register domain names only at `www.network solutions.com`, but the service is now available through hundreds of sites. These services connect to the same master databases that track all the domain names on the Web, but they charge different amounts for domain registration. Many of these services also offer Web site hosting (covered in detail in Chapter 4), e-mail, and more. If you do a Web search on *domain registration*, you'll find thousands of matches. My favorite domain registration service for price and options has been `www.godaddy.com`, which boasts that it has registered more domains in the last few years than any other company. I also recommend `www.1and1.com`, an international company that offers competitive domain registration services and claims to be the largest Web hosting service in the world.

Unfortunately, common domain names were taken long ago. But even if your first choice for a domain name is unavailable, don't give up. With a little trial and error, you're likely to find a variation that will work fine. (You'll find suggestions for finding a domain name in the "Naming tips" section that follows.)

To search for and register a domain name for your family, follow these steps:

1. **Use a Web browser to visit a domain name registrar.**

   As mentioned, I recommend `www.godaddy.com`.

2. **In the search area on the registrar's site, type the name you want to register.**

   In Figure 3-1, I'm searching for *warnerfamily*.

3. **Click to begin your search.**

   The results of your search are displayed. (If you use `godaddy.com`, for example, you would click the Go button.) My results are shown in Figure 3-2.

4. **If the name you want is not available and you don't like the alternatives offered, try another name.**

Most registration services provide a list of recommended alternatives if the name you want is taken. If you still need a little help, read on.

If you register a domain name at `www.godaddy.com`, you'll be offered many additional products and services during the registration process. I don't like this aggressive sales technique, which makes you scroll through pages of product offers before you can complete your registration, but I do like the low prices at Go Daddy and their excellent, 24-hour customer support. So let me just reassure you that you don't *need* any additional products or services, such as Web hosting and Spam blocking software, to register a domain name. You can simply skip through these product pages by clicking "no thanks" until you get to the final checkout page to complete your registration.

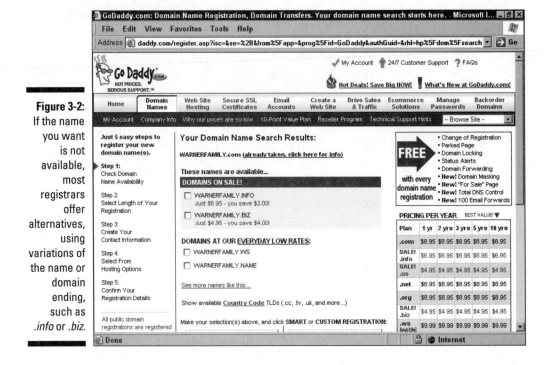

Figure 3-2:
If the name
you want
is not
available,
most
registrars
offer
alternatives,
using
variations of
the name or
domain
ending,
such as
.info or *.biz*.

Naming tips

Don't get frustrated if you find that your family name is already taken. You
can almost always find a variation on your name that will serve you well. Try
one of the following tricks:

- ✔ Add a word or phrase that indicates geographic location, for example,
  www.michiganwarners.com or www.thecanadasmiths.com.

- ✔ Sometimes a different but equally appropriate name can work. For example, my Uncle David's family has always been referred to as The David's
  because there were too many McCains (my mother's last name) to refer
  to everyone by their last name. A good name for my uncle's Web site
  would be www.thedavids.com

- ✔ Try something playful, such as the www.funfrinkles.com or www.
  lovinggibsons.com.

- ✔ Although you may use a hyphen or an underscore in your name, the
  best choice is a word or a combination of words run together. For example, you could register www.the-sunshine-family.com, but that's
  harder to convey verbally because you have to explain the hyphens. If
  you simply use www.sunshinefamily.com, you can say, "My address is
  SunshineFamily dot com, all one word."

> ✔ The best domain names are easy to remember, easy to convey (can be said in one simple sentence), and easy to spell.
>
> ✔ Don't choose a name that's too close to someone else's if they have a site you'd be embarrassed to be associated with. (Always check the site of the name you want before you choose a close variation.)

I searched for `www.warnerfamily.com`, `www.thewarners.com`, and `www.thewarnerfamily.com`, but none were available. At that point, I was thinking about how *our* Warner family deserved to be able to use our own name — and sure enough, `www.ourwarnerfamily.com` was still available. With a little persistence, I'm sure you'll find the right domain name for your family, too.

Naming rules

As you consider what you want to use for a domain name, remember the following rules. Note that these rules are based on technology requirements and laws, so there aren't any good ways to get around them:

> ✔ Make sure your domain name doesn't violate a trademark. (You can do a simple trademark search at `www.uspto.gov`. If you're starting a business or concerned about violating someone's trademark, consult an attorney.)
>
> ✔ The only punctuation allowed is the hyphen and the underscore — no spaces, periods, apostrophes, or other punctuation.
>
> ✔ Domain names are not case sensitive. For example, you can get to my Web site by entering `www.janinewarner.com` or `www.JanineWarner.com`. Because people are accustomed to seeing capital letters in a person's name, I often capitalize the J and W when I type my domain name.
>
> ✔ Anything that comes after a domain name (after the dot-com part of the address) *is* case sensitive. For example, `www.JanineWarner.com/books` takes you directly to the page on my site where I list my books. You can't get there if you capitalize the *B* in *books*.

Buying a name from someone else

Buying and selling domain names has become big business in a world where your name is your front door, your street address, and much of your identity. Web businesses dedicated solely to the sale of domain names have sprung up around the world.

Your virtual image

I tell my friends that they should register their own names as domain names because I consider that an important way to protect what I call your *virtual image*. I registered www. JanineWarner.com years ago and I use it as a place to showcase everything I want the world to know about my books, speaking engagements, and more. A personal Web site serves as a great way to promote yourself, whether you are job hunting, developing a consulting business, or simply want to share your story with the world. After you've registered a domain name for your family, consider registering names for each member of the family individually.

I've heard a few sensational stories about domain names being sold for exorbitant prices. However, for the most part, many names and variations on names are still available for the registration price, so few people offer huge amounts of money for a domain name anymore, even if it's a great one. If you have your heart set on a name and find that it's already taken, contact the owner and try negotiating.

You can find out to whom a domain name is registered by going to

```
www.NetworkSolutions.com
```

and clicking the WHOIS Lookup button at the top of the home page. The registration listing includes the street address and e-mail address of the person who registered the domain name, as well as information about the server or service provider that hosts the domain.

Searching the WhoIs database at Network Solutions is free, but if you want to register a domain name, I suggest you use a lower-priced registration service. Network Solutions was once the only place to register domain names and remains one of the most expensive ones.

If you want to keep your own name and address out of the domain database at WhoIs, use the Private Domain Registration option, available exclusively at www.godaddy.com. It costs $9 per year in addition to the $8 registration fee, but it will keep your personal information out of the public database.

Disputing a domain name

Almost as soon as it became possible to register domain names, people started fighting over who had the right to own *their name*.com. Recognizing a potential bonanza, many early Web users registered dozens of names they thought they might be able to sell later. Country names, product names, and many common terms (such as www.toothpaste.com) were snatched up early. Not surprisingly, ownership of some of those names came into dispute when a company that thought it had a legal right to the name tried to take it from the person who registered it.

Registering multiple domain names

Excerpted from Janine's Business Technology column, originally published in The Miami Herald

Can anyone find your Web site?

I am amazed when I type a business name into a browser and don't find the site I'm looking for. I must confess, sometimes it's because I've typed it wrong, or assumed they were using their full name when they were using some alternative. I eventually find what I'm looking for, but don't count on all your visitors to be as persistent as I am.

A shortened version of your business name may seem like a better domain name because it requires less typing, but if your customers know you by your full name, they may be confused. For example, the official site for American Airlines is www.aa.com, but they've been smart enough to register more than one name, so if you type in www.americanairlines.com, you go to the same site.

My best advice: Register every variation and misspelling of your name you can think of and direct those domain names to your Web site. (Just because some people didn't do well in the third-grade spelling bee doesn't mean they don't have money to buy your products or services online.)

Directing more than one domain name to the same Web site is a relatively simple technical detail you can arrange through your Internet service provider or the company where you register the name. And it's not that expensive. Some of the new registration sites, such as godaddy.com, charge as little as $8 per year. (You'll pay $29 at www.register.com and $16 at www.buydomains.com.)

Also consider registering the same name with different domain endings, such as .org, .net and, most importantly, .com. The Seattle Ballet, for example, registered seattleballet.org (the domain ending used by most nonprofits), but they should also consider registering seattleballet.com because many people will assume that's the address.

Consider whitehouse.gov. The .gov at the end of that name distinguishes it as an official government site. You can't register a .gov site as an individual, but anyone can register .com (which stands for commercial) and .org (which stands for organization).

I don't recommend visiting the .com version of Whitehouse. It's a hard-core porn site, and provides a dramatic lesson in the importance of protecting your domain name. I'm sure that site receives many visits from unsuspecting people who type .com instead of .gov. The .org version of Whitehouse isn't an official government site either, although it does at least have a picture of the White House. It also has lots of critical commentary on the U.S. government.

The moral here is that if you are a nonprofit, a government organization, or a university (usually distinguished by .edu), you should also register *your name*.com, just to make sure that people don't end up at a site that's trying to get traffic from your name recognition.

Similarly, if the .com version of a name you want is unavailable, registering the .net, .biz, or .info versions may be a fine alternative. But make sure that the site that has the .com version is not a direct competitor or something you'd be embarrassed by if your visitors found it by accident.

The courts seem to be applying the same laws to domain names that they apply to trademarks. For example, if you have a legal trademark such as Levi and someone registers `www.levi.com` before you do, you can probably go to court and force the person to give you the domain name. If you don't have a trademark, you may have no other alternative than to try and buy it from the person or choose an alternative.

Even if you have a strong case, domain name disputes can be lengthy and expensive. In many cases, you're better off avoiding names that may be deemed suspect by large, established companies. If your last name is Disney, you may have a strong case for registering `www.disney.com` (if it were still available), but you still might lose in court and would undoubtedly run out of money before Disney Enterprises, Inc. would in the legal battle.

If you think you have a case against someone who has taken your name, don't bother Godaddy or Network Solutions with your complaint. They don't handle domain name disputes; they just register names on a first-come, first-served basis. Instead, talk to the guilty party directly. If that doesn't work, take it court. If you can get a judge to rule that you're right, the domain registration service will revoke the name and let you have it.

Understanding Domain Name Endings

When you search for a domain name, you need to determine not only the first part of the name but also the ending. Table 3-1 provides a list of common domain name endings, their purposes, and any restrictions.

Table 3-1	Domain Name Endings	
Domain ending	**Purpose**	**Restrictions**
`.com`	Commercial organizations	No restrictions; by far the most popular domain ending
`.net`	Internet services	No restrictions; used increasingly by people who didn't get the `.com` name they wanted
`.org`	Nonprofit organizations	No restrictions
`.biz`	Businesses	No restrictions; one of the newer domains, and it is increasingly used by businesses when they can't get the `.com` domain name
`.name`	Individuals	No restrictions

Domain ending	Purpose	Restrictions
.info	Informational sites	No restrictions
.pro	Professionals, such as doctors and attorneys	No restrictions; in the process of being established
.aero	Air-transport industry	Restricted
.coop	Cooperative associations	Restricted
.museum	Museums	Restricted
.gov	United States government	Restricted
.edu	Accredited colleges and universities	Restricted
.mil	United States military use	Restricted

The .com domain has emerged as the most valuable because it is the best recognized and the one people are most likely to remember. However, all these domains work the same way in terms of directing users to a Web site address. For example, www.smith.com, www.smith.net, and www.smith.org work the same way on the Internet.

Country domains

Nearly every country in the world now has its own domain. Country domains include domains such as .am for Armenia, .br for Brazil, .uk for the United Kingdom, .sa for Saudi Arabia, and .zw for Zimbabwe.

What about .tv and .ws?

A few foreign country codes have become popular in the United States because they represent common acronyms, such as .tv, which many assume stands for television but is really the domain for the county of Tuvalu. Similarly, .ws is assumed to mean Web site (and is even listed that way on some registrar sites), but it is the country code for Western Samoa. You can register a name with the .ws or .tv domain even if you don't live in one of those countries, but these domain codes are not as common as the ones listed in Table 3-1.

Although you can register a domain name with a country code from any-where in the world, it's generally more expensive to register a country domain. The price ranges from $10 to $80 per year, depending on the price set by the particular country.

Creating E-mail Addresses for the Family

After you've registered a family domain name, you can set up e-mail addresses at that domain. (See Figure 3-3.) For example, if you register www.moscowitz.com, you can then set up an e-mail address such as frank@moscowitz.com or a more general address such as family@moscowitz.com. Most domain regis-trars also offer e-mail services for as little as $10 per year.

If you're hosting your Web site by using a different company from the one you used to register your domain name, you may prefer to set up an e-mail address at the Web hosting company. There is no right or wrong choice in this matter. Make your decision based on which service you find easiest to use, most reliable, or most cost effective.

Figure 3-3: After you've registered a domain, it's easy to create an e-mail address by using your own domain name.

Chapter 4

Choosing a Web Hosting Service Provider

*I*f you've ever heard the phrase, "Wherever you go, there you are," you may appreciate how the Internet works. There is no one "there" in the Internet, no master computer that holds all the information in the world. Instead, you find innumerable "theres," each represented by a computer connected to another computer to make up a network, which is connected to other networks connected to networks of networks. Essentially, the Internet is a bunch of computers and wires strung together all across the globe.

When you visit a Web site, you are essentially viewing pages stored on another computer's hard drive, and it generally doesn't matter if that computer is across the office or thousands of miles away. What does matter is what kind of computer it is, what software it uses, and how it's connected to the Internet. In this chapter, you discover how Web servers work, why you need one to host your Web site, and how to choose one that best fits your needs and your budget.

Understanding Web Servers

A *Web server* is a computer with a permanent connection to the Internet and special software that enables it to communicate with Web browsers, such as Internet Explorer or Netscape. As a general rule, you create a Web site on your computer's hard drive, using a program such as FrontPage or Dreamweaver, and then transfer the completed site to a server when you're ready to publish your site on the Internet.

Plain old telephone service

Many different kinds of phone lines exist. Most homes have a basic phone line, a twisted copper wire the phone company still calls POTS, or plain old telephone service (yes, that's really what they call it). Many homes and businesses have upgraded to DSL (Digital Subscriber Line), which supports multiple phone lines and provides higher bandwidth and better signal quality than a POTS line. For a higher price, some businesses get T1 lines, which are high-speed, dedicated connections that transmit digital signals at 1.544 megabits per second and can handle many phone lines and Internet connections at a time. At the top of the heap, a T3 line transmits digital data at 44.746 megabits per second (trust me, that's really fast).

To help you compare the differences in bandwidth, visualize them as if they were running water:

56K modem — garden hose

DSL or cable modem — fire hose

T1 line — small waterfall

T3 line — Niagara falls

Most Internet service providers use T1 or T3 lines, which afford them a permanent connection to the Internet with lots of bandwidth that they then split up among customers. A single T1 line is the equivalent of about 24 phone lines. The bandwidth that you can transfer across such a line can be divided and shared among many users. Thus, when you pay an ISP for a connection to the Internet, you're paying for a small portion of the high-speed line that the ISP shares among many users.

Most Web servers are connected through special high-speed Internet lines with odd names such as T1 and T3. These lines afford greater bandwidth, so they can transport more information more quickly (much faster than a cable modem or a DSL line).

Bandwidth measures the carrying capacity of a connection on the Internet. Compare it to a garden hose and its capacity to transport water. The larger the diameter of the hose, the more water it can carry. Bandwidth works the same way: The greater the bandwidth, the faster the transmission of information. On the Internet, information is digital data, measured in kilobytes and megabytes (the same way it's measured on your hard drive). The larger the file, the more bandwidth is required to transport the file across the Internet. For example, most short text files (1 to 20 pages) are only a few kilobytes in size so they take only a few seconds to send, even over a 56K modem (the equivalent of a garden hose in this analogy). Sending the entire manuscript of, say, *War and Peace* will take a little longer. But the kinds of files that take the most bandwidth — the ones that warrant a fire hose, or a high-speed connection such as a cable modem or a DSL line — are video and animation files, PowerPoint presentations, and large color images, which can be many megabytes in size.

A number of companies, such as Microsoft and Netscape, make software for Web servers as well as the browsers used to look at the pages they serve. Each system has its own features and limitations, but all of them do essentially the same thing: serve files from a Web site to its visiting audience.

Web servers use the Hypertext Transfer Protocol (HTTP) to deliver Hypertext Markup Language (HTML) and other files to a client, usually a browser. At the low end, a Web server can be set up on almost any desktop computer with a connection to the Internet. If you use a 56K modem, the connection is slow, but setting up a Web server at the low end doesn't cost much, as long as you have the technical expertise — and you need a lot of that to run a Web server. At the high end of the Web server spectrum, a powerful computer with a fast and dedicated Internet connection and the staff to keep everything working costs many thousands of dollars.

Some servers are designed to handle only one Web site; others handle many sites simultaneously. Universities, government organizations, and private companies generally operate the latter. Internet service providers usually have one or more large servers capable of hosting 100 or more Web sites on each server. When you set up your site with an ISP, you essentially rent a small section of the hard drive on one of their servers. ISPs can section off a server and provide you with access to only the part of the server that you're using to manage your Web site, even though many other Web sites may be hosted on the same computer.

Many people who are setting up Web sites for the first time think that they need to run their own Web servers to put their sites on the Internet. Let me reassure you that you don't have to run a server to publish a Web site. This is a good thing because maintaining a server can be complicated and expensive, requiring skills that are quite different than the ones you need to develop Web pages. Unless you're building a large and complex Web site, setting up your own server is not necessary — and definitely not recommended! Let the ISPs take care of that part and dedicate your time and resources to building a great Web site for your family.

Choosing a Service Provider

So you've established that you definitely don't want to run your own server. Now, how do you find an Internet service provider? And what exactly does a service provider do?

Internet service providers sell accounts that let you connect to the Internet, host a Web site on their server, or both. To log onto the Internet to check e-mail or to surf the Web, you want a *user account*, a service provided by your ISP (unless you log on through a university, a large company, or another private service). To build a Web site, you want a *Web hosting account*, which is usually sold separately from a user account. For example, you may like using AOL as your service provider to log onto the Internet but choose a company such as XO, shown in Figure 4-1, for Web hosting.

Although you don't have to use the same service to host your Web site that you use to access the Internet, sticking with the same company may be a good choice if you're happy with your user account and like the customer service your provider offers. Most ISPs, such as XO, lease Web space to customers and can set up an account for you in a few days.

If cost is your biggest concern, you may want to select one of the free Web hosting options featured later in this chapter in the "Comparing Free Hosting Services" section.

The big-ticket items at ISPs are bandwidth, disk space, and security. Bandwidth gets expensive if lots of people visit your site, because more visitors mean more use of the connection.

The bigger your site — the more images and especially the more sound files, video, and animation files you include — the more you'll pay for the disk space to host it. Because video files are much larger than images or text files, video takes up much more hard drive space and requires more bandwidth to be viewed. As a result, providing many hours of video on your site can be expensive. Most people limit their sites to a few short video clips (30 seconds to a few minutes each) to save on hosting expenses.

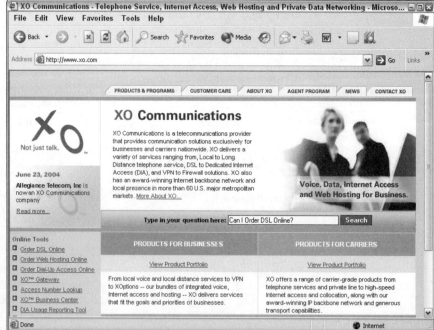

Figure 4-1:
Web hosting services offer many packages. The basic level of service is more than enough for most family sites.

Some Web hosting packages include secure e-commerce capabilities and sophisticated programming options. Unless you're planning to create a commercial site (maybe a family business?) or to put large amounts of video or sound files on your site, you'll probably do fine with the simplest or lowest-level Web hosting package your service provider offers.

Shop around; many service providers offer basic Web hosting services for $5 to $10 per month. Some services also offer discounts if you pay for a year in advance.

Finding an Internet service provider

The best place to look for an ISP is also the most obvious: Look online! Also, ask around and get references from people you trust.

If you want to find a server anywhere in the world, The Directory (`www. thedirectory.org`) claims to list more Internet service providers and bulletin board services than any other such registry in the world. The main page of the site may not look like much, but it's been around for almost ten years and boasts a comprehensive list of service providers.

If you use the Web design program FrontPage 2003, which is featured in this book, you may want a service provider that supports FrontPage extensions, which are advanced features included in the program that require special support on the server. Microsoft's Web site at `www.frontpage2003.com` includes a list of companies that provide FrontPage hosting.

Asking the right questions

Running a Web server is an increasingly competitive business, and not all companies offer the same features. Before you select an ISP, consider what you want on your Web site and make sure that you find a service that meets your needs. The goal is to find the provider with the best collection of services within your budget. Here are a few questions you may want to ask when considering which service provider to use to host your Web site.

How much do you charge?

Choosing an ISP is a little like choosing a cellphone company or a long-distance service. In theory, all phone companies provide the same ability to make a phone call, but as you've probably discovered, they offer a wide variety of rate plans and special services.

My best advice is to get a good start on the development plan for your site so that you know what kinds of services you'll need before you shop around for a service provider. (You can find more information about planning a Web project in Chapter 2.) You may decide, for example, that you want 24-hour technical support so you can get help at night after work, but you don't want to pay extra for secure financial transactions because you don't plan to sell products online.

Two of the biggest factors in cost are how much hard drive space you need and whether you want a secure server. As a general rule, the more server space you need, the more you pay. Most family sites shouldn't need more server space than is included with most basic plans, which range from about 50MB to 500MB. In a world where new computers often come with 100GB hard drives, you may think that 50MB of space doesn't sound like much. But remember that, on the Web, you want your files to be small so that they load as quickly as possible. A site with a few hundred pages and graphics may be less than 10MB if the images are optimized and you don't include multimedia, such as video and audio files which take up much more hard drive space than text and image files).

It's a good idea to make sure your service provider will let you add more space if you need it. However, you can always move to another server if you need to. And if you register a domain name (covered in Chapter 3), you can redirect your domain to the new server and your URL never has to change.

In addition to the cost of server space, most ISPs charge a fee based on how much bandwidth you use (measured by the amount of traffic on your site). This fee is like paying rent based on the number of people who walk through your door. Most Web sites created by families don't get enough traffic to worry about added bandwidth costs, and the standard amount included in your basic plan should be plenty. But be aware that many service providers do charge for excessive bandwidth use, so you may see additional bandwidth as an option among their offerings.

Do you provide e-commerce services?

Most Web server accounts that support secure e-commerce transactions, such as `Storefront.net` shown in Figure 4-2, charge extra for the service. If you're thinking of starting a family business, you may want to make sure your service provider can handle e-commerce transactions. If you plan to sell a lot of products, I also recommend a shopping cart system, a program that enables visitors to add products to a checkout page that tracks and tallies selected items as a visitor moves through your site. (You can buy shopping cart systems separately, but many service providers include these programs as an added feature.)

Figure 4-2:
Some Web hosting services provide e-commerce capabilities.

Do you provide security?

Security is a complicated issue on the Web, but mostly it deals with *encryption*, a process of encoding and decoding messages so that they're harder to intercept by people who might want to steal confidential information, such as credit card numbers. A *secure server* is called *secure* because the data being transmitted between the browser and the server is encrypted. No system is 100 percent secure, but as a general rule, the stronger the encryption, the more it costs. If you're trying to keep credit card numbers private, you may be willing to pay a premium for security, but if you're creating a family Web site, you probably don't need to pay extra for a secure server.

Do you provide technical support?

Because each service provider is different, you can't find everything you need to know about your server in this, or any other, book. If you run into trouble uploading or maintaining your site, you need to contact your hosting company to find out more about the specifics of connecting to their Web server. If you want to use more advanced services, such as an e-commerce system, you're even more likely to need their help. The bottom line: Technical support is important, and it's always a good idea to make sure you can get help when you need it.

Some ISPs have knowledgeable technical support staff on call 24 hours a day; others may never answer the phone (especially those with the lowest rates). Before you even sign up for service, call the tech support line of the service providers you're considering to see how long it takes each one to respond to your initial questions. If you have trouble finding out how to buy an ISP's services, you'll probably have even more trouble getting help after the ISP has your money.

Most ISPs post FAQs (frequently asked questions) on their Web sites. FAQs can be a great place to get answers to common questions and to find out about common problems other users are having — before you even sign up.

Expect your ISP to give you basic assistance, such as helping you understand the specific aspects of how to log on to their server and upload your pages. However, few ISPs provide help with actual Web design and development, so don't judge them badly if they won't give you advice about the design or graphics for your site.

What kind of backup systems do you have in place?

Backup systems are crucial on the Internet — technical problems are common, servers go down, and the contents of a Web server can be lost if its not backed up regularly. Any reputable service provider should have a regular backup system in place. If they balk when you ask about their backup system, they're probably not reliable or well run.

Protecting yourself with clever passwords

An extraordinary number of people use the same word for their user ID and password. That may seem like a good idea because using the same word makes your password easier to remember, but it's also the easiest password for someone to guess if they find your user ID.

Other common passwords are the name of your pet, your spouse's name, or a birthdate. Those are fine options if you're not too worried about security, but if you want to make it harder for someone to break into your computer system, use more than just a name or a common word.

Adding punctuation and mixing the case in your password makes it much harder to guess, but not necessarily harder to remember if you're

clever. For example, if your dog is named Spot and you live at 44 Maple, you can add the number to your dog's name to create a great password such as spot44. The goal is to come up with a password that is easy for you to remember, but hard for someone else to guess, even if they use a software program designed to try random names as passwords.

Mix numbers and words together, and you make it much harder for anyone to break into your computer system. Add a random capital letter, and you make it even harder. Oh, and don't leave your password on a sticky note next to your computer, unless you want anyone who walks into your home or office to have access to your system.

Always keep a backup of your Web site on your own computer. You're probably doing this already if you created the site on your hard drive, but it's a good idea to keep an extra copy of the site on a disk or a CD. If you use consultants to do any of the work for you, get copies of their work. Similarly, if other members of your family are working on the site, make sure you collect their work in one place and keep it backed up.

Where are you located?

When you look for a Web hosting service, keep in mind that it doesn't need to be in your geographic location. You can send files anywhere on the Internet, so your Web site can be almost anywhere. If you're in a small town or an isolated area where few companies provide Web hosting, you may want to look beyond your neighborhood to find a better deal. For example, I live in Los Angeles, but I use Internet hosting services in Michigan (www.nexcess.net) and Canada (www.tera-byte.com). Although California has reputable service providers, these two came highly recommended and I've had great experiences hosting Web sites with both companies.

Can I host more than one domain name?

As you compare options, you may notice that some providers charge more for packages that enable you to host multiple domain names. You might choose a package that supports multiple domain names if you want each member of the family to be able to register their own domain name and set up their own site separately. For example, you could set up www.Jean Doherty.com, www.JoshDoherty.com, and www.TheDohertyFamily.com as separate sites on the same account. Although a Web hosting package that supports multiple domain names is more expensive, it may save you money compared to the cost of setting up a different Web hosting account for each family member's Web site.

Note that there is a difference between hosting multiple domain names that point to different Web sites, as in the example in the preceding paragraph, and pointing two or more domain names to the same site. If you want two names, such as www.TheDohertyFamily.com and www.TheDohertys.com, to both direct visitors to the same site, you can manage that with your domain name registrar and save the cost of a premium Web server account that supports multiple domain names. Check with your domain name registrar for more information on how to direct multiple domain names to the same Web server.

Publishing a Web Site to a Server

After you build your Web site on your own computer, you transfer the site's files to your Web server by using a technology protocol called *FTP*.

The *File Transfer Protocol* (FTP) describes the system used to transfer any files from one computer to another on the Internet. The term is often used as a verb, as in, "Can you FTP that graphic to the Web server?" A number of freeware and shareware programs have been designed for file transfers, such as Fetch for the Macintosh and WS_FTP for Windows.

FTP might seem like computer magic at first, but it's simple and easy to do. To upload — or FTP — your site, you just copy files from your computer to your server. FrontPage 2003 has built-in FTP capabilities, making this process almost automatic. In Chapter 8, I provide step-by-step instructions on how to use FrontPage 2003 to FTP your Web site to your server.

If you're not using FrontPage 2003 or you want an alternative, I recommend the WS_FTP program. You can download a trial version of WS_FTP from www.ipswitch.com.

You also find a copy of the WS_FTP program on the CD that accompanies this book.

To use an FTP program like WS_FTP, follow these steps:

1. **Open your FTP program.**

   FTP programs are relatively simple utilities designed to move files from one computer to another. Usually they have two windows: One displays the contents of your computer's hard drive, and the other displays the files and folders on your Web server, as shown in Figure 4-3.

2. **Enter the information for your service provider.**

   As you see in Figure 4-4, you need to enter your server's host name, as well as your unique user ID and password to connect to your Web server.

3. **Click to select the files or folders you want to transfer.**

4. **Click the arrow that points from the window that represents your computer to the window that represents the Web server.**

   The files are automatically transferred from your computer to the server. This process can take a few minutes depending on the size of the files you're transferring.

You can also use an FTP program to transfer files from your Web server to your computer. Simply select the files in the window that represents your server and click the arrow that points to the window that represents your computer.

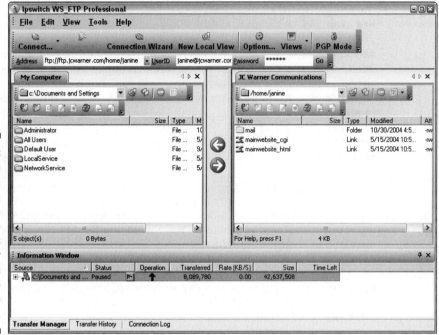

Figure 4-3:
You can use a program like WS_FTP to transfer files from your computer's hard drive to your Web server.

Figure 4-4:
When you set up your FTP program to connect to your Web server, you need to enter your server's host name and your user ID and password.

Moving to a New Server

As you consider which ISP is best for you, remember that you can always move to a new server later if your situation changes. Transferring your Web site to a new ISP is a relatively painless process, but it does require some organization if you want to move without your site going down in the process.

One of the biggest advantages of having your own domain name is that you get a permanent address. That means your visitors will always use the same address to find you, even if you move to a server on the other side of the world.

If you don't have your own domain name, your Web address will include the name of your service provider. That means if you change service providers, you have to change your address, too. (You can find more information about domain names in Chapter 3.)

Follow these general steps to move your site to a new service provider and redirect your domain name:

1. Set up an account with a new service provider.

2. Transfer the files from your site to the new server and test your site on the new server to make sure everything works properly.

3. Notify the service where you registered your domain name that the name should be redirected to the new server. You can usually make the request to redirect your domain name yourself by filling out a few forms on your registrar's Web site.

4. After you request that your domain be redirected, your service provider will send you an e-mail message to verify that you really want to make the change. This ensures that you haven't made the request by accident and that no one else is trying to steal your domain name by redirecting it to another server without your permission. The request may expire if not confirmed, so respond to this verification e-mail promptly.

5. After your domain name is safely directed at the new server and everything is in working order, notify your old service provider to close your account.

Comparing Free Hosting Services

The word *free* makes many people skeptical. You may be wondering what's the catch, so before I tell you about some free hosting sites on the Web, let me tell you what you can expect from them.

First, you'll face many design limitations. You can't just upload your own Web site to their server as you can with a commercial service provider. Instead, you're generally limited to using the templates and designs provided by the free site. So the first thing you give up is design control and options.

Second, you'll be limited in the size of your site and the amount of bandwidth you can use. If you want to put lots of big photos online, you may quickly run out of space or exceed the bandwidth limitations. When that happens, your viewers might be greeted with an error message instead of your pages.

And finally, you'll have to share your pages with advertising — that's the real catch. These free sites make money by selling advertising that they display across the pages they host, and you won't have any control over the ads that may appear on your pages. Across the top of your family Web site, you may find a car ad one day and an ad for diet pills or an online gambling site the next day.

If you don't mind these limitations or think they're worth it because the price is right, keep reading. Just remember, Web site hosting can cost as little as $5 per month, so you may not be saving much with a free site. (Also beware of bait-and-switch tricks. Many of these sites try to attract users with free server space and then sell premium services for a fee. Before you pay for these added services, shop around. You may find comparable services for a much better price elsewhere.)

The following services provide free, basic Web hosting services:

- **Yahoo! Geocities (**www.geocities.com**):** This popular one-stop solution to e-mail and Web page hosting also provides PageBuilder, PageWizard, and SiteWizard. These programs enable you to use basic click-and-drag techniques to arrange your photos and text, and provide some simple templates into which you can insert your content.

- **Angelfire (**www.angelfire.com**):** Especially popular among young people, Angelfire, shown in Figure 4-5, offers free, basic Web site hosting, if you don't mind sharing your pages with their advertisers. Owned and operated by Terra-Lycos, this site features a variety of other options (prices vary by service), including a blogging program, as well as premium services that let you store up to 100MB of images and MP3 music files. (If you want to know more about blogging, see Chapter 15.)

- **Tripod (**www.tripod.com**):** Also owned by Terra-Lycos, Tripod is designed to reach a more mature market than Angelfire, but it features a similar suite of options, including basic Web site hosting for free (with ads), and the option to upgrade to more advanced services, such as their blogging software, for a fee.

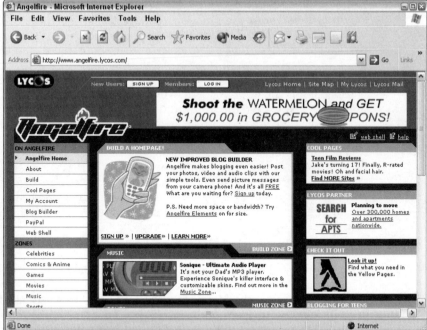

Figure 4-5:
Angelfire
features
free basic
Web
hosting, as
well as
many
premium
services you
can
upgrade to
for a
monthly fee.

Although none of these free services will let you set up a site with your own domain name (instead, they assign you a name like www.geocities.com/yourusername), you can register a domain name at a site such as www.godaddy.com and then use the services offered by your domain registration service to forward your domain name to your address at the free Web server. Then when visitors type your domain name, they'll be directed to the free site by your domain registrar.

Part II
Lookin' Good: Images and Design

The 5th Wave   By Rich Tennant

"THAT'S A LOVELY SCANNED IMAGE OF YOUR SISTER'S PORTRAIT. NOW TAKE IT OFF THE BODY OF THAT PIT VIPER BEFORE SHE COMES IN THE ROOM."

In this part . . .

This part is all about making sure you have the best-looking images on your Web pages while ensuring that they download quickly for your visitors. In Chapter 5, I show you where to find premade images, such as clip art and royalty-free photos, and how to download images from the Internet. You also find out how to retrieve photos from a digital camera and how to scan photos, drawings, and anything else you can fit on a scanner.

In Chapter 6, you find an introduction to Photoshop Elements 3 and discover how to crop, reduce, and edit images, as well as how to optimize them so they download as fast as possible. In Chapter 7, you discover the advanced features in Adobe Elements that help you keep track of all your images and automatically create a photo album or image gallery for your Web site.

Chapter 5

Gathering Images: Scanning, Downloading, and Finding Clip Art

*W*hat would your family Web site be without pictures? Adding images, such as vacation photos and old family portraits, can make your Web site more attractive and bring family stories to life. But how do you get those great images on your computer so you can add them to your Web site? Consider scanning your children's artwork and keepsakes, as well as the great prints you've taken over the years. And if that's not enough, add clip art and royalty-free photos (professional pictures can enhance the overall look of your site and compliment your snapshots).

In this chapter, you discover how to download images from Web sites through a browser, such as Internet Explorer or Netscape, and where to purchase clip art and photos on CDs. You also find out how to scan printed materials, such as artwork and photos, with Adobe Photoshop Elements 3 and a scanner, and retrieve images from a digital camera. In Chapter 6 you find an introduction to editing photos and preparing them for the Web, and in Chapter 7 you find tips for organizing images and using Elements 3 to create Web photo galleries and photo album pages.

Click! Using Images You Find Online

So you've surfed to a site that has an image on it that you'd love to use on your Web site. Maybe it's a still image from your favorite movie, or a photo of the Sydney Opera House, which is exciting for you because your family went to Australia last year. Maybe it's a picture of a cartoon character that bears a strong resemblance to your spouse. Whatever the image and whatever your reason for wanting to use it, can you just grab it from the Web site and use it on your site? Well, although it's technically possible to save the image to your hard drive, it may not be legal to use it.

Before I show you how to download images from the Web I have to include a little legal disclaimer. When you publish something on the Internet, you are in the same category as publishers who produce books or magazines. That means you have the same legal obligations to respect copyright. Be careful not to copy images or graphics from other people's Web sites without asking permission. You find a few guidelines about copyrighted material in the following section.

How do you know what you can and can't use? Most commercial photos, taken by professional photographers or journalists, are copyrighted. When an image is copyrighted, the person who owns the rights has the right to determine who can use it. Generally, you need to either purchase the right to use a photo or obtain written permission. Simply giving credit to the photographer by name or citing the source of the image is usually not enough.

The same goes for cartoons, drawings, artwork, and clippings from newspapers and magazines. For example, scanning a greeting card and using the image on your Web site would almost surely violate the copyright of the greeting card company.

The exceptions? Images you find on Web sites that offer copyright-free images, images you purchase with the expressed right to reuse the images, and images that are considered public domain, such as vintage photos where the original photographer is unknown or where the subject of the photo is a person, place, or thing that's considered public property. For example, you can find many freely available photos of the Statue of Liberty, presidents, Mount Rushmore, and other common subjects.

So, now that the attorneys are happy, here are the steps to follow if you do have the right to use an image and want to copy it from a Web site:

1. **In a Web browser, open the Web page containing the image you want.**

2. **Place your cursor directly over the image and right-click (in Windows) or click and hold (on the Mac).**

   A pop-up menu appears, as shown in Figure 5-1.

3. **Choose Save Picture As from the drop-down menu.**

   The Save Picture dialog box opens, as shown in Figure 5-2.

4. **If you want, type a new name in the File name box.**

5. **Click Save.**

   The image is saved to the specified location.

Figure 5-1:
You can easily copy images from Web pages to your hard drive.

Figure 5-2:
You can change the name of an image file when you save it to your hard drive.

After you've saved the image, you can use it as you would any other image you create or capture on your hard drive.

If you follow these steps and the Save Picture As command is dimmed, the site's designer has protected the images from copying and saving, and you won't be able to save the image to your hard drive.

Searching for Photos and Clip Art

Now where do you find professional photos, artwork, cartoons, and more for your site? On the Web, of course, and also on CD.

For the most part, *clip art* refers to graphic images, such as cartoons, drawings, and sketches, and the word *stock* is used when referring to photographs. An image that's royalty free isn't necessarily free. *Royalty free* means you don't have to *continue* to pay royalties for the right to use an image or graphic.

When downloading free images, purchasing images from a Web site, or using clip art or photos from a CD, be sure to check the fine print for any restrictions. For example, some images are free to use on only noncommercial sites. If you sell products or services through your family site, you may have to pay a higher fee for commercial use.

Finding royalty-free images and clip art online

If you're looking for a specific image, such as a drawing of a duck for a baby site, try an online search (for example, type *ducks + free clip art* in Google). You can find an extraordinary amount of free images on the Web, but you often get what you pay for.

If you're willing to invest a little in quality images, I recommend the following. Some of these sites provide free images, but most charge a usage fee, especially for the highest quality images.

Most of the sites listed here offer the same images at high, medium, and low resolution, and some charge more for the highest resolution. When you're talking about images, *resolution* refers to the amount of detail in an image. The higher the resolution, the bigger the file size and the better the quality of the image. As a general rule, you'll want high-resolution images only if you plan to print them (especially if you want to make large prints). On the Web, low resolution is preferred because the file size is smaller and the file downloads faster.

Most image sites enable you to search through photos and other graphics by keyword (for example, you could search for *photos of Paris* to find professional photos to complement your travel pictures). Some of these sites also have images organized in categories you can browse. All these sites make it easy to download pictures immediately:

✔ **Public Domain Images** (www.pdimages.com): As the name implies, this site provides access to a wide range of images considered to be in the public domain because the photographer is either unknown or has relinquished the copyright. Although they do charge for some of the images on this site, many are available for free.

✔ **Getty Images, Inc.** (www.gettyimages.com): Getty Images is the largest supplier of royalty-free digital imagery on the Web, specializing in photographs and illustrations of a wide variety of subjects, including film footage. Pay for images and footage as you go.

✔ **Stockbyte** (www.stockbyte.com): Stockbyte is a great source for international royalty-free photos. You can purchase photographs at a high or low resolution.

✔ **Photos.com** (www.photos.com): Photos.com is a subscription-based service for royalty-free stock photography and photo objects. A 1- to 12-month subscription gives you unlimited access and use of its collection.

✔ **ImageSource** (www.imagesource.com): You can register on this site for free and search through a vast array of professional photos, paying only for what you select to download.

✔ **Clipart Connection** (www.clipartconnection.com): A great source for free clip art and animations designed for the Web.

✔ **Clipart.com** (www.clipart.com): This subscription-based site boasts the largest collection of clip art on the Web, but you have to pay a weekly, monthly, or annual fee.

✔ **Web Promotion** (www.webpromotion.com): A great source for animated GIFs and other Web graphics. Artwork on this site is free.

Purchasing photos and clip art on CD

Photo and clip art CDs are available in most office supply stores and copier or printer stores, and you can often get a big selection of images for $10 or less. CDs with hundreds of images on them are not hard to find, and many come with images in several popular categories. You can also buy specialized collections, such as ocean images, nature scenes, pictures of animals, cars, homes, famous locations, or people.

A search for *photos on CD* (using Google, Yahoo, or another search site) will result in a long list of sites that sell images on CD. Here are a few sites where you can order clip art and photo CDs:

✔ **Photos for Me** (www.photosforme.com): This site offers CD collections of photos, graphics, and even video.

✔ **PunchStock** (www.punchstock.com): Boasting 550,000 images from more than 30 vendors, you're sure to find what you're looking for at this CD site.

Working with Scanners

Scanners have had a huge effect on the types of images you can include on a Web site. In the past, you had to use a professional copier service to turn printed artwork, photos, and drawings into electronic images. Now, with the widespread use of scanners, capturing digital images for your Web site has never been easier.

Scanning printed images for your site

Now that scanners are available for less than $100, many families are investing in these seemingly magical devices. You can scan not only old photographs and printed materials, but also just about anything you can fit on the glass plate of your scanner. Some newer scanners, such as the HP Scanjet 4670, make it possible to scan oversized artwork with a detachable glass plate that can be moved across a large image or object.

Use your imagination — scan your hand to show far-away relatives your engagement ring, scan a piece of china to show off a special pattern, scan the lid of a painted box to create a beautiful abstract image, or scan fabrics to create textured images (great for background images and buttons). Just be careful not to scratch the delicate glass on the scanner.

Some scanning suggestions:

- ✔ You can scan only the area that interests you or that will fit within the intended display or print space. This works well if you want to eliminate some people in a group photo or want to select only the flower bed from a picture taken in someone's back yard.

- ✔ You can scan in color or in black and white, regardless of the nature of the original. In fact, it's often best to scan black-and-white photos as color because it gives you more image content to work with when you're editing the image later. Scanning in color is especially important if you want to use a program such as Photoshop Elements to add color to a black-and-white image after it's scanned.

- ✔ You can scan your images at a high resolution, creating a very large file and preserving as much detail as possible, or you can scan at a low resolution, creating a smaller file with less fine detail. If you plan to do any editing of the image before it finds its way to your Web site, scan it at a higher resolution (300 ppi or higher) so that you have lots of content to work with. As you find out in Chapter 6, you can reduce the image resolution later, after the desired edits are completed, by optimizing the image.

Setting up your scanner

Scanners have become exceptionally easy to use. Modern scanners are plug and play, meaning all you have to do is connect the scanner to your computer and install the scanner software. Although your scanner software should enable you to scan, fax, and e-mail images, I generally prefer to scan images with an image editor, such as Photoshop Elements.

Every scanner is different so you should follow the instructions that come with your system. Many manufacturers instruct you to simply connect the scanner and restart your computer. Others direct you to install the software on the CD before you connect the scanner. Either way, it's a relatively pain-less process. Unless you run into conflicts or have faulty equipment, you should be able to get a new scanner up and running in a matter of minutes.

The installation process informs not only the operating system, but also all your applications, that a scanner is now available. This means if you start Photoshop Elements after installing your scanner, the File⇨Import menu will include your scanner by name, as shown in Figure 5-3.

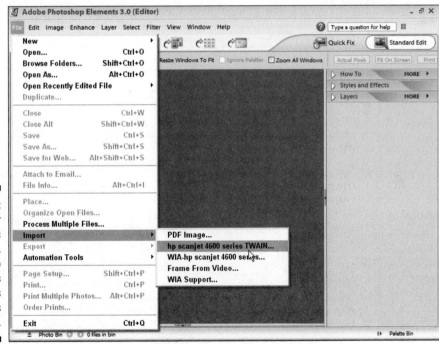

Figure 5-3:
When your scanner is installed, Photoshop Elements recognizes it and makes it available.

Scanning an image

When you're ready to scan an image, place it so it faces the scanner's glass plate. Position the image or object you want to scan by following any symbols (such as arrows or dots) or picture instructions (icons that look like a sheet of paper) that appear along the edges of the plate. Don't worry too much about making sure the image is facing the right direction, you can always rotate it later in an image program such as Elements by choosing Image⇨Rotate).

Most scanners have a "sweet spot" that gives you the best scan possible. See the instructions that came with your scanner or do some experiments to find the best placement for your scanner. (The sweet spot is usually in the middle.)

You have two primary options for scanning in Photoshop Elements 3. If you want to use your scanner's software, start from the Editor view in Elements and choose File⇨Import, and then select your scanner's name from the list of options (refer to Figure 5-3). Elements launches your scanner software and imports the image after the scan is complete.

If you want to use the scanning features built into Elements 3 (which I prefer), you start from the Organizer view and use the scan dialog box, as shown in Figure 5-4.

Figure 5-4:
When you
install a
scanner, it
becomes
available in
the list of
import
options in
Photoshop
Elements 3.

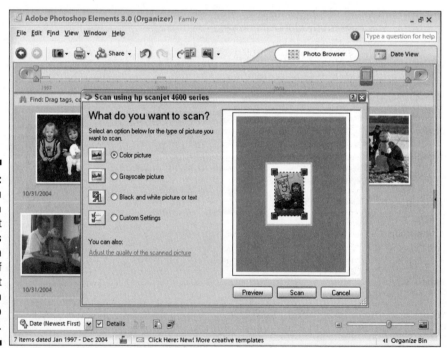

To scan an image from the Organizer view in Elements, follow these steps:

1. **From the Organizer in Photoshop Elements, choose File⇨Get Photos⇨From Scanner, as shown in Figure 5-5.**

   Note: To open Organizer view, click the Photo Browser button at the top of the Editor workspace or choose the View and Organize Photos button on the Welcome screen when you first launch Elements.

2. **In the Get Photos from Scanner dialog box, select the scanner you want to use.**

   If you've connected your scanner properly, it should appear in the list. If your scanner is not visible, consult the scanner's manual.

3. **Use the Browse button to select the folder where you want to save your scanned images.**

   Elements saves scanned images in its `Scanned Photos` folder, but you can specify any folder available on your computer system.

4. **Specify the format and adjust the quality settings.**

   You can choose to save your scan as a JPEG, TIFF, or PNG file. As a general rule, JPEG is best for photographs for the Web, TIFF is best for print, and PNG is best for line art, such as drawings. Your choice doesn't matter too much at this stage because you can convert the image to any format available in Elements after you finish the scan.

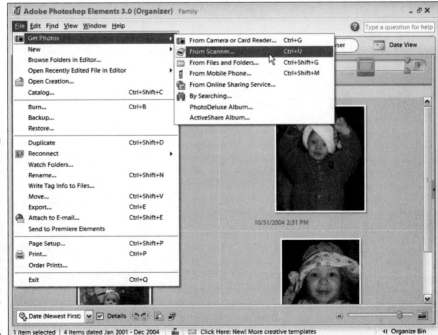

Figure 5-5:
To use scanning features in Photoshop Elements 3, use the Get Photos option from the Organizer view.

The quality settings apply to only JPEG — the higher the quality, the more detail you will get in the scan and the larger the file size. As a general rule, choose a mid to high quality to get the best scan. (See Chapter 6 for instructions on reducing and optimizing images for the Web, an important final step before placing an image on a Web page.) In the example shown in 5-6, I've chosen to scan my image as a JPEG at the Maximum quality setting.

Figure 5-6:
You can scan your image at high or low quality and save it anywhere on your computer system.

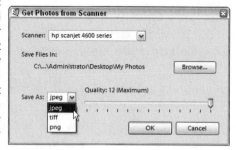

5. **Click OK.**

   The Scan dialog box opens.

6. **Select the scan option that corresponds to the type of image you're scanning.**

7. **Click the Preview button.**

   A preview of the image appears in the dialog box.

8. **Click a handle at the edge of the preview and drag to adjust the preview to cover only the area you want to scan.**

   In the example shown in Figure 5-7, I dragged the handles to select only the photograph in the middle of the scanner plate, eliminating the white border around the image and the remainder of the scanner plate.

9. **Click the Scan button to scan the image.**

   The scanner makes a final pass over the image and the final scanned version appears in the New Photos window in the Organizer.

To use Elements edit features, click to select the image in the New Photos window and then click the Edit Your Photo button at the top of the screen. You find further instructions for editing, resizing, and optimizing images for the Web in Chapter 6.

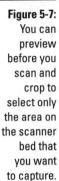

Figure 5-7:
You can
preview
before you
scan and
crop to
select only
the area on
the scanner
bed that
you want
to capture.

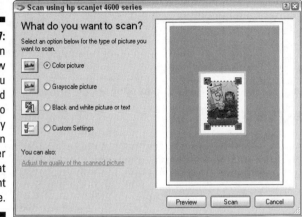

If you want to scan several photos at once, say three or four photos from a batch of prints, you can lay them on the scanner's plate side by side and scan them as a group. You can also place them all on the scanner bed and then use the preview and resizing process to scan them one at a time if you want to capture each one separately. Either option is likely to save you time replacing images between scans.

Downloading Images from a Digital Camera

In the early days of digital cameras, downloading images was a complex process that involved connecting your camera to your computer with a special cable and then using a software program to download the images to your hard drive. You can still use that option with most digital cameras, but today there are simpler ways to get your images on your computer. The options described in this section can be used with most digital cameras (consult the manual that came with your digital camera for details about your system).

Copying images from a memory card

If you have the right card reader in your computer or printer, you can simply remove the memory card from your camera, slide it into your computer, and copy the files to your hard drive as you'd copy images from a CD or floppy disk. Most digital cameras use CompactFlash cards, SmartMedia cards, or some other kind of removable storage device. Many computers now come with all these card readers built in. However, if your computer doesn't have what you need, you can buy adapters that will let you use a PCMCIA slot or USB port. (Check with your local computer store to find the right adapters for your system.)

Importing images directly into an image program

If you've installed the software that came with your digital camera and you have an image program such as Photoshop Elements 3 you can import images directly into your image editor. This option may help you keep track of your images and save you the step of opening them in the editor or adding them into the Organizer after you've copied them from the camera. This option also works for retrieving images from a cellphone or other device.

To import images into Elements from a digital camera or other device, make sure Elements is in the Organizer view and follow these steps:

1. **Insert your camera's memory card into the appropriate slot on your computer or plug your camera into the computer with the cable that came with your camera.**

   Consult the camera's manual for more detailed instructions, if necessary. Note: If Photoshop Elements is open when you connect your camera or insert a memory card, the Get Photos from Camera or Card Reader dialog box may open automatically. If so, skip the next step.

2. **Choose File⇨Get Photos⇨From Camera or Card Reader.**

   The Get Photos from Camera or Card Reader dialog box appears.

3. **Click to deselect any images you *don't* want to import.**

   Elements automatically selects all the images on the camera or memory card, but you can click to uncheck any images you don't want to import.

4. **Specify where you want to save your images.**

   Elements saves your images in a new subfolder named with the date you are saving the images. As you see in Figure 5-8, I'm saving these images on 10-31 — and yes, I've been interrupted many times tonight by trick-or-treaters. If you prefer, click the New Name option; you can change the name of the subfolder to anything you like, or use the Browse button to specify a folder on your hard drive.

5. **Select the Rename Files option and enter a name in the text field.**

   Elements will use the name you enter, followed by sequential numbers, beginning with 001. If you don't select the Rename Box, Elements will save your files with their current names; if you're copying files from a digital camera, those current names are probably a long number that has no meaning to you.

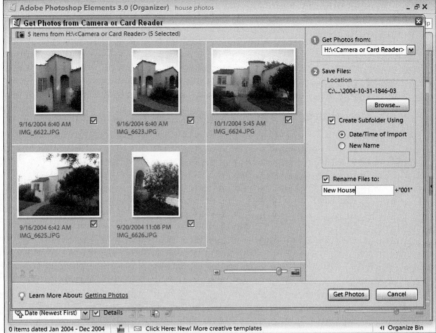

Figure 5-8:
You can
retrieve
photos from
a digital
camera with
Photoshop
Elements.

6. **Click the Get Photos button.**

   Elements copies your images from the camera or card to your computer's hard drive, saves them in the specified folder, and displays them
   in the New Photos window. When the download is complete, the Delete
   Files on Device dialog box opens.

7. **In the Delete Files on Device dialog box, choose Yes to delete the files
   from your camera or card reader or No to leave them untouched.**

   To retrieve images from a cellphone, choose File⇨Get Photos⇨
   From Mobile Phone, and then follow Steps 3 through 7.

After your images are downloaded from a camera, a cellphone, or another
device, you can work with them as you would any other image. In Chapter 6,
you find instructions for editing, cropping, and optimizing your images so
that they load quickly and look their best on your Web pages.

Chapter 6

Creating and Editing Images for the Web

*I*n the old days, my grandmother carefully cut printed pictures into clever shapes to create designs for her holiday letters and photo album pages. If she were still with us today, she'd be amazed by all the ways you can edit, alter, and restore photographs with a computer.

In this chapter, you leave the scissors and glue behind and discover some of the extraordinary things you can do today with a program like Photoshop Elements 3. You find out how to correct red eye (if the flash makes your subjects look like zombies), how to resize images, and even how to restore old pictures.

Perhaps most important in this book about creating Web sites, the last part of this chapter helps you understand the differences between the main image formats that work on the Internet — JPEG and GIF — and how to optimize your images so that they download more quickly.

You can use a number of competing image editing programs to complete the tasks described in this book. I recommend Adobe Photoshop Elements 3 because it's based on the industry standard in image editing, Adobe Photoshop CL, but is a lot easier to use. And at about $100, Elements is also a great value.

Introducing the Elements Workspace

Although Photoshop Elements 3 is a stripped-down version of its big sister program Adobe Photoshop CL, it's still a powerful tool. The workspace, shown in Figure 6-1, is clean and simple, and its myriad tools and palettes can be moved and resized so you can customize the program to fit your work style.

To help you get familiar with the program, this section introduces you to the four primary components of the workspace: the toolbox, options bar, menu bar, palettes.

The toolbox

Shown in Figure 6-2, the Elements toolbox has 22 buttons and the primary color picker. You can use these tools to alter, copy, crop, and retouch images, select portions of an image, paint in the image, and enter text.

Menu bar

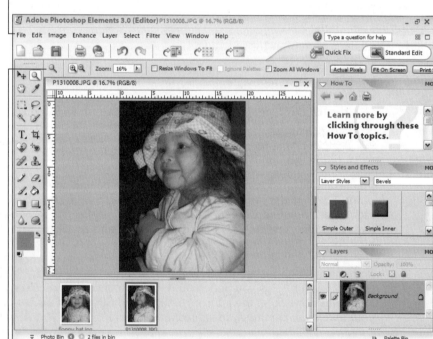

Figure 6-1:
You can alter the Photoshop Elements' interface to match your preferences.

Options bar

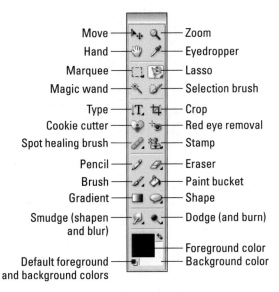

Figure 6-2: The toolbox gives you a comprehensive set of weapons for your image editing arsenal.

Move — Zoom
Hand — Eyedropper
Marquee — Lasso
Magic wand — Selection brush
Type — Crop
Cookie cutter — Red eye removal
Spot healing brush — Stamp
Pencil — Eraser
Brush — Paint bucket
Gradient — Shape
Smudge (shapen and blur) — Dodge (and burn)
— Foreground color
Default foreground and background colors — Background color

Many toolbox buttons have a small triangle in the lower-right corner, indicating that multiple tools are accessible from the button. To view these alternate tools, simply click and hold the button for a moment, until a small fly-out menu appears, as shown in Figure 6-3.

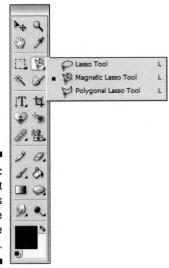

Lasso Tool   L
Magnetic Lasso Tool   L
Polygonal Lasso Tool L

Figure 6-3: The fly-out menus provide even more options.

The options bar

Running across the top of the Elements workspace is the options bar (labeled in Figure 6-1), containing drop-down lists, check boxes, and radio buttons, each controlling how the currently selected tool will work. For example, when the paint brush tool is active, options are available for changing the size and shape of the brush. Switch to the text tool, and the options bar features font and size options, much like a toolbox in a word processor.

The menu bar

No program is complete without a menu bar (labeled in Figure 6-1). Click the menu names and you can choose from a list of commands. If an ellipsis (...) follows the command name, the command launches a dialog box with additional options. Otherwise, the command kicks in automatically.

If you do something to your image you don't like, the greatest menu command ever created (for this program and any other) is Edit⇨Undo. If you're a keyboard shortcut fan, that's Ctrl+Z in Windows and ⌘-Z on the Mac.

The palettes

Like every Adobe application, the Elements workspace is filled with palettes, small windows that hold formatting options and other setting. The various palettes provide tools to help you edit and examine your image. To open a palette, select its name from the Window menu. For example, Window⇨ Color Swatches opens a palette with color options. Note that each palette has a More button. Clicking More displays a list of additional commands.

Palettes can be left in their column on the right side of the workspace or dragged out into the workspace, as shown in Figure 6-4 where I'm applying a bevel to a small image to create a button. To move a palette, drag it by its tab, and release it where you like. After you detach a palette from the main application window, it gains its own title bar for easy moving and identification.

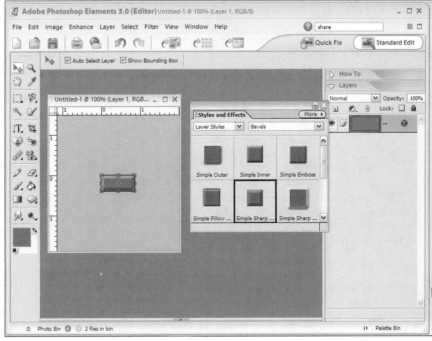

Figure 6-4:
You can move a palette so that it's closer to what you're working on.

Cropping and Resizing Images

Cropping and resizing images are two of the most important things you should do when you prepare an image for the Web. Resizing is important for two reasons. One, you want images to be small enough to display well on a computer monitor. Two, the smaller you make the image, the more you reduce the size and the faster the image downloads to your user's computer.

When you *crop* an image, you cut off the top, bottom, or sides, reducing the overall size of the image. Cropping is especially important on the Web because it's harder to view an image on a computer screen. Figure 6-5 is a good example of how cropping can help focus attention on the subject of an image while removing distracting background elements, such as the lamp to the left. In addition, cropping results in a smaller image, a bonus when you then go to resize the image.

Crop tool

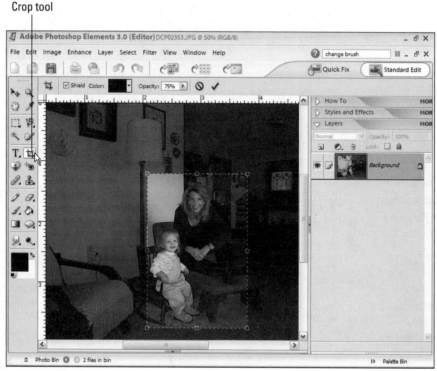

Figure 6-5:
You can
crop an
image to
reduce its
size and
remove
distracting
background
elements.

To crop a photo in Photoshop Elements, follow these steps:

1. **With the image open in Elements, select the cropping tool from the Tools palette (labeled in Figure 6-5).**

2. **Click and drag within the image to designate the area you want to crop.**

   To increase or decrease the size of the cropping box, drag the handles at the corners or edges of the crop area.

3. **Double-click in the middle of the selected area to complete the crop.**

   (You can also click the cropping tool again to complete or cancel the crop.) The cropped area disappears.

To resize a photo in Photoshop Elements, follow these steps:

1. **With the image open in Elements, choose Image⇨Resize⇨Image Size.**

   The Image Size dialog box opens, as shown in Figure 6-6.

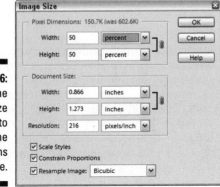

Figure 6-6:
Use the
Image Size
dialog to
change the
dimensions
of an image.

2. **Specify the height or the width.**

   Although you have multiple options for changing image size, I think the simplest option is to adjust the image size in the Pixel Dimensions area at the top of the screen and use the percentage setting. If you keep the Constrain Proportions box selected, you need to change only the height or the width. Elements automatically adjusts the corresponding setting to maintain the original proportions of the image.

3. **Leave the other settings unchanged.**

   Unless you know that you want to change the resolution, scale, or proportions, leave those at the default settings. Although you will probably want to change your image resolution (72 dpi is optimal for the Web), it's best to make that change in the Save for Web dialog box described in the "Optimizing Images for the Web" section, later in this chapter. Making other adjustments in this dialog box gets complicated and it's easy to distort the image.

4. **Click OK.**

   The image is resized.

When you view an image in Elements, you can display it at full size, or you can use the zoom tool (labeled in Figure 6-2) to increase or decrease the size in which the image appears on your screen.

By changing the display size, you can figure out how much you want to change the actual size of your image. Here's how: Click to select the zoom tool from the toolbox, and then click anywhere on the image to increase the display size. Alt+click (on a PC) or Option+click (on a Mac) to decrease the display size. When the image is the size you want, look at the percentage (displayed at the very top of the screen next to the file name). Then enter that percentage in the Image Size dialog box.

To redisplay the image in its actual size on your monitor, double-click the zoom tool.

Adjusting the size of a digital image is more complicated than many people imagine because you have to consider the physical dimensions of the image in relation to its resolution. Resolution is affected by the number of dots per inch in the image (the dpi) and the size and number of the dots depend on many factors. If you're looking at a picture on a computer screen, for example, the image can be displayed only at 72 dpi, the resolution of the average monitor. If you're printing the image on a printer, where the resolution can vary from about 300 to 1200 dpi or more, the image may print much smaller than it looked on the screen because of the higher dpi.

In the Image Size dialog box (refer to Figure 6-6), the Pixel Dimensions area represents what you see on the screen. If you set the width to 500 pixels, the image should span 500 pixels across the screen at 72 dpi no matter what because the computer monitor display is set at 72 dpi. The Document Size area represents the size you expect your image to be when you print it, but only if you print it at the specified resolution. If the Document Size is .8 inches at 216 dpi (refer to the example in Figure 6-6) and you print the picture on a 1200 dpi printer, it won't print at .8 inches.

I can't possibly explain the intricacies of image resolution and printing in this book. If you want to find out more about Photoshop Elements, I recommend *Photoshop Elements 3 For Dummies* by Deke McClelland and Galen Fott (published by Wiley).

Replacing and Editing Content

Do you have an image in which something is just a bit out of balance? Maybe the family's too close to the left edge of the photo, and you have a big gap on the other side. Perhaps Uncle Mike has a lamp sticking out of his shoulder. Whether it's a small object, multiple objects, or entire members of the family, moving (or removing) them is no big deal.

Selecting content

Before you can manipulate or change something in an image, you have to select it. Photoshop Elements has various selection tools but the primary ones are the marquee tools, the lasso tools, and the selection brush.

The marquee tools

To see both the rectangular and the elliptical marquee tools, click the downward-pointing arrow at the corner of the marquee tool (labeled in Figure 6-7). You use these tools to select squarish or circular regions of your image. Simply click to select either tool, and then move your cursor into the image to see the cursor's crosshairs. Then click and drag with your mouse to mark off the desired region, as shown in Figure 6-7.

To make a perfectly square or perfectly round selection, hold down the Shift key while dragging with a marquee tool.

The lasso tools

Located next to the marquee tools are the three lasso tools: the lasso, the magnetic lasso, and the polygonal lasso (refer to Figure 6-3). The lasso tool is used to make freehand selections. Simply click the tool, move your cursor to your document, and draw a selection around what you want. In Figure 6-8, the lasso tool is being used to select just the barn.

Rectangular marquee tool

Figure 6-7: A moving dashed line, which Adobe refers to as *marching ants,* delineates your selected region.

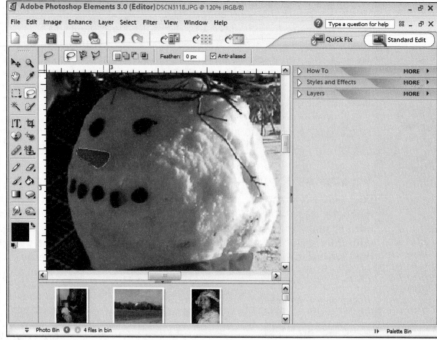

Figure 6-8:
The lasso tool is best for making selections around irregularly shaped objects, like the carrot nose on a snowman.

The magnetic lasso tool snaps itself to pixels that have a high degree of contrast to neighboring pixels, such as a dark object against a light background. Simply click the magnetic lasso where you want to begin and move the cursor around the object, and the selection line snaps to the object's outline.

The polygonal lasso tool enables you to snap to straight selection lines, one click at a time. Simply click in one location with your cursor to start, move to a new location, and click. Elements sets down a straight line between these points.

The selection brush

For my money, the selection brush is the greatest addition to the toolbox yet. With this selection tool, you simply choose your brush size and then drag your cursor over the area you want to select, as if you were painting it with a paintbrush.

Cutting, copying, and pasting

After you have something selected, you can cut, copy, or paste that selection anywhere in your document. These three commands are found on the Edit menu. They can also be implemented by using keyboard shortcuts, as shown in Table 6-1.

Table 6-1	Keyboard Shortcuts for Cut, Copy and Paste	
Command	*Windows*	*Macintosh*
Cut	Ctrl+X	⌘-X
Copy	Ctrl+C	⌘-C
Paste	Ctrl+V	⌘-V

After you make a selection in an image (as detailed in the preceding section), you're ready to delete, copy, move, or change your image by using the steps in the following exercise. This is a great way to move one element in an image closer to another, remove an object (or a person) from an image, or even replace one part of an image with a section you've copied from another image.

Selecting layers and tools in Photoshop images

If you find yourself trying to edit or alter part of your image but the program won't let you, here are a few tips that may help cut down on your frustration.

Photoshop Elements is a complex program with many tools and options, and if you don't choose just the right one, you may run into trouble. This can be confusing until you get used to it, but keep in mind that each tool in the Tools palette is designed to do just one job, For example, if you're entering text with the text tool and then you decide you want to move that text to another part of the page, you have to first select the move tool.

Another confusing feature is the concept of layers in Photoshop Elements. Essentially, layers enable Elements to separate an image into different parts, making it possible to manipulate those parts independently. This is useful, for example, if you create an image, fill it with the color blue, and then add text on top of it. The

blue area becomes the background layer and the text is added as a new layer on top of it. Because Elements treats the text as a new layer, you can move the text anytime without affecting other parts of the image.

To select a layer, simply click the layer name in the Layers palette (available by choosing Window⇨Layers). The active layer is shaded grey and appears darker than the other layers. You can switch from one layer to another by clicking the desired layer, and you can even move layers in the Layers palette by clicking and dragging. If you want a layer to cover another layer, for example, move it higher up the list.

If you're trying to do something in the program that you think should work but doesn't, you probably haven't selected the correct tool or layer. Keep this is mind, and you can save yourself a lot of grief as you find how to use this truly great program.

To cut and paste a selected area of an image, follow these steps:

1. **Using the selection tool of your choice, select the content you want to reposition.**

   See the preceding section for details on the different selection tools.

2. **Choose Edit⇨Cut.**

   The content disappears from the image, shown in Figure 6-9, where I've cut one of the seals out of this image. (Don't worry, you'll paste it back in to make it reappear in the next step.)

3. **Move your cursor to the part of the image where you want the content to be moved and choose Edit⇨Paste.**

   You can also move your cursor onto any other image open in Elements and paste the selection into a different image file. The part of the image that you selected and cut is inserted into the image on a new layer, as shown in Figure 6-10, where you can see that I've moved the seal a little away from its original location.

4. **Click the move tool (labeled in Figure 6-10).**

Figure 6-9:
You can cut
a section
out of an
image and
move it to
another
place in the
same image
or paste into
a different
image.

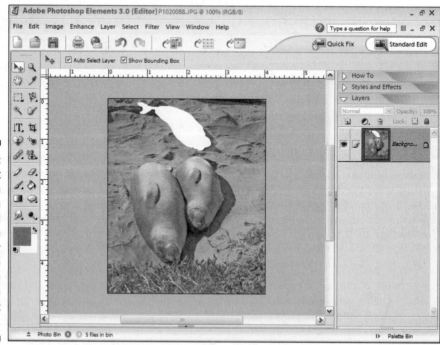

Move tool

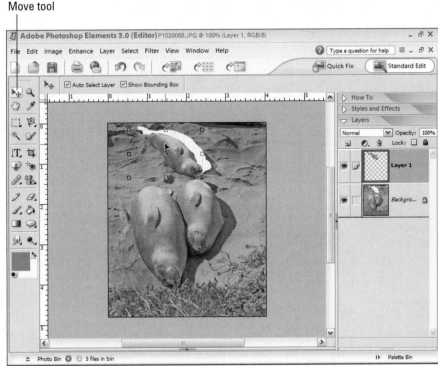

Figure 6-10:
The pasted
content is
inserted on
its own
layer so it
can be
moved to
any position
in the
image.

5. **Click and drag to reposition the pasted section, as shown in Figure 6-11.**

   The pasted content moves as you drag it around the screen. You can
   also use the arrow keys on your keyboard to move a layer (a good trick
   for making more precise adjustments). When you move the image, make
   sure to click in the middle of it; if you click a handle on the edge you risk
   resizing or rotating the pasted section.

   When you use the paste function, the newly created layer becomes active
   by default. However, it's easy to click another layer area and lose track of
   the layer you want to be manipulating. To make sure that the desired layer
   is active, check the Layers palette. The active layer is shaded grey and
   appears darker than the other layers. To select a layer, simply click the
   layer name in the Layers palette.

6. **To resize or rotate the pasted section, use the handles that appear
   around it.**

   If you want to resize a layer, click and drag a corner handle. To rotate the
   layer, place your cursor slightly beyond a corner handle until it changes
   to a curved, two-headed arrow. Using the curved arrow, drag your cursor
   clockwise or counterclockwise to rotate the image section. In the example, shown in Figure 6-11, I rotated the seal slightly so that it would line
   up better next to the other two seals.

Adobe Photoshop Elements 3.0 (Editor) seals rotated.psd @ 100% (Layer 1, RGB/8)

File   Edit   Image   Enhance   Layer   Select   Filter   View   Window   Help

Type a question for help

Quick Fix   Standard Edit

How To
Styles and Effects
Layers

Normal   Opacity: 100%

Lock:

Layer 1

Backgro...

Photo Bin   5 files in bin   Palette Bin

Figure 6-11:
Click the middle of the pasted section and drag to reposition the layer.

Working with the clone stamp tool

If you've deleted content or moved content from one spot to another, you probably have a hole that needs filling. The clone stamp tool (visible in Figure 6-1), copies content from one part of an image to another. You can use this tool to cover up unwanted items, such as a zit on someone's nose, by copying one area and pasting it over the item you want to remove. This is an amazing tool because it makes a precise replica of the pattern in the selected area, creating such a perfect patch that even your mother won't notice that you've cleaned up your acne.

To use the clone stamp tool, follow these steps:

1. **Select the clone stamp tool (labeled in Figure 6-12).**

2. **Position the cursor over an area of the image you want to sample.**

3. **Alt-click (Windows) or Option-click (Mac) to designate the sampling point, the portion you want to copy from.**

4. **Move your cursor to the area you want to cover, and click and drag to begin painting.**

   The sampled area fills the area you're painting, providing an ideal way to replace a pattern, such as the sand in Figure 6-12.

Clone stamp tool

Figure 6-12:
You can use
the clone
stamp tool
to copy a
pattern and
fill in or
replace
areas of an
image.

You can change the clone stamp tool options, such as size and opacity, by adjusting the tool options in the options bar at the top of the screen.

Repairing the Signs of Wear, Tear, and Age

If you have old photos stacked in drawers or boxes, chances are the images are getting cracked, scratched, ripped, torn, spotted, or stained. Perhaps entire sections of the image are destroyed.

If you find your favorite images have suffered this fate, don't panic. You can solve many of these problems by using Elements, after you can the images into your computer. The images probably can't be restored to their perfect original condition, but in most cases they can be salvaged so that you aren't reduced to heaving them on the dustheap of family history.

Scratches, tears, or cracked edges can be restored easily by replacing missing content with other content from the same image (or another image), as we've just seen. With a little ingenuity, you can bring back lost details, as well as remove stains and spots. No, this isn't an ad for a household cleaning product. Using the brush, smudge, dodge, and burn tools, by themselves or in concert, you can correct just about anything that's happened to your old photos. (Too bad we don't have tools like that in real life.)

Scratches, scuffs, and tears (along edges or even right down the middle of the image) are easily repaired with the following tools:

- ✔ **The Dust & Scratches filter:** Use this filter to remove scratches and scuff marks.

- ✔ **The smudge tool:** Blend away small blemishes, tiny scratches, spots, holes from a thumbtack, and more with the smudge tool.

- ✔ **The dodge tool:** This tool lightens dark regions and shadows to bring out detail lost to fading and stains.

- ✔ **The burn tool:** The reverse of the dodge tool, the burn tool darkens the region you apply it to. This is handy for scuff-marks and some types of stains.

Using the Dust & Scratches Filter

The purpose of the Dust & Scratches filter is apparent in its name. When you scratch the surface of a photo, you typically get a white line. Dust tends to form dark splotches on the photo's surface. The Dust & Scratches filter attempts to compensate for these defects by locating adjacent pixels with a high degree of difference in contrast and color. It then reduces those differences, resulting in a smoother, more even distribution of color and contrast. This filter is not the solution for really big scratches and tears, but it's just the thing for an image covered in multiple tiny scratches that has a beat-up, dusty look.

To use the Dust & Scratches filter, follow these steps:

1. **Select the portion of the photo that you want to correct.**

   If you're not sure how to make a selection, see the "Replacing and Editing Content" section, earlier this chapter. If you don't make a selection, the entire photo will be filtered.

2. **Choose Filter➪Noise➪Dust & Scratches.**

   The Dust & Scratches dialog box appears, as shown in Figure 6-13.

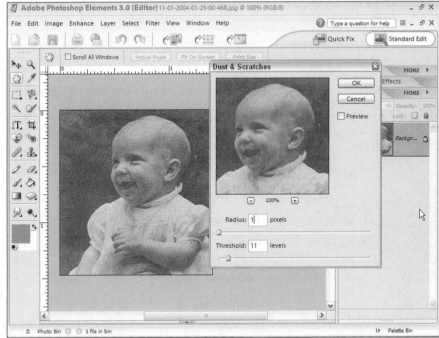

Figure 6-13:
To remove
visual
"noise"
such as
scuffs
and tiny
scratches,
use the
Dust &
Scratches
filter.

3. Adjust the Radius for the filter, as desired.

This setting determines the size of the pixel groups to be compared and their differences in contrast and color. You'll probably want to keep this setting on a low number, such as 1 or 2, and use the Threshold settings to balance it. Click to select the Preview option and your changes are applied to the image in real time so you can see the effect and find the best setting. I've left it unchecked in the example so you can see the difference between the original image and the preview of the altered image.

4. Adjust the Threshold setting, as desired.

This setting determines how great the disparity in contrast and color should when making adjustments to the pixels within the given radius. You shouldn't need to go over about 10 or 15 on most images but, again, use the preview window to find the best setting for your image

5. Check out the results in the Preview window.

Use the (+) and (-) buttons beside the Preview window to zoom in and out. Drag with your mouse inside the Preview window to reposition and view different sections of the image.

6. To apply the filter, click OK.

Working with the smudge tool

Small marks, stains, or other little blemishes can be smoothed away with the smudge tool (labeled in Figure 6-2). For example, you might use the smudge tool on freckles or small scars on a face, tiny imperfections on furniture, or a dot on a picture that came from dirt on the camera's lens, the scanner bed, or the original image's surface.

To smudge away small spots, stains, and image imperfections, follow these steps:

1. **Select the smudge tool.**

2. **Click to insert the cursor where you want to work in the image.**

3. **Drag a very small distance at a time.**

   You want to smudge pixels from the clean area around your imperfection onto the area to be smoothed away.

4. **Repeat this process, smudging in tiny increments, until the imperfection is gone.**

If this action doesn't produce the desired effect (for example, the smudging effect is too pronounced or in some other way too obvious), try switching to the clone stamp.

You can always start over again in Elements by using the Undo command to reverse your actions — such as a failed attempt at smudging away a blemish. You can choose Edit⇨Undo as many times as you want. (Elements has unlimited Undo capabilities and will reverse any actions taken since the last time a file was saved.)

I often find that using the clone stamp and the smudge tool in combination is the best strategy. First use the clone stamp to replace the content, and then use the smudge tool to smooth out any rough edges. Trial and error is again the best way to find the right balance for your image. Finding the right tool depends on the quality of your original image and how you want the final result to look.

Using the dodge and burn tools

Instead of replacing, covering, or blending pixels, the dodge, burn, and sponge tools (labeled in Figure 6-2) change brightness, contrast, and color. Based on real-world darkroom procedures, the dodge and burn tools work in tandem, having opposite but related effects on pixels. The dodge tool lightens, and the burn tool darkens.

To use the dodge or burn tool, follow these steps:

1. **Select the tool of your choice: dodge to lighten, or burn to darken.**

2. **Place your cursor over the area you want to lighten or darken.**

3. **Click and drag to dodge or burn.**

   The area of the image becomes lighter or darker accordingly.

You can adjust the size and exposure of the dodge and burn tools by changing the brush tool options in the options bar at the top of the screen. Use the Set the Brush Size option to increase or decrease the area affected by the dodge or burn tool. Use the Exposure option to increase or decrease the effect. Lowering the setting can soften the effect; raising the setting can strengthen the effect. For example, if you're trying to dodge a dark area in an image so that it becomes lighter and more of the details are visible in the shadows, lowering the Exposure setting can make the effect less dramatic, so you can lighten the area without making it look too light or underexposed.

 When I'm using tools such as burn and dodge I often use the Undo command (my favorite trick in Photoshop Elements). I try something, and if it doesn't look right, I choose Edit➪Undo (or press Ctrl+Z on a PC and ⌘-Z on a Mac) and then try again. With this technique, you can experiment with an image without worrying about doing irreparable damage to it. Photoshop Elements has unlimited levels of undo, so you can back up multiple steps.

Eliminating Red Eye

Red eye in an image occurs when the light generated by a camera's flash unit bounces off the retina of the subject being photographed. It's a common problem that has been turning friends and family members into red-eyed monsters for years. Fortunately, Elements has a special tool dedicated to this common problem: the red eye removal tool (labeled in Figure 6-2).

To use the red eye removal tool, follow these steps:

1. **Click to select the red eye removal tool in the Tools palette.**

2. **Click and drag the cursor over the red area of an eye.**

   As soon as you release the mouse button, the red is removed. In Figure 6-14 I have selected the center of the eye, but not yet released it to take the red out.

3. **Repeat Steps 1 and 2 as necessary.**

Figure 6-14:
You can remove the red glow from the eyes of your loved ones, pets, and any other creatures who get captured in your flash.

Sometimes the red eye removal tool does too good a job and not only removes the red but also blackens any reflective highlights on the pupils and leaves eyes looking lifeless and unnatural. You can compensate for this by using the dodge tool to lighten any highlights left behind or, if necessary, using the paintbrush to paint the highlights back in. And, as with any tool in Elements, don't forget you can always undo your work with the Edit⇨Undo command and try again.

Correcting Colors and Contrast Fast

The color and contrast in your photos can be out of whack for a multitude of reasons. Time, temperatures, sunlight, and grimy fingers are the usual suspects. Accidents can happen in the darkroom, camera, or film canister as well.

Regardless of the path your image took to its current condition, Elements offers quick fix mode to help you out. This new editing mode places a series of the most common photo correction tools in a handy sidebar, allowing you to choose option buttons or manual sliders to repair your image.

You don't want to go hog-wild with the quick fix tools, applying three or four of them at a time. In most cases, color and contrast issues can be corrected with one or maybe two tools. If your first choice doesn't solve the problem, click its corresponding reset button and give another option a try.

To use the quick fix tools, click the Quick Fix button at the top of the main application window. The Quick Fix sidebar appears, as shown in Figure 6-15.

The following options are available in the Quick Fix sidebar:

✔ To improve color balance, shadows, and highlight details, click the Auto button next to the words Smart Fix in the General Fixes section. Use the Amount slider below the Smart Fix Auto button to vary the amount of the adjustment made to your image.

✔ To improve contrast and color in your image, click the Auto button next to Levels in the Lighting section. Auto Levels improves contrast and color by looking at the lightest and darkest pixels in your image and compensating when the variance is not sufficient

✔ To improve the image's contrast without affecting color, click the Auto button next to Contrast in the Lighting section. Use the Lighten Shadows, Darken Highlights, and Midtone Contrast sliders to make manual adjustments.

Just below the Lighting section of the Quick Fix sidebar is a Color section. Elements claims that the Auto button in the Color section improves color and contrast automatically, but you'll have more control if you use the sliders in the Color section to make manual changes. It's easy to overdo color correction and dramatically change the natural colors of an image.

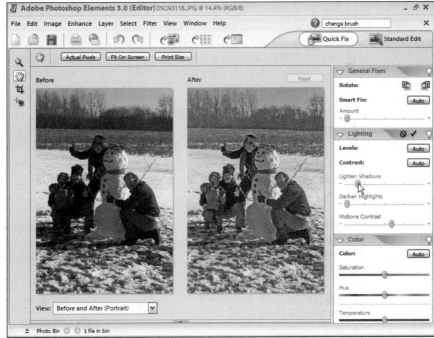

Figure 6-15: Element's Quick Fix tools make it easy to make many adjustments, including lightening the shadows in an image with too much contrast.

Choosing the Best Format for the Web

Before you put your images on your Web pages, you need to make sure that they're in the right format and *optimized*, a process of compression and reduction designed to give an image the highest possible visual quality at the smallest possible file size.

Why optimize? To provide the best experience for your site visitors, you want them to see your images quickly. To view an image on a Web page, a browser has to first download the image file to the local computer. The bigger the file size, the longer it takes to download. The better an image is optimized, the faster it will appear.

Fortunately, this is an area where Elements excels. In the Save for Web dialog box, available from the File menu, you can make a wide range of adjustments to an image and convert it to any Web format, all in one easy-to-use interface. You can even preview your image — complete with file size and estimated download time — as you adjust the settings. This makes it easy to see the effects of your compression and reduction adjustments in real time and experiment until you get the results you want. The trick is to make the image as small as you can while keeping the image at an acceptable quality.

One of the benefits of using the Save for Web dialog box is that Elements creates a copy of your image when you're finished, leaving your original file untouched and creating a new file ready for your Web site. (It's a good idea to save your high-quality original because any edits you make in Photoshop later will work better on a higher resolution version of the image.)

Today's Web browsers support three file formats: GIF (Graphics Interchange Format), JPEG (Joint Photographic Experts Group), and PNG (Portable Network Graphics). You want to choose the format that's best for the type of image you're working with. In general, use JPEG for multicolored images such as photographs and GIFs for line art and drawings. PNG is not commonly used on the Web but I cover it here because it's included in Elements and may be used more on the Web in the future.

Using GIF for art

GIF is an 8-bit format that can have a maximum of 256 colors. When you're preparing a GIF file for the Web, the more you limit the number of colors, the smaller the file size becomes.

If you've ever enlarged a digital image, you know that it's made up of lots and lots of tiny dots. And if you look closely, you'll see that the dots are different colors and even shades of colors that blend on the computer screen to create the illusion of a solid image. When you reduce the colors in a GIF file, you're essentially taking away some of the colored dots. Often the change is imperceptible when you look at the image at full size, but you have to be careful. If you take away too many colors, the change can be dramatic and may not be worth the reduction in file size. In the upcoming optimization section, you see how the Save for Web dialog box makes it easy to compare how an image looks with different color settings before you save your changes.

GIFs can also be compressed, a process that further reduces file size. GIFs use a compression method called LZW, after its creators, Lempel, Ziv, and Welch. When you compress an image, you essentially remove unused space within the file. This a lossless compression method that causes little change in the appearance of the image but can greatly enhance download speed.

Because GIF supports a maximum of only 256 colors in an image, you shouldn't use this format to optimize an image with thousands of colors. GIF is best suited for images with a limited number of total colors, preferably with a high degree of contrast where the edges at which two colors meet are sharply defined. The logo in Figure 6-16 is a prime candidate for GIF optimization.

Figure 6-16:
The GIF format is best for logos, cartoons, and other images that use only a few colors.

Using JPEG for photos

JPEG stands for the Joint Photographic Experts Group, an organization of companies and academic institutions around the world. The JPEG format is designed for continuous tone images that contain a nearly unlimited range of colors and shades of grey.

JPEG is a 24-bit format, giving it a color depth of 2 to the 24th power — or 16,777,215 maximum colors. This compression method is designed to favor changes in brightness and contrast over changes in color hue, an approach that mimics the limitations of our own eyes. Unlike GIF, JPEG uses a compression method that removes information from the image, but it does so in a clever way, taking advantage of the fact that most of us are better at noticing brightness and contrast differences than minute changes in color tone.

Because JPEG compression removes data from a file it's called a lossy compression method. The challenge with JPEGs is to compress them as much as possible without losing too much quality. In the optimizing section that follows, you see how the Save for Web dialog box makes it easy to compare the effects of compression settings until you have the best balance of size and quality for your Web image.

The second letter in the JPEG acronym — *P* for *Photographic* — is a telling clue as to what types of images are best saved in this format. JPEGs are preferred for photographs, photo-realistic images, and any graphics that use millions of colors and lots of color gradation, or shades of gray, like the image shown in Figure 6-17.

Figure 6-17:
The JPEG
format is
best for
photographs
and other
images with
millions of
colors or
gradients.

Understanding PNG

PNG, like GIF, uses a lossless compression method. It also has both 8-bit and 24-bit options. The 8-bit version is comparable to GIF in producing quality images with low file sizes. PNG can often produce slightly large files, but only by a kilobyte or two.

Unfortunately, the 24-bit version of PNG doesn't compete well against JPEG. Because the PNG compression method is lossless (removing no additional data from the image), files optimized in the 24-bit format are typically double the size than when optimized in the JPEG format. This format is not widely used on the Internet and I generally recommend you stick with GIFs or JPEGs for your images.

Optimizing Images for the Web

The process of optimizing an image for the Web involves several steps, all of which can affect the appearance of an image as well as its file size. To help you sort through these settings to find the best combination for your images, Elements includes a special dialog box just for converting images for the Web.

Make sure you do your cropping, editing, and resizing before you use the Save for Web dialog box. You get better results when you edit an image at the highest quality.

In the Save for Web dialog box, you can preview your image and select your optimization settings, choosing the format, amount of compression, and color options. To display the Save for Web dialog box, open any image in Elements and choose File⇨Save for Web.

The dialog is broken into separate panes so you can compare your original image (on the left) with the optimized results (on the right) to decide which settings give the best results. Below the original image, you see its file name and file size. Below the optimized image, you see the effects of the optimization settings and the new file size and estimated download time.

Download time is calculated by using an estimated Internet connection. You can change the setting by right-clicking the file size and optimization time text. This displays the Preview pop-up menu, shown in Figure 6-18, from which you can select the access speed of your choice. (These days most people have at least a 56K modem, so I prefer that setting.)

Optimizing GIF images

If you're working with a graphic, such as a logo, a cartoon character, or some other drawing that has less than 256 total colors, you should use the GIF options in the Save for Web dialog box and reduce the colors as much as possible. To help make up for the degradation in image quality that can happen when colors are removed, GIF uses a trick called dithering. *Dithering* involves alternating pixels in a checkerboardlike pattern to create subtle color variations, even with a limited color palette. The effect can smooth the edges in an image and make it appear that the image uses more colors.

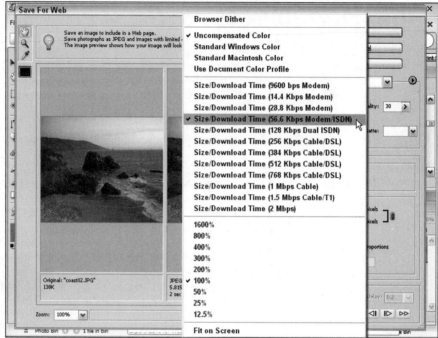

Figure 6-18:
The Preview
pop-up
menu lets
you to
choose
between
multiple
modem,
ISDN, cable,
or DSL
speeds.

To convert an image to a GIF with the Save for Web dialog box, follow these steps:

1. **Open the image that you want to use on your Web site in the Editor window of Photoshop Elements.**

   Choose File⇨Open, locate the photo on your hard drive, and double-click to open it.

2. **Choose File⇨Save For Web.**

   The Save For Web dialog box appears.

3. **In the Optimized File Format list, choose GIF.**

   GIF is the preferred image format for line art, such as a logo shown in Figure 6-19.

4. **Set the number of colors in the Colors box.**

   The fewer colors you use, the smaller the file size and the faster the image will download. For an even smaller file size, reduce the number to 4 or 8, but be careful. The ideal number depends on your image; if you go too far, you'll adversely affect the image's appearance.

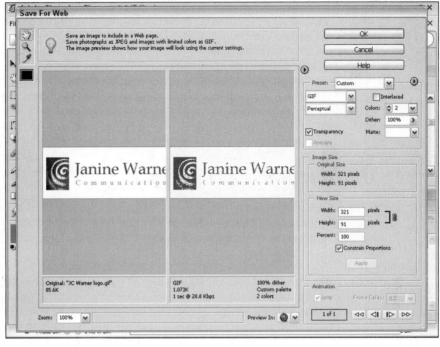

Figure 6-19:
You can see
the effects
of reducing
colors in a
GIF image
so you don't
reduce too
much.

5. **Click the Transparency box if you want to maintain a transparent area in your image.**

   Any area of the image that was transparent when you created the image in the editor appears transparent in the preview window. If you don't have a transparent area in your image, this setting will have no effect.

   Transparency is a good trick for making text or another part of an image appear to float on a Web page because the transparent background won't display on the Web page. You can select transparency as a background option in the New File dialog box when you create an image.

6. **Leave the other settings unchanged.**

   Unless you have a lot of experience with creating images for the Web, leave the remaining settings unchanged and trust that Elements has made the best choices for you.

7. **Click OK.**

   The Save Optimized As dialog box opens.

8. **Enter a name for the image and save it into the images folder in your Web site folder.**

9. **Repeat these steps for each image you want to prepare for your site.**

Trial and error is a great technique in the Save for Web dialog box. In Figure 6-19, for example, I reduced the image to only two colors to see what it would look like and to show you that the preview window provides a good way to test your settings. (Don't reduce your images as dramatically as I did in the example.) As you can see in the preview image on the right, reducing the image to only two colors made the text almost unreadable because it removed the black that was used in the lettering. When I increased the setting to eight colors, it looked fine and was still only 2.1KB, so that's the setting I finally saved it in.

Optimizing JPEG images

If you have an image with lots of colors, such as a photograph or a highly complex drawing or painting, convert it to the JPEG format. This format is ideal for optimizing continuous tone images and is capable of supporting some 16.7 million colors.

With JPEGs, instead of choosing a number of colors, you choose how much compression should be applied, a process that removes data to make the image smaller. In the Save for Web dialog box in Elements, you can compare compression levels on the same image and see how the quality is affected. Essentially, the lower the quality of the image, the faster it will download. However, don't go too low or the image won't look like much when it's viewed.

If you have a digital photograph or another image that you want to prepare for the Web, follow these steps to optimize and save it:

1. **Open the photograph that you want to use on your Web site.**

   Choose File➪Open, locate the photo on your hard drive, and double-click to open it.

2. **Choose File➪Save For Web.**

   The Save for Web dialog box appears, as shown in Figure 6-20.

3. **In the Optimized File Format list, choose JPEG.**

   JPEG is the preferred image format for photographs and other multicolored images.

4. **Set the compression quality.**

   Use the preset options: Low, Medium, High, Very High, or Maximum from the pull-down list. Or use the slider in the Quality field to make more precise adjustments. Lowering the quality reduces the file size and makes the image download more quickly.

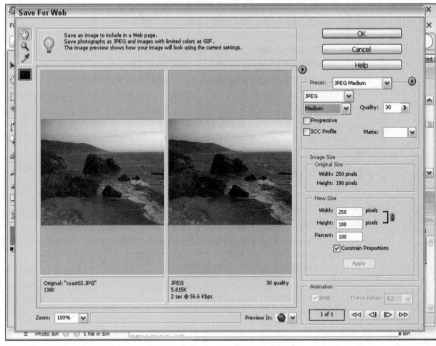

Figure 6-20:
You can preview the effects of different compression settings to find the best combination.

Elements uses a compression scale of 0 to 100 for JPEG, with 0 the lowest possible quality (the highest amount of compression and the smallest file size) and 100 the highest possible quality (the least amount of compression and the biggest file size). You can use the slider in the dialog box to make smaller adjustments until you reach the best balance between image quality and file size.

I prefer to change compression levels manually, as described in Step 4, because I like being able to make minute adjustments to get the best balance of quality and file size. If you prefer a quick fix, use the Preset pull-down list. The three JPEG options — Low, Medium, and High — automatically sets compression to 10, 30, and 60, respectively.

5. Leave the other settings unchanged.

Unless you have a lot of experience with creating images for the Web, let Elements make the choices for you.

6. Click OK.

The Save Optimized As dialog box opens.

7. Enter a name for the image and save it into the images folder in your Web site folder.

8. Repeat these steps for each image you want to prepare for your site.

Creating Banners and Buttons

You can enter text directly into a Web page and format text with any font on your computer. Unfortunately, for the text to display in the font you desire, that font has to be on your user's computer also. Using text on a Web page works fine when you aren't too concerned about the font or you're using common fonts, such as Times or Arial, but if you want to create beautifully designed banners with more unusual fonts, such as Papyrus (shown in Figures 6-21 and 6-22), you're better off creating a banner or button as an image. That way, you can guarantee that your text will display on a visitor's computer exactly as it did when you created it. You can also use colored backgrounds, or even images as backgrounds, as shown in the examples in this section.

Why not create all the text for your Web pages as images? For one thing, it takes a lot more time to create images than to just type your text into a page in a program such as FrontPage. But more important, images take longer to download than text. You should use this trick sparingly and save it for text that really matters, such as the banners at the top of your pages or the buttons that you use to navigate your site.

Before you start creating a banner or button, select the color you want for the background in the default foreground and background box at the bottom of the toolbox (labeled in Figure 6-2). When you create a new file, you can apply only the Background color choice.

To create a button or banner graphic for your Web pages, follow these steps:

1. **If it's not already open, launch Photoshop Elements.**

2. **Choose File⇨New⇨Blank File.**

   The New dialog box appears.

3. **In the Name box, enter a name for the button or banner.**

4. **Specify the width and height.**

   If you're creating a banner graphic, most Web designers recommend that you create a banner that is 700 pixels or less wide because it will display well on most computer screens at that size. If you're creating a button, consider making it 150 to 300 pixels wide, depending on the design of your page. In Figure 6-21, I created an image that is 200 by 80 pixels.

   The height of your banner and buttons can be anything you like, but remember you're using up real estate on your page, and the bigger you make these images the longer they take to download.

5. **Set the resolution to 72 pixels/inch.**

   If you're creating an image for print, you should use a much higher resolution. When you're creating an image for the Web, however, the graphic will be viewed on a computer monitor, and most computer monitors display only 72 pixels/inch. The more pixels, the larger the file size and the longer the file takes to download.

6. **If you haven't already set the background color (see the tip preceding this set of steps), specify the color now.**

   Your options are White, Background Color (which uses the background color selected in the toolbox), or Transparent (which creates an image with no background). The Transparent option is a good choice if you want your words to look like they float on a page. (Don't worry if you haven't preselected the color you want for the background color; you can change it in Step 12.)

7. **Click OK.**

   The blank image is created with the background color specified in Step 6.

8. **Select the text tool in the Tools palette.**

9. **Use the text formatting options in the options bar at the top of the screen to specify the font face, size, style, and color.**

10. **Click to insert your cursor on the new blank image, and begin typing to enter the text you want on your button or banner.**

   If you want to change the font or other text formatting options after you add text to an image, make sure the text tool is selected from the Tools palette, click and highlight to select the text you want to change, and then make an adjustments in the options bar at the top of the screen.

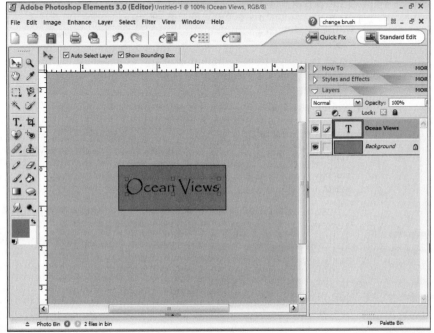

Figure 6-21:
You can use Elements to create custom banners and buttons for your Web site.

11. If the Layers palette is not already open, choose Window⇨Layers.

Notice that the text appears on its own layer, separate from the background of the image, unless you created a transparent background, which is not treated as a separate layer.

12. Edit the background and the text layers independently.

Click a layer to select it. For example, if you want to change the background color, select the background layer and choose Edit⇨Fill. In the Fill Layer dialog box, use the pull-down menu in the Use box to specify the background color (the color represented by the swatches at the bottom of the toolbox). A transparent background can't be edited independently, so you can't fill it with a color without affecting the text, but you can edit the text without altering the transparent background.

13. Choose File⇨Save For Web.

The Save for Web dialog box appears.

14. In the Optimized File Format list, choose GIF.

GIF is the best format for images that use only a few colors, such as logos or banners.

15. Set the number in the Colors box.

Limiting the number of colors helps reduce the file size and make the image download more quickly. For an even smaller file size, reduce this number as much as you can without affecting the appearance of the image too adversely.

16. Save the button or banner and give it a new name.

Repeat these steps for each button or banner you want to create.

Make sure you save the original Photoshop Elements image as well as the optimized GIF or JPEG image you create for the Web. When you save an image for the Web, the layers are compressed. If you keep the original, layered image, you can make changes later more easily.

As you see in Figure 6-22, you can also create banners or buttons by inserting text over a photograph. Simply open an existing image, and follow Steps 4 through 15. If you use a photograph, also change Step 13 to save your image as a JPEG and Step 14 to specify your preferred compression option instead of reducing the number of colors.

Figure 6-22:
Add text to a
photograph.

Chapter 7

Organizing Images and Creating Photo Albums and Galleries

. . . .

In This Chapter

▶ Working with the Organizer

▶ Viewing your organized images

▶ Creating photo albums and Web galleries

. . . .

*1*f your household is anything like mine, you have a few catchall areas, where things accumulate without much order. Among these, you probably have a drawer or box full of photos and other memorabilia you've been intending to arrange in a photo album or scrapbook. Often, it seems you don't even realize how disorganized you are until you need a particular photo, drawing, or clipping and can't find it.

If you're tired of digging around boxes and opening every folder on your hard drive when you want to find an image, you'll appreciate the features in Photoshop Elements 3 that make it easier to keep track of images and turn folders full of digital pictures into well-designed photo album pages and Web galleries.

In addition to being a great photo editing program, Elements 3 includes a feature called Organizer. In the first part of this chapter, you discover how to create catalogs and collections of digital photos, drawings, and scanned documents with Organizer so you can find them more easily in the future. In the second part of this chapter, you find instructions for using the creation tools in Elements 3 to build photo album pages and Web photo galleries that you can add to your Web site.

Getting Organized

Elements has three main work areas:

- **Editor,** where you resize and alter images (covered in Chapter 6)
- **Organizer,** where you select images and organize them in catalogs and collections
- **Creator,** where you can use automated tools to create a variety of projects, including photo albums, calendars, and Web galleries

In the following sections, I cover Organizer and Creator with a series of exercises that begin with selecting images in Organizer and culminate in a complete Web photo gallery generated by Creator. (Photo galleries are ideal additions to sites like the ones you can create with the templates in Chapters 11 through 14.)

Starting Organizer

Knowing where your images are is an important first step to creating any image project. Taking time to get your photos and other images into collections before you start creating projects such as photo albums will save you time later and help ensure you have all your images handy, even if they come from different sources.

You can open Elements' Organizer window in a couple of ways. The simplest way is to select View and Organize Photos on the Welcome screen (see Figure 7-1), which appears when you first launch Elements. To open Organizer from the Editor window, click the Photo Browser icon at the top of the screen.

If you've already opened Elements, you can start Organizer by clicking the Photo Browser button on the shortcuts bar, as shown in Figure 7-2. Opening the Organizer can take a few seconds, so be patient.

Touring the Organizer workspace

Before you begin using Organizer, it's a good idea to take some time and get to know the environment. At the top of the screen is the title bar, which tells you that you're in the Organizer (see Figure 7-3). Below that are some familiar menus, including File and Edit.

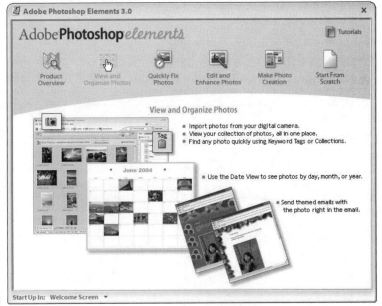

Figure 7-1:
The Welcome screen features links directly to the main environments in Elements, including the Organizer.

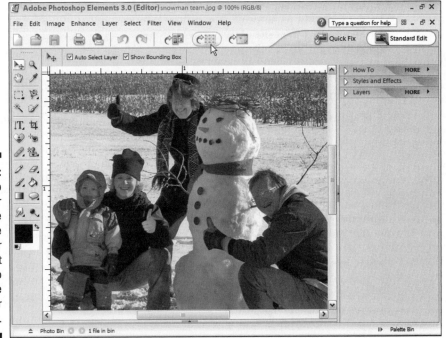

Figure 7-2:
The Photo Browser icon at the top of the Editor makes it easy to open the Organizer window.

Figure 7-3:
The
Organizer
makes it
easy to look
at several
images at
once.

On the right side of the workspace in Photo Browser, you see two tabs labeled Tags and Collections (these are not available from Date view):

- ✔ The Tags tab features six categories: Favorites, Hidden, People, Places, Events, and Other, for images that defy categorization.

- ✔ The Collections tab enables you to view the images you've collected and stored in named groups by using the organizational options, described in the following section.

In the top-right corner is the Help box, where you can type a question and press Enter (or click the little question mark button) to query the help files. Just below the Help field, you find two icons that enable you to control how your images are displayed in the Organizer: Photo Browser and Date View. If you prefer to organize your images according to when they were taken, you'll like Date view, as shown in Figure 7-4. If you prefer to organize images according to what they contain, the main Photo Browser window (refer to Figure 7-3) is your best choice. Note that not all the Organizer options are available in Date view.

Figure 7-4:
Use Date
view to
organize
your
images
in a
calendar
window
based on
the date
they were
taken or
saved.

Gathering Your Images

Elements offers a number of ways to group and organize images. You start with a *catalog*, Adobe's name for its system for managing images. As you create a catalog, Elements gathers information about each image (including its file name, location on your computer, size, and date) and stores the information in a database. Elements doesn't actually move your images anywhere; it just records their location on your system and stores other relevant information about them to help you keep track of images and create projects in the future.

You can further organize your images into *collections*, which makes it easier to select only the pictures you like best from a large group. You can create a collection by choosing specific images from multiple catalogs, or a subcategory of a catalog. For example, if you take 100 pictures at a family reunion, you probably want to show about 10 or 20 of them to family and friends. By gathering images into a collection, you can easily select a subset of images from a catalog or a group of catalogs and then use them to make a *creation*, such as a Web gallery (covered in the "Creating a Web gallery" section at the end of this chapter).

Creating a catalog

To help you stay organized, you can create different catalogs for different groups of photos. You can also create collections within a catalog, as you see in the following section. The first step is creating a catalog.

Follow these steps to create a catalog in Elements:

1. **With the Organizer window open in Elements, choose File➪Catalog.**

   A prompt appears, as shown in Figure 7-5 with the New, Open, Save As, and Recover buttons.

Figure 7-5: Creating catalogs for different collections of images is a great way to stay organized.

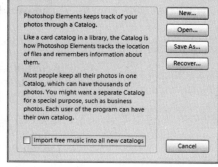

2. **Click the New button to start a new catalog.**

   The New Catalog dialog box opens.

3. **In the File Name box, type a name for the catalog.**

   You can call the catalog anything you want, but it's helpful to make it something you'll remember so you can keep track of multiple catalogs. I like to use descriptive names, such as Jenny's Wedding or New House.

4. **Click Save.**

   The catalog is created and opened, ready for you to add photos.

Follow these steps to add your photos to the catalog:

1. **To open a catalog, choose File➪Catalog and then click the Open button.**

   If you have just created a catalog, it should be open and empty in Organizer.

2. Choose File➪Get Photos.

You can select images from a camera, a scanner, a folder on your computer, or a mobile phone — or by searching if you don't know the location of the images. The search option lets you quickly identify images on any available hard drive, CD, or other storage device connected to your system.

You can always add more images after a catalog is created. This is a good way to retrieve images from different places on your computer system or from different storage devices. Each time you add more photos, you can choose from the full list of options, including From Camera, From Scanner, and From Files and Folders. However, if you add images from a removable storage device, such as a memory card or a CD, that source will have to be inserted into the computer when you want to retrieve those images again.

3. To add images that are already on your computer, choose From Files and Folders.

The Get Photos from Files and Folders dialog box opens.

4. Navigate around your hard drive to find the folder containing the photos, and then click the folder name or the names of the individual files you want to select.

You can click and drag to select multiple images, or use Ctrl-click (on a PC) or ⌘-Click (on a Mac) to select nonconsecutive images. If you select a folder name, all the images in the folder are added to the catalog.

If you're using Windows, you can choose how you want to display your files in the Get Photos from Files and Folders dialog box to make it easier to identify the images you want to add to your catalog. In Figure 7-6, I selected the Thumbnails option, which displays small versions of the images so I can see what they look like. Use the List option if you prefer to view your images by file name, or use Details to see the creation date, size, and file type. These options are available from any folder on your system and from all the dialog boxes you use to open or get images in Elements.

5. Click the Get Photos button.

The images you selected are added to your open catalog and are displayed in the work area, as shown in Figure 7-7.

6. To add more images, repeat Steps 2 through 5.

When you add additional images to an existing catalog, the new images are displayed in their own window when you click Get Photos. To view the entire catalog, click the Back to All Photos button at the top of the work area.

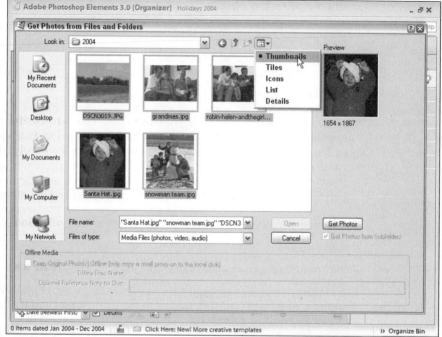

Figure 7-6:
It's easy create a catalog with photos from your computer, a CD, or another connected device.

Figure 7-7:
You can always add more images to a catalog after it's created.

Want to see larger thumbnails of your images in Photo Browser? Click and drag the slider (located in the lower-right corner of the work area) to make the images larger or smaller.

Creating collections

One of the best ways to further organize your images is to create collections within your catalogs. You can create as many collections as you want within each catalog. Collections can be used to create a variety of projects, such as calendars and photo albums.

The first step is to create a collection and give it a name. Follow these steps:

1. **With the Organizer open in Elements, click the Collections tab.**

2. **Click the New button.**

3. **In the drop-down list, choose New Collection to create a single collection.**

   The New Collection Group option in the list lets you organize multiple collections into a group that can be managed collectively.

4. **In the Create Collection dialog box, enter a name for the collection.**

   You can call your collection anything you like, but it's always good practice to use a descriptive name that will help you identify its contents later, such as "Photos of dad acting goofy." In the example shown in Figure 7-8, I created separate collections for three groups of images and named them Halloween, New House, and Nieces.

   If you want to assign your new collection to an existing collection group, use the Group pull-down list to make the association. You can also add notes in this dialog box to describe the collection.

5. **Click OK.**

   The collection is created and its name is added to the list of collections in the Collections tab.

6. **Add your images to the collection.**

   Drag an image from the open catalog in the Organizer work area and drop it on the collection name in the Collections panel. Or right-click an image, choose Add to Collection, and select the name of the collection from the drop-down list. Collections are automatically saved and associated with the catalog.

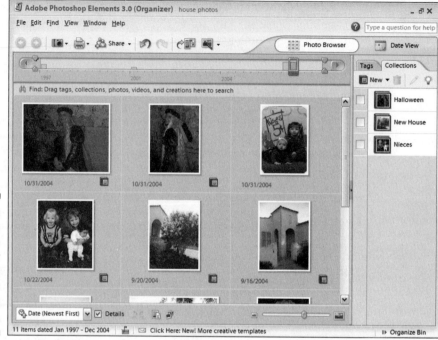

Figure 7-8:
You can
organize
images by
creating
collections
within a
catalog.

Assigning tags to identify images

After your images are in a catalog, you keep track of and prioritize them by assigning tags to them. To assign a tag, simply right-click an image in the Organizer window, choose Attach Tag, and then select from a list of categories and subcategories. For example, if you choose People, as I have in the example in Figure 7-9, you can then further categorize the image as Friend or Family. You can create as many categories and subcategories as you like. In the example, I created a subcategory called Warner Family.

To create a category or subcategory, click the arrow next to New at the top of the Collections tab, enter a name in the Create Category or Create Subcategory dialog box, and specify any relevant associations. For example, when I created the Warner Family subcategory, I associated it with the Family subcategory of the People category.

Elements then lets you view images in groups based on any category or subcategory. For example, if you click the People option in the Tags tab, all images tagged as People appear in the work area. If you choose Family, only images tagged as People with the subcategory Family are shown.

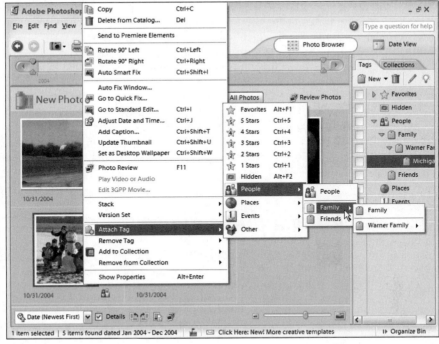

Figure 7-9:
You can tag
your images
to organize
them in
categories
such as
People or
Places —
and even
give them 5-
star ratings.

The Star options (shown in the list in Figure 7-9) are for rating images. For example, you can tag all your best pictures from all your family gatherings with 5 stars and then view only images with 5 stars to see all your best shots at once.

You can even use tags in combination. For example, you can tag photos to identify them as Family photos and rank them with star ratings. Then you can search for only your best family images.

Creating Photo Albums and Web Galleries

After all the organizing in the first half of this chapter, it's time for the fun part, turning those images into a photo album or Web gallery so you can show them off to family and friends. After all, what good are all those great pictures if you keep them hidden on your computer's hard drive?

This is where Element's Creator features come in. The Create button is on the shortcuts bar at the top of the screen in both the Organizer and Editor views in Elements. When you click the Create button, the Creation Setup window opens, as shown in Figure 7-10, and you can choose from a list of Creation types, including Photo Album Pages, Postcards and Wall Calendar.

In this section, you find step-by-step instructions for creating a photo album and a Web photo gallery. The Postcard and Wall Calendar options are best suited for creating designs that will be printed, so I don't cover them in this book. If you want to add a calendar to your Web site, try one of the online calendar services featured in Appendix A, such as the free calendars at `calendar.yahoo.com`.

Creating a photo album

When you create a photo album in Elements, you organize your images onto pages that can be printed or saved as a PDF file and attached to an e-mail message or linked to a Web site.

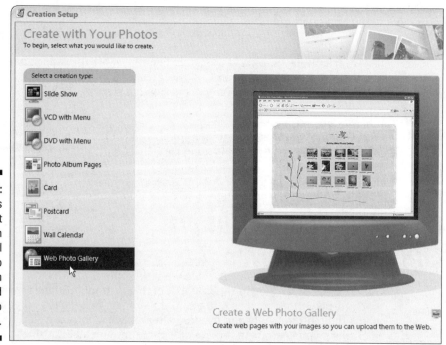

Figure 7-10: Elements makes it easy to turn digital images into photo album pages and Web galleries.

You can't create a photo album until you have created a catalog (a good first step to organizing your images anyway). The instructions in the "Gathering Your Images" section, earlier in this chapter, show you how to create catalogs and collections.

To create a photo album, follow these steps:

1. **Click the Create button or choose File➪New➪Creation.**

   After a few seconds, the Creation Setup window appears.

2. **In the Select a Creation Type list, double-click Photo Album Pages.**

   The Create Photo Album Pages wizard opens.

3. **Specify the style of your album and choose from a list of options:**

   a. **Click to select the style you want to use for your photo album.**

      The panel on the right side of the window features a long list of style choices, with thumbnail samples of each option. If you click the style name once, you can view a sample of the style in the main portion of the window, as shown in Figure 7-11.

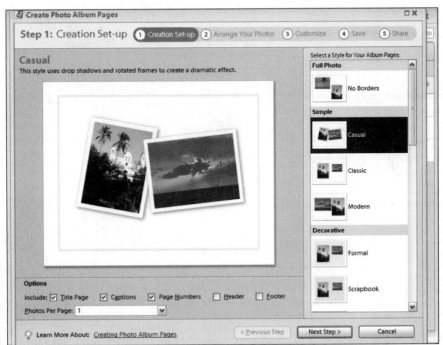

Figure 7-11: Choose a style for your album pages.

 b. **At the bottom of the window, select the page options you want to include.**

  Click to select the options you want, such as page numbers, headers, and footers. If you click the Captions option, you can add captions in the Customize dialog box later. You can also choose how many images you want to include on each page by selecting a number from the Photos Per Page list.

 c. **Click the Next Step button.**

  The Arrange Your Photos window opens

4. **At the top of the Arrange Your Photos window, click the Add Photos button.**

 The Add Photos dialog box opens, as shown in Figure 7-12.

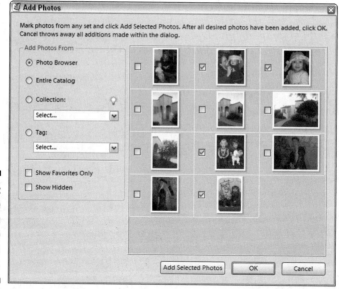

Figure 7-12:
Select the photos you want to include in your album.

5. **Add photos from a combination of sources:**

 a. **Use the options under Add Photos From to view photos in your catalogs or collections.**

  When you select an option from the left pane, such as Entire Catalog, the images are displayed as thumbnails in the right pane.

 b. **Click to select the check box next to each photo that you want to include on your album pages.**

c. Click OK.

The Add Photos dialog box closes and the Create Photo Album Pages window becomes fully visible again.

6. In the Create Photo Album Pages window, click and drag to change the order in which your photos will appear in the album, and then click Next Step.

Note that each image thumbnail (one for each image that you added to the album) has a page number. You can use your mouse to drag the thumbnails to another position in the album. As you drag, a vertical line follows your mouse, indicating the location where the image will end up when you release the mouse button.

7. In the Customize window, double-click the title area to edit the text, and then click Done.

Replace the words *Double-click to Insert Title* with your caption, and use the options in the dialog box to specify the font, size, alignment, and style of the title text. In the example shown in Figure 7-13, I've changed the title to *Our Family Tree.*

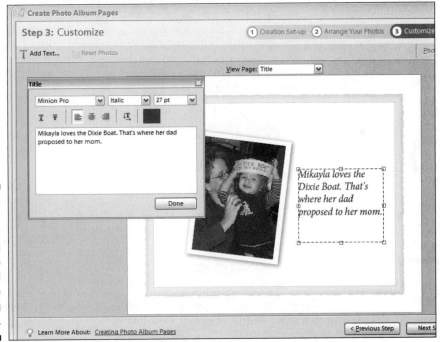

Figure 7-13:
You can add titles and captions to your photo album and change the formatting of the text.

8. **Use the View Page pull-down list at the top of the Customize window to view and edit the pages in your photo album, and then click Next Step.**

   You can edit a caption on your album pages, just as you edited the title on the first page, by double-clicking the caption area and using the options in the Caption dialog box to specify the font, size, alignment, and style of the text. You can write captions as long as you like, but if you want your images to appear on one page, limit yourself to no more than a sentence or two for each image.

9. **In the Album Pages Name box, name your album and then click Save.**

   You can type a name or use the title page for the name by clicking the Use Title for Name option.

10. **In the Share window, click to select the option that corresponds to what you want to do with your album.**

    Your options are as follows:

    - **Create a PDF:** Shown in Figure 7-14, this option saves your album in portable document format (PDF), a common format for sharing documents on the Internet. If you choose this option, you are prompted with three quality options. Optimize for Viewing Onscreen makes the PDF file as small as possible (the best option if you want to e-mail your photo album or add it to a Web page). Optimize for Printing is the best option if you want to print your file (you can e-mail a PDF at this quality setting, but it will take longer to download). Use Full Resolution if you want to leave your images untouched.

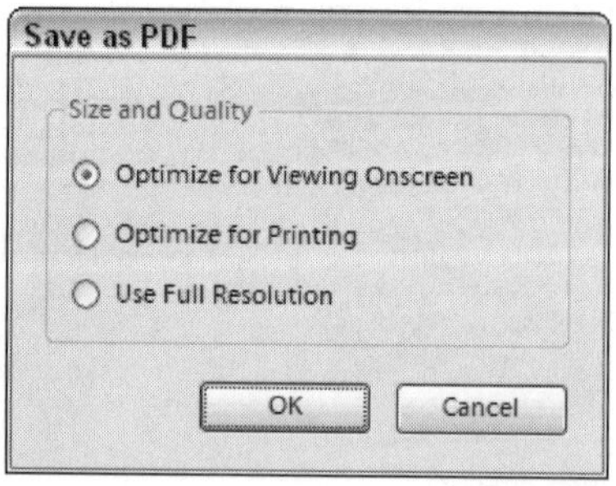

Figure 7-14:
You can save your album as a PDF file.

Save as PDF

Size and Quality

⦿ Optimize for Viewing Onscreen

○ Optimize for Printing

○ Use Full Resolution

OK   Cancel

    - **Print:** This option opens the Print dialog box, where you can specify how you want to print your pages.

    - **E-mail:** This option creates a PDF file and also automates the process of sending that PDF file as an attachment to an e-mail message. When you select E-mail option, the Attach Creation Items to E-mail dialog box opens, and you can enter the e-mail address of the person you want to send the album to and specify the quality you want for your images. (Unless you and the person you are sending the photo album to both have fast Internet connections, choose the Optimize for Viewing on a Screen option so that the file will download more quickly.) Elements takes care of everything: It creates a PDF file of your album, launches your e-mail program, composes a message to the address you entered, and attaches the PDF file to the message. All you have to do is add a personal message to the e-mail and click the Send button.

11. **When you're finished, click Done.**

    Elements saves your creation.

PDF, which stands for Portable Document Format, is a common format for documents that contain text or graphics and is especially useful when you want to preserve formatting. You can add a PDF file to a Web page as you would to any other page in your Web site — by creating a link. (You can find instructions for creating links in Chapter 8.)

If you want to use your PDF file on your Web site, make sure to give it a Web-friendly name, meaning don't use special characters or spaces. To view a PDF file, your visitors must have Adobe Acrobat Reader, a free viewer that can be easily downloaded from www.adobe.com and is now built into most Web browsers.

Creating a Web gallery

One of my favorite features, the Web Photo Gallery option enables you to quickly and easily design an online photo gallery that you can add to your Web pages. Adobe Elements not only resizes your images and optimizes them for the Web but also creates the HTML pages, inserts your images into them, and links the pages. It's an incredible timesaver, especially if you're creating a large photo gallery for your site.

Creating a Web gallery is similar to creating a photo album. You identify the catalog or collection you want to use, select the images, and then make a few formatting choices before saving your work.

If you want to make changes after you've created a gallery, you have to start over and generate the gallery again. But don't worry, this doesn't take as long as you may think because Elements saves your settings and generates new galleries in a matter of seconds. You can always go back and re-create your gallery, changing any of the settings to alter the final result. Each time you create a Web gallery, Elements creates new copies of all your images and new pages to display them on, according to the settings you specify in the Creation Wizard.

To create a Web gallery in Elements, follow these steps:

1. **Open Photoshop Elements and choose File➪New➪Creation.**

   After a few seconds, the Creation Setup window appears.

2. **In the Select a Creation Type list, double-click Web Photo Gallery.**

   The Adobe Web Photo Gallery dialog box appears, as shown in Figure 7-15.

3. **At the top of the Photos area (on the left), click the Add button.**

   The Add Photos dialog box appears. If you started the Web photo gallery wizard with a catalog open, the images are added automatically.

4. **Use the options under Add Photos From to select the images you want to include in your Web photo gallery, and then click OK.**

   The Add Photos dialog box closes and the Adobe Web Photo Gallery window becomes visible again.

5. **Specify formatting as follows:**

   • **Gallery Style list:** You can choose from a variety of layout designs, such as Baby Boy and Space. To see what a style looks like, select it from the pull-down list. A preview of the style is displayed at the top of the dialog box. In the example in Figure 7-15, I selected the Winter style.

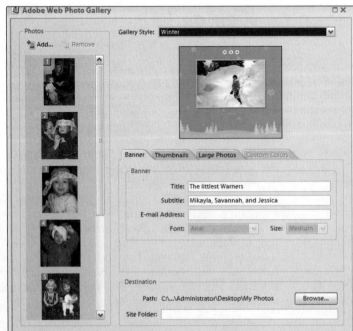

Figure 7-15:
You can customize the appearance of your Web photo gallery.

- **Banner tab:** The *banner* is the text that appears at the top of your gallery pages. You can leave this option blank or fill in the boxes to add a title, a subtitle, and an e-mail address (which automatically creates an e-mail link to the specified address on all your pages). You can also specify the font face and font size for the title and subtitle text. Use the Destination Site Folder box at the bottom of the dialog box to specify a name for your gallery, and browse to choose where you want the files to be saved on your hard drive. If you want to add the gallery to your Web site, I recommend that you save the gallery in a subfolder within your Web site folder.

- **Thumbnails tab:** The settings on this tab affect the size and style of the thumbnail images displayed on the gallery pages that Elements creates. You can choose Small, Medium, Large, or Extra large. As you generate your Web gallery, Elements creates a copy of each of your images in the specified thumbnail size, leaving your original images untouched. If you're not sure what size you want, try Medium; you can always change your mind later and generate a new Web gallery with thumbnails in another size.

  At the bottom of the Thumbnails tab are options for captions you might want to appear with your images. Specify the font face and size and then choose what you want Elements to use to generate the text for your caption. Your options are Filename, which adds captions based on the name of the image file, Date, which inserts the creation or save date of the image, and Caption, which inserts caption text you added to the General image properties. (You open the Image Properties dialog box by right-clicking an image in the Organizer and choosing Show Properties). You can select any combination of these options.

- **Large Photos tab:** When a visitor clicks a thumbnail-sized image on the main page of the photo gallery, a new page with a larger photo appears in its stead — in whatever size you specify here. You can also adjust the image quality by dragging the slider. (The lower the quality, the faster the image will download.) The Caption options are the same as those described for the Thumbnails tab.

- **Custom Colors tab:** You can change the colors of the text and pages in your gallery by using the color pickers next to each option: Background, Banner, Text, Link, Active Link, and Visited Link. For best results, use light-colored text on a dark background or dark text on a light background.

6. **When you've specified the settings and format options for your Web photo gallery, click Save to create it.**

Elements creates your Web photo gallery and displays the pages in the Elements viewer. The viewer mimics a Web browser, as shown in Figure 7-16.

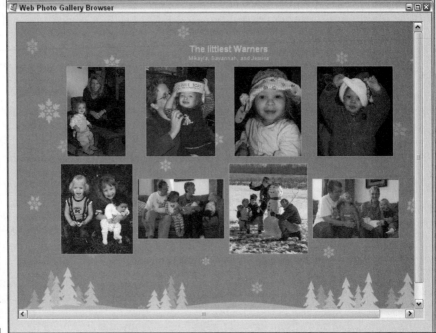

When creating a Web photo gallery, which takes remarkably few seconds, Elements creates copies of all your selected images, converts them to JPEG format, and saves them as thumbnails and as larger images. Then Elements does something most image programs couldn't dream of — it creates HTML pages and links everything for you.

When the gallery is completed, it includes a main HTML page (or pages, depending on how many images you selected), which displays the thumbnail images in the style you chose in the creation wizard. Each thumbnail is linked to a different page, which displays the larger version of that image. To view a Web gallery on your own computer, open any of the pages with a Web browser by choosing File⇨Open and finding the main page of the gallery site, which should be called index.html.

After the photo gallery folder is generated (with whatever name you entered), it contains three subfolders named images, pages, and thumbnails. You can add a Web photo gallery to any Web site by saving or copying the folder and its subfolders (with all the images, thumbnails, and pages) into your Web site folder (the folder I recommend you create to hold all the images and pages of your entire Web site).

You can open any of the HTML files in the pages folder with a Web design program such as FrontPage or Dreamweaver to edit them further. You find instructions for editing pages and creating links in FrontPage in Chapter 8.

Part III
Creating Web Pages and Adding Multimedia

The 5th Wave — By Rich Tennant

RURAL WEB DESIGN

"What you want to do is balance the image of the pick-up truck sittin' behind your home page with a busted washing machine in the foreground."

In this part . . .

In Part III you discover how easy it is to build Web pages, work with templates, and add sound, video, and animation. Beginning in Chapter 8, you find an introduction to Microsoft FrontPage 2003, a Web design program that makes creating a new site almost as easy as creating a document in Microsoft Word. Chapter 9 explains the various ways you can create and use templates in FrontPage 2003, and Chapter 10 provides an overview of the many multimedia formats in use on the Internet today and instructions for adding audio, video, and more to your Web pages.

Chapter 8

Working with Microsoft FrontPage

• •

In This Chapter

▶ Introducing FrontPage

▶ Using FrontPage's Open Site features

▶ Creating a page

▶ Adding links to your Web page

▶ Changing the properties of your Web page

▶ Using tables and layers to create page designs

▶ Previewing your Web page

▶ Publishing your Web page to a server

• •

Considered the most popular Web design program for people who are not professional designers, FrontPage 2003 combines a familiar interface (it looks a lot like Microsoft Word) with sophisticated tools. You can use FrontPage to build a simple Web site or a complex one, even if you're new to the world of the Web.

FrontPage 2003 can help you with every aspect of Web development, from creating pages, to setting and correcting links, to publishing your pages on a Web server. In this chapter, you get an introduction to this Web design program, an overview of some of the most important features, and step-by-step instructions for creating a simple Web page.

The features covered in this chapter can be applied to your work whether you're creating a custom page or using predesigned templates, such as the ones featured in Chapters 11 through 14, and want to edit or add to a page design. In the next chapter, you find a guide to using and creating templates in FrontPage.

Introducing the Many Components of FrontPage 2003

FrontPage can be overwhelming at first, with its many features, menu items, and display options. To help you get familiar with the program, this section introduces you to the interface and provides an overview of the basic functions of FrontPage. In the sections that follow, you find out how to create a page in FrontPage, add text, insert an image, and even create links.

Starting with the workspace

You have more than one option for creating Web pages in FrontPage. You can

- Create a blank page
- Edit an existing page
- Use one of the many FrontPage templates or themes
- Load your own template (from this book's CD or a number of other sources)

If you choose to create a blank page, FrontPage starts a new blank HTML page in the main workspace. The *workspace* consists of a main window that shows the page you're working on and menus and toolbars across the top of the screen. Figure 8-1 shows the FrontPage workspace with a blank HTML page open. You can type text directly onto a page in the workspace and apply basic formatting, such as bold and italics as you would in a program like Microsoft Word.

Figure 8-1:
The
FrontPage
workspace
includes a
document
window, a
menu bar,
and optional
toolbars.

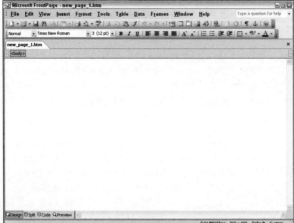

The big, open area in the main area of the workspace is the *document window,* which is where you work on new and existing pages. Four display options are accessible through small icons at the bottom left of the screen: Design, Split, Code, and Preview. You can switch from one display setting to another by clicking the respective icon at the bottom of the page.

You can choose from the following four display options in the FrontPage workspace:

- **Design view:** By default, FrontPage presents new pages in Design view, which displays the page much as it would appear in a Web browser, except links are not functional. To select Design view, click the Design icon at the bottom left of the screen (this is the option selected in Figure 8-1).

- **Preview:** If you want to test your links, click the Preview icon. The workspace is transformed to function like Microsoft's Web browser, Internet Explorer.

- **Code view:** If you want to see the HTML code behind the page, click the Code icon to change to Code view. If you're not accustomed to looking at programming code, the page may look like hieroglyphics.

- **Split view:** If you want to find out how to read or write HTML, try the Split view, which enables you to see HTML code in both Code and Design views simultaneously, as shown in Figure 8-2.

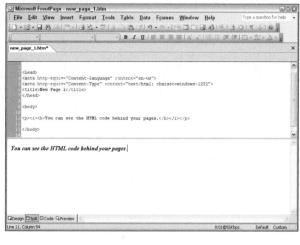

Figure 8-2:
The Split view lets you see the HTML code behind the page while you work in Design view.

Pages viewed on the Web may not always look exactly the way they do in FrontPage because not all browsers support the same HTML features or display them exactly the same way. For best results, always test your work in a variety of Web browsers and on different computers. The best way to make sure that your pages are displayed consistently on different machines (such as your cousin's Macintosh or your grandfather's 8-year-old computer) is to simplify the design.

Meandering through the menu options

FrontPage has many menu options that probably look familiar, especially if you use other Microsoft products such as Microsoft Word. Click the File menu and you'll find the same Save and Print options you'd find in Word. You'll also find a few new options, such as Open Site, which enables you to open an entire Web site rather than just a single page, and Preview in Browser, which enables you to open the page you are working on in a Web browser to see how the page will appear on the Web.

The Edit menu contains the well-known Cut, Copy, and Paste options, plus some new ones. For example, the Check In and Check Out options are helpful if you're working with a team of developers; when someone is working on a page on the Web site, these options keep track so that no one else overwrites that person's work.

The View menu provides access to some helpful design features, such as grids and rulers, which you can use as guides when designing a page. The Tracing Image option enables you to insert an image into the background of a page and use it to guide your design work. Many professional designers use this feature to create a design in a program such as Photoshop and then re-create the design in FrontPage for the Web.

The Task Pane option opens a pane on the side of the workspace, as shown in Figure 8-3. The task pane gives you easy access to help files, as well as links to training information, online discussion areas, and recommended downloads.

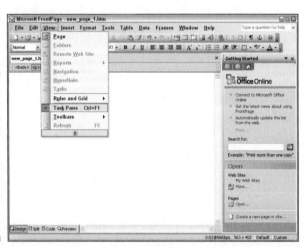

Figure 8-3:
The task pane, on the right side of the screen, provides easy access to help files and other resources.

As you get started working with FrontPage, take a few minutes to click the other menu options. For example, the Format menu provides font, numbering, and bullet options, and the Tools menu is where you'll find spell check.

If you're not sure what an option does, you can look it up quickly in the FrontPage Help features, available in the task pane (use the Ctrl+F1 shortcut for quick access).

Toddling across the toolbars

At the top of the screen in the standard interface, you'll find the standard and formatting toolbars. In FrontPage, as in word processing programs, these two toolbars hold the most commonly used features, such as bold, italics, and alignment options. To add or remove a toolbar, choose View⇨Toolbars and select an option. The Pictures toolbar, for example, provides quick access to many of the program's image formatting features.

The Insert Table, Insert Layer, and Insert Picture icons are located on the standard toolbar, which appears at the top of the work area. In Figure 8-4, I used the Insert Picture icon to add a photo to a Web page. (Special thanks to Chris and Natalie, as well as photographer Jessica Verma, for letting me feature their photos in this chapter.) You find detailed instructions for adding images in the "Adding an image" section later in this chapter.

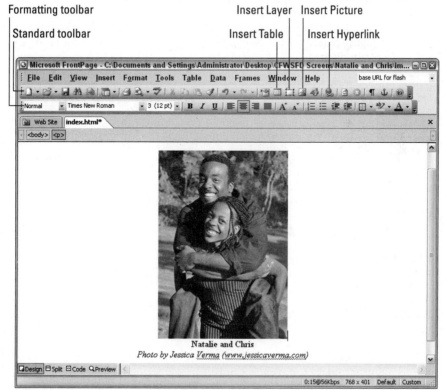

Figure 8-4:
The Insert Picture icon makes it easy to add a photo or a graphic to your Web page.

Formatting toolbar · Insert Layer · Insert Picture
Standard toolbar · Insert Table · Insert Hyperlink

Natalie and Chris
Photo by Jessica Verma (www.jessicaverma.com)

Before You Create or Edit Pages

When you work with a program such as FrontPage, you create your Web pages on your own computer and then transfer them to a Web server when you're ready to publish them on the Web.

To ensure that your Web pages and related files transfer correctly to the server, it's important to store all the files for your Web site in one main folder on your computer. That's because links are created based on where pages, images, and other files are in relation to each other. You can create subfolders within the main folder to better organize your files, but just make sure that everything is stored within one main folder before you start creating links or inserting images.

FrontPage includes special site management features to help you organize your Web site, but these features work only after you have identified your main Web site folder in FrontPage. In this section, I describe three ways you can open an existing Web site or create a site in FrontPage.

When you create files or subfolders in a Web site, it's important to name those files and folders without any spaces or special characters. But when you create the main folder for your Web site, you can name it anything you like because the main folder is used to store your site only on your hard drive and won't be transferred to the Web server when you publish your Web site. For more tips on naming files in a Web site, see Chapter 2.

Opening an existing site in FrontPage

If you want to edit an existing Web site in FrontPage or are using one of the predesigned template sites featured in Chapters 11 through 14, you should first open in FrontPage the main folder that contains your Web site files.

Follow these steps to open in FrontPage an existing Web site or one of the predesigned templates from the CD:

1. **Choose File⇨Open Site.**

   The Open Site dialog box appears.

2. **Navigate your hard drive until you locate the main folder of your Web site.**

3. **Double-click to select the folder name.**

4. **Click Open.**

   Because your new folder was not created in FrontPage, a dialog box appears, stating: "FrontPage needs to add information to your folder in order to help manage your Hyperlinks and other Web site content."

5. **Click Yes.**

The Web site folder is opened and the files and subfolders in your main site are displayed in the FrontPage work area (as shown in Figure 8-5).

Creating a Web site folder

Although you can create a site from within FrontPage, I prefer to create a new main site folder myself on my hard drive and then open it in FrontPage. This option enables me to save my Web site folder wherever I want to on my hard drive, instead of being limited to the default folder FrontPage uses. FrontPage's site management features will work the same.

To create a Web site folder and then open it in FrontPage, follow these steps:

1. **Create a folder on your hard drive as you'd create any new folder.**

On a PC, you can choose File⇨New Folder in Windows Explorer to create a new folder anywhere on your hard drive. On a Mac, choose File⇨New Folder from within any existing folder. You can name the main folder of your site anything you like, but I suggest using a name that means something to you, such as Baby Web Site.

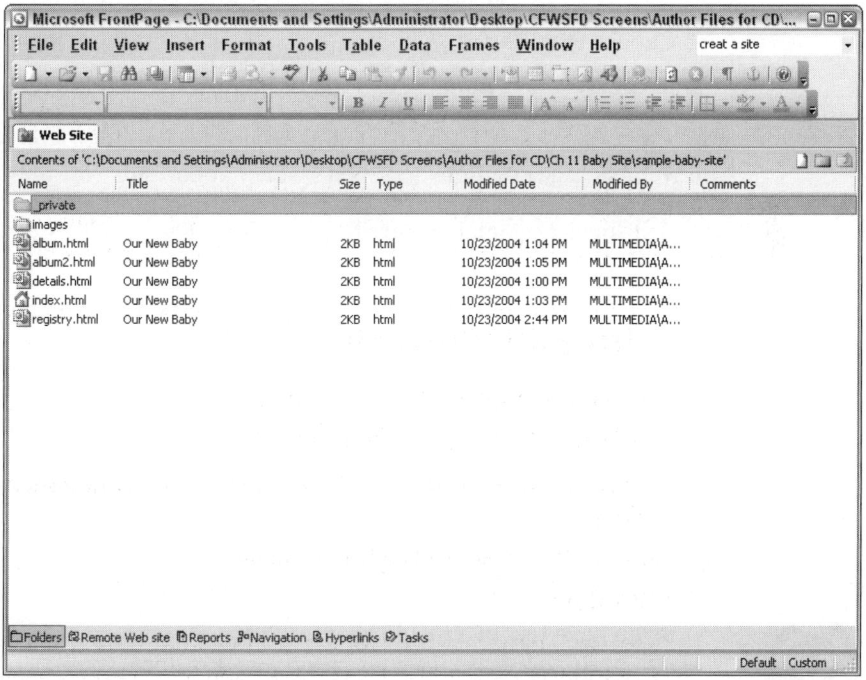

Figure 8-5:
When you open a site in FrontPage, the files and subfolders are displayed in the main FrontPage work area.

2. **In FrontPage, choose File⇨Open Site.**

   The Open Site dialog box appears.

3. **Navigate around your hard drive until you locate the new folder you created for your Web site.**

4. **Double-click to select the folder name.**

5. **Click Open.**

   Because your new folder was not created in FrontPage, a dialog box appears, stating: "FrontPage needs to add information to your folder in order to help manage your Hyperlinks and other Web site content."

6. **Click Yes.**

   The Web site folder is opened and the files and subfolders in your main site are displayed in the FrontPage work area (refer to Figure 8-5).

Creating a New Web Page

Whether you're working on a new site or an existing one, after you've opened your main site folder in FrontPage, you're ready to create new pages.

To create a page in FrontPage, follow these steps:

1. **Choose File⇨New.**
2. **In the New task pane, select Blank Page, as shown in Figure 8-6.**

Many other features are accessible from the New task pane, such as templates and Web package solutions, but don't worry about those for now. In this chapter, you create a simple HTML file. In Chapter 9, you find out how to use predesigned templates and other automated features.

Creating a headline

Suppose that you want to center a headline and make it big and bold, such as the one shown in Figure 8-7. Follow these steps:

1. **Click to insert your cursor at the top of the blank page and type some text.**

   Type anything you like — you just need something that you can format so you can follow the formatting instructions in this section.

   If you have text in a word processor or another program, you can copy and paste that text into your FrontPage document.

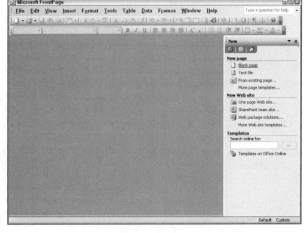

Figure 8-6:
Select the
Blank page
option to
create a
new page in
FrontPage.

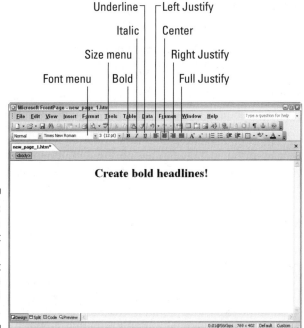

Figure 8-7:
FrontPage
makes it
easy to
format text
to create
bold
headlines.

2. **Highlight the text you want to format.**

3. **On the formatting toolbar, do the following:**

   a. **Click the Bold icon.**

   This icon and the others in this set of steps are labeled in Figure 8-7.
   The heading becomes bold.

b. Click the Center icon.

The text is centered.

c. Use the Size pull-down menu and choose 36.

The text changes to font size 36.

Indenting text

If you want to add more text to your page, you can simply continue typing or you can copy and paste to move text from a Word document or other file into your Web page. To add more text to a page and indent the text, follow these steps.

1. **Press the Enter key to create a paragraph break.**

   To create a line break rather than a paragraph break, press Shift + Enter (on a PC) or Shift + Return (on a Mac).

2. **Type a little more text after your headline text.**

   A single sentence or a couple of short lines is enough.

3. **Highlight the text you want to indent.**

4. **Choose Text⇨Indent.**

If you want to add more text that's not indented, make sure no text is selected and then choose Text⇨Outdent to transition back to plain text mode. You can also use the Increase and Decrease Indent buttons on the toolbar at the top of the page.

Adding an image

Using FrontPage to add an image to your Web page is simple. The challenge is to create a good-looking image that loads quickly in your viewer's browser. You need another program, such as Photoshop Elements or Fireworks, to create and edit images. You find out more about editing images in Chapters 5 and 6, but for now, I assume that you have a GIF or JPEG image file ready to load on your page.

The only image formats that will display on a Web page are GIF and JPEG. If you don't have an image handy for this next exercise, use one of the sample image files on the CD-ROM.

PNG is also an accepted image format on the Web, but Web designers rarely use it because browsers do not support PNG as well as they support GIF and JPEG.

Before you insert an image on your page, you should do two important tasks. First, choose File⇨Save to save your new HTML page in your Web site's folder on your hard drive (even if the page is still blank). This step is important because FrontPage can't properly set the link to your image until it identifies the relative locations of the HTML page and the image. Until you save the page, FrontPage doesn't know what folder the page is in, so it won't be able to set the link properly.

For this same reason, the second task is to make sure that the image file is stored in the same main folder you created for your Web site. Many designers create a subfolder called `images` so that they can keep all their image files in one place.

If you move the page or image to another folder on your hard drive after you insert the image on your page, you risk breaking the link between the page and the image, and an ugly broken image icon appears when you view your page in a browser. If you want to move files and folders without breaking links, make sure your site is open in FrontPage (as described in the "Before You Create or Edit Pages" section) and make your changes from the Web site folder view (refer to Figure 8-5).

If you do break a link to an image, you can correct it by clicking the broken image icon and then clicking the Insert Picture icon on the standard toolbar and selecting the image again.

Follow these steps to place an image on your Web page:

1. **Click the Insert Picture icon on the standard toolbar (labeled in Figure 8-4).**

   The Picture dialog box appears, as shown in Figure 8-8.

2. **Navigate to the folder that has the image you want to insert.**

3. **Double-click to select the image you want.**

   The image appears on your Web page.

4. **Double-click the image on your page.**

   The Picture Properties dialog box appears, as shown in Figure 8-9.

5. **Specify image attributes, such as alignment, horizontal and vertical spacing.**

   The Picture Properties dialog box enables you to specify many options for how your images are displayed on your Web page. These various options are described in Table 8-1.

6. **Click OK to close the Picture Properties dialog box.**

Figure 8-8:
Simply
select an
image here
to add it to a
Web page.

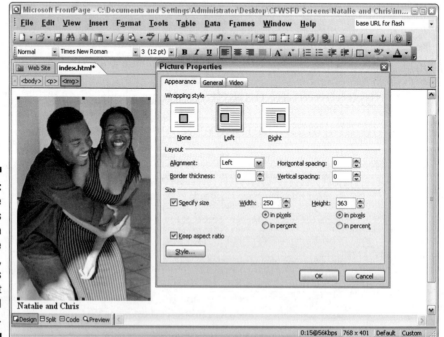

Figure 8-9:
You have
easy access
to common
image
attributes,
such as
alignment
and
spacing.

Table 8-1   Image Options in the Picture Properties Dialog Box

Appearance Tab	
Option	*What It Does*
Wrapping Style	Wraps text around an image.
Alignment	Wraps text aligned to the right or left around the image. The other options — Baseline, Top, and Middle — control the horizontal alignment of text or other objects next to the image.
Border Thickness	Adds a border, specified in pixels, around an image. FrontPage makes 0 the default setting, so if you don't want a border you can ignore this option. (I nearly always use 0.)
Horizontal Spacing	Inserts blank space, measured in pixels, to the left and right of the image.
Vertical Spacing	Inserts blank space, measured in pixels, above and below the image.
Width	Alters the width of the image in pixels or by a percentage. FrontPage automatically specifies the width of the image based on the size of the image file.
Height	Alters the height of the image in pixels or by a percentage. FrontPage automatically specifies the height of the image based on the size of the image file.
Keep aspect ratio	Adjusts the height or width automatically to maintain the original proportions of an image when either the height or width is changed.
Style	Opens the Modify Style dialog box, where you can create and apply preset formatting options, called styles.
General Tab	
Option	*What It Does*
Picture	Specifies the file name and path to the image. FrontPage sets this automatically when you insert an image.
Browse Button	Opens the Picture dialog box.

(continued)

Table 8-1 *(continued)*

General Tab	
Option	*What It Does*
Edit Button	Opens the image in an image editor.
Picture File Type Button	Opens the Picture File Type dialog box, where you can specify the image format. Options are GIF, JPEG, PNG-8, and PNG-24. If your image file includes an extension, such as `.jpeg` or `.gif`, you do not need to use this dialog box. (See Chapter 2 for more on image extensions and Chapter 6 for more on image formats.)
Low-Res	Inserts a second image in the same place on a page. The low-resolution image loads first and is then replaced by the primary image. This option is useful when you have a large image file because you can set a smaller image file (such as a black-and-white version) as the Low-Res image and it will display while the main image downloads.
Text	Displays the words you enter only if the image doesn't appear on your viewer's screen because the viewer has images turned off or can't view images. Special browsers for the blind "read" this text so visitors can identify images even if they can't see them.
Long Description	Inserts a longer text description in the code behind your image.
Default Hyperlink Location	Displays the address or path if the image links to another page. (For more about linking, see "Setting Links" later in the chapter.)
Target Frame	Specifies where the page that you're linking to should open. This is important when you're using an HTML frameset or when you want a link to open a new browser window.

The options in the Video tab do not apply to still images. For instructions on adding video, see Chapter 10.

To resize an image in FrontPage, you can drag the edge of the image or change the Height and Width values in the Picture Properties dialog, but those are not the best methods. When you change the dimensions of the image in FrontPage, you change not the size of the image but the way it appears on the page. That's a bad idea because it distorts the image. In addition, if you use this method to make the image smaller, you make your visitors download a larger file than necessary.

You're always better off using an image editor, such as Photoshop Elements, to change the physical size of an image. You find out how in Chapter 6.

Setting Links

Creating links on a Web page is much easier than most people imagine. After you've opened or created a Web site in FrontPage, the Insert Hyperlink option takes care of just about everything for you. FrontPage keeps track of the locations of your files and folders and inserts the necessary information to create a link from one page to another or to any other file in your site. (If you haven't already opened your site in FrontPage, you find instructions for doing so in the "Before You Create or Edit Pages" section, earlier in this chapter.)

If you're creating a link to another Web site or to an e-mail address, you need only the address; FrontPage takes care of the rest. This section includes instructions for creating all three of these common kinds of links.

Linking pages within your Web site

Linking from one page to another page in your Web site is easy. The most important things to remember are to save your pages before you start setting links and to make sure that all your Web page files are in your main Web site folder.

Creating pages makes it easier to set links

When you start working on your family Web site, consider creating a bunch of "holder" pages right away. Doing so enables you to organize the structure of your site before you start setting links. After all, you can't link to a page that doesn't exist. If you plan to have, for example, three main links on your front page to the family history page, the baby page, and the photo album, go ahead and create pages for each of those sections, even if you don't have anything to put on them yet. With these initial pages in place, you benefit from having an early plan for organizing the site and can start setting links among the main pages right away.

Here's how you create a link to a page within your Web site:

1. **In FrontPage, create a new page or open the page on which you want to create a link.**

   Remember, always save the page you're working on before you set links.

2. **Select the text or image that you want to serve as the link.**

   That is, select the text or image that will open another page when a user clicks it.

3. **Click the Insert Hyperlink icon on the standard toolbar.**

   (The icon is labeled in Figure 8-4.) The Insert Hyperlink dialog box appears.

4. **Navigate around your hard drive to find the page to which you want your image or text to link.**

5. **Click the file name to select the page, and then click OK.**

   The link is set and the dialog box closes. If you selected text, the words appear underlined and in a different color. If you selected an image, you will not see any change in the way the image appears unless you have added a border to your image, an option I don't recommend. (For more on using image borders, see the Border Thickness option in Table 8-1.)

 It's always a good idea to test your links. To do so now, click the Preview icon at the bottom of the screen and your links will become active. Simply click the linked text or image to open the page it links to. Click the Design icon at the bottom of the screen to edit your page or create additional links.

Linking to pages outside your Web site

Linking to a page on another Web site is even easier than linking to another page within your site. If you have the URL of the page to which you want to link, you're most of the way there.

To create an external link, follow these steps:

1. **In FrontPage, create a page or open the page from which you want to link.**

2. **Select the text or image that you want to serve as a link.**

3. **Click the Insert Hyperlink icon on the standard toolbar.**

   The Insert Hyperlink dialog box opens.

4. **In the Address box at the bottom of the dialog box, enter the URL of the page you want to link to.**

   Alternatively, you can click the arrow to the right of the Address box and choose any link from the list. FrontPage collects your recently visited URLs in this list.

   If you're not sure of the URL or you don't want to type it, you can click the Browse the Web icon (the small icon that looks like a globe with a magnifying glass over it at the top of the Insert Hyperlink dialog box). FrontPage launches Internet Explorer and, if you're connected to the Internet, lets you browse the Web. When you find the page you want to link to, leave it displayed in the browser, switch back to FrontPage, and the URL is automatically inserted in the Address box.

5. **Click OK.**

   The Insert Hyperlink dialog box closes and the link is set.

Although you don't have to type the `http://` at the beginning of a Web site address to get to a site in most browsers, you need to use the full URL, including the `http://`, when you create an external link. Otherwise, the browser may think that `www.whatever.com` is the name of a folder on your Web server rather than an external site address, and you'll get a `404, Page Not Found` error.

See Figure 8-10 for an example of how you set a link to the Wiley Publishing Web site, using its full URL.

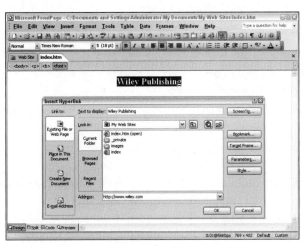

Figure 8-10: To set a link to another Web site, highlight the text or image you want to link and type the URL in the Address box.

Setting a link to an e-mail address

Another common link option is to link directly to an e-mail address, making it easy for visitors to send you a message. I recommend that you invite visitors to contact you because getting feedback on your Web site is half the fun.

Setting a link to an e-mail address is almost as easy as setting a link to another Web page. Before you start, make sure you have the e-mail address to which you want to link handy because you'll have to insert that into the link field in the Insert Hyperlink dialog box.

To a visitor to your Web page, text linked to an e-mail address looks just like text linked to a Web page, so it's a good idea to identify e-mail links. Unlike links to other Web pages, which simply open a page in the browser window, an e-mail link launches an e-mail program on the user's computer and inserts the e-mail address. E-mail links make it easy to send you an e-mail, but clicking one can be disconcerting if a visitor isn't expecting to open his or her e-mail program.

To create an e-mail link in FrontPage, follow these steps:

1. **In FrontPage, create a page or open the page on which you want to create an e-mail link.**

2. **Click to highlight the text or image where you want to create the link.**

3. **Click the Insert Hyperlink icon on the standard toolbar.**

   The Insert Hyperlink dialog box appears.

4. **Select the E-mail Address option, at the bottom left of the dialog box.**

   The Insert Hyperlink dialog box changes to display e-mail link options.

5. **In the Text to display box, enter or edit the text you want to use to represent the link on the page.**

6. **In the E-mail address box, enter the e-mail address you want to link to.**

   For example, in Figure 8-11, I'm creating an e-mail link to `Janine@jcwarner.com`. The `mailto:` is inserted automatically when you enter an e-mail address.

7. **If you want to add a subject line to the user's e-mail when the user clicks your e-mail link, enter some text in the Subject box.**

If you're creating links to the same e-mail address repeatedly, you may appreciate that FrontPage stores e-mail addresses after you link to them. You can find them in the Recently used e-mail addresses area of the Insert Hyperlink dialog box. Simply click the e-mail address you want to reuse and it's inserted into the E-mail Address box.

8. **Click OK and the e-mail link is set.**

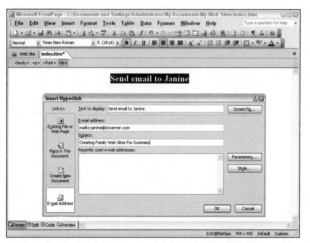

Figure 8-11:
To set a link
to an e-mail
address,
highlight the
text or
image you
want to link
and type the
address in
the Address
box.

Changing Background Colors and Other Page Properties

In the Page Properties dialog box, FrontPage provides access to many of the features that apply to an entire page, including the page's background color, link and text colors, and page title. (The page title appears at the top of the browser, next to the browser name, and is also the text saved in a user's bookmarks list.)

The Page Properties dialog box has multiple tabs across the top, each containing options that apply to the entire page. You can make many adjustments to a Web page, but to keep things simple, the following steps show you how to change the most common elements on your pages: the background color, text color, and the title.

Follow these steps:

1. **Right-click the page and choose Page Properties, or choose File⇨ Properties.**

   The Page Properties dialog box appears.

2. **In the Title field of the General tab, enter a title for your page.**

   The title of your page appears at the very top of the browser window. Page titles are important because they're used by many search engines and by browsers to identify your page when it's bookmarked by a user. If you don't enter a title, FrontPage titles your pages with the words "New Page."

3. **Click the Formatting tab.**

   The Background, Text, and Hyperlink color options become visible, as shown in Figure 8-12.

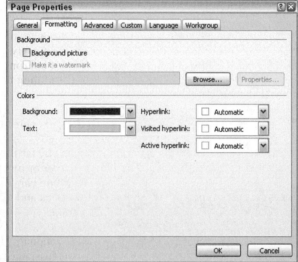

Figure 8-12:
You can change text and link colors, as well as specify a title for the page.

4. **In the Background pull-down list, select a background color.**

   Select any color you like from the displayed colors in the pull-down list, or select More Colors to open the More Colors dialog box and click to select any color from the color wheel. The color you select fills the color swatch box in the Background box in the Colors area. The color does not fill the background of your page until you click the OK button, which also closes the dialog box. If you want to alter the text color or other options, don't click OK until you've made all your changes.

   Make sure that the background and text colors you select look good together and, more important, that the text color is readable against the background color.

5. **In the Text pull-down list, select a text color.**

   The process is similar to setting the background color. Select any color you like from the displayed colors in the pull-down list, or select More Colors to open the More Colors dialog box and click to select any color from the color wheel. The color you select fills the color swatch box in the Text box in the Colors area.

6. **After you've made your changes, click the OK button to close the Page Properties dialog box.**

   Your changes are applied to the page.

Creating Complex Page Designs with Tables and Layers

One of the most frustrating aspects of Web page design is that you can't just place pictures and text anywhere you want on a page. If you drag an image to the bottom-left corner of a Web page, for example, the image pops back up to the top and aligns itself to the left of the page, unless you specify another alignment option. This annoying limitation is not the fault of FrontPage or Dreamweaver or any other Web design program; it's a limitation of HTML and the way that Web design works.

Sure, you can align images and text with the left, right, and center alignment options, but when you want to create more complex designs, you're best served by using HTML tables or HTML layers. Layers are by far the easier option. You simply insert a layer by choosing Insert➪Layer or by clicking the Layers icon on the toolbar. After you've created a layer, you can insert an image, text, or other content into the layer, and simply click and drag to place the layer and its contents anywhere you want on the page.

Unfortunately, layers are still a relatively new formatting option in HTML and are not supported by all browsers, which is why many professional designers still use HTML tables to create complex page designs even though they're much harder to work with. If you know that all your visitors are using one of the latest versions of Internet Explorer or Netscape, you should be able to use layers without concern. But if someone visits your site with an older browser, beware that content inserted into a layer may not appear on that visitor's screen.

Because all browsers do not support layers, I chose to use HTML tables to create the designs in the templates for Chapters 11 through 14. If you use one of these page templates, you may notice the dotted lines within the page designs that represent the edges of the tables. You can click and drag the edges of a table to resize the cells, and you can add, merge, split, and delete table cells in the Tables Properties dialog box to adjust the cells in a table. To open the Table Properties dialog box, choose Table➪Table Properties and then select Table to edit the entire table or Cell to edit a selected cell within the table.

Like most designers, when I create tables to control page design, I set the border value of the table to 0 so visitors don't see the table I use to keep images and other content in place. You can create a table by clicking the Insert Table icon on the toolbar.

Working with layers and tables can get complicated, and covering them in detail is beyond the scope of this book. To discover more about creating complex page designs by using tables and layers, consult the help files in FrontPage or pick up a copy of *FrontPage 2003 For Dummies* by Asha Dornfest (published by Wiley).

Previewing Your Page in a Browser

FrontPage displays Web pages much like a Web browser, but it doesn't let you follow links. Also, different browsers display pages differently. So, to check links and to see how your Web page looks, it's important to check your work in multiple Web browsers (at least Netscape and Internet Explorer) regularly.

The simplest way to preview your work and test your links is to save the page you're working on, and then choose File⇨Preview in Browser. FrontPage provides multiple options so that you can view your page at different screen resolutions and in different browsers.

When you install FrontPage, it automatically finds a browser on your computer and uses that browser as the default in the Preview in Browser option. If you want to test your work in other browsers (and you should), add more options to the list. Choose File⇨Preview in Browser⇨Edit Browser List, and then navigate around your hard drive to find the icon for the browser you want to add to the list. The browser must be on your hard drive for you to add it to the list.

Publishing Your Pages to a Web Server

When you build a Web site with FrontPage, you create all the pages on your computer. Then when you're ready to publish your site on the Internet, you transfer all the pages, images, and other content to a Web server. The advantage of this method is that you can edit your pages on your computer and work out any problems before going "live."

You can publish a single page or an entire site full of pages all at once. After you publish your site for the first time, updating or revising your site is as easy as replacing the page or images you've added or changed.

Follow these instructions to set up FrontPage to connect to your Web server and publish your Web site:

1. **Choose File⇨Publish Site.**

   The Remote Web Site Properties dialog box appears.

2. **Specify a Remote Web server type.**

   FTP is the most common method for transferring files to a Web server. If you use a commercial service provider to host your Web site, select the FTP option. If you use a server that supports FrontPage extensions and you're using these advanced features (which are not covered in this book), choose the FrontPage or SharePoint Services option. Don't worry about the WebDAV system, unless you know that your system uses this advanced development option. If you're publishing your Web site to a server within your company, university, or organization and you're on the same network, you may use the File System option. If you're not sure which option to use, check with your service provider or system administrator.

3. **Enter a Remote Web site location.**

   If you are using a commercial service provider and selected the FTP option in Step 2, enter the FTP location, which is usually your domain name preceded by *ftp* (for example ftp.mydomain.com. Beware, however, that the location address can vary depending on the kind of Web server you're using and how it was set up. Again, check with your service provider or system administrator if you're not sure how to access your Web server.

   If you selected one of the more advanced Web server types in Step 2, check with your system administrator for connection information required in this step and the following steps.

4. **Enter an FTP directory.**

   This is usually a long address to a directory on the server, and it will look something like: /web/users/jcwarner.

5. **Click to select the Publishing tab at the top of the Remote Web Site Properties dialog box.**

6. **Click to select the Changed pages only option.**

   This ensures that only the pages you have updated on your site will be published. If you're publishing your site for the first time, all pages will be transferred to the server. After that, only pages that you have changed will be transferred.

7. **Click OK.**

   The User Name and Password dialog box appears.

8. **Enter your user name and password.**

   If you don't know your user name and password for your server, your service provider or system administrator should be able to provide you with that information.

9. **Click OK.**

   FrontPage automatically accesses your Web server, displaying the contents of the server on the right side of the window and the contents of your site on your hard drive on the left, as shown in Figure 8-13.

10. **In the Local Web site window, select the files and folders that you want to publish on the server.**

    To select multiple files, Shift+click (on a PC) or ⌘+click (on a Mac) as you select the file names, or click and drag to select multiple files at once. You can also use Ctrl+click (PC and Mac) to select noncontiguous files.

Figure 8-13:
FrontPage
displays
your Web
files in the
Local Web
site and
Remote
Web site
windows,
making it
easy to
transfer files
from your
computer to
the server.

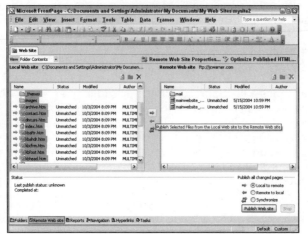

11. Click the single, right-facing arrow between the Local Web site and Remote Web site windows to transfer the files.

FrontPage copies the selected files to your Web server, replacing any older versions with the same file names.

The built-in FTP features in FrontPage make it easy to publish your Web site to a server and to update your site. After you transfer your files to the server, it's always a good idea to test your work by viewing your published pages with a Web browser. If you find any errors or want to make further changes, simply edit the page in FrontPage and then replace the page on the server with your corrected page.

In Chapter 9 you find an introduction to working with FrontPage templates. And in Chapters 11 through 14 you find instructions for using FrontPage to customize the various predesigned Web pages included on the CD to create a baby site, wedding site, sports site, and travel site. Using the instructions in this chapter, you can edit any of the predesigned sites on the CD — even altering them to create different kinds of Web sites. For example, you can turn the predesigned travel site or wedding site into a more general family Web site.

Chapter 9

Timesaving Templates

● ●

In This Chapter

▶ Introducing FrontPage templates

▶ Discovering where to find templates

▶ Using templates to create new pages and sites

▶ Saving templates in FrontPage

▶ Creating new FrontPage templates

● ●

*W*ant to create a personalized Web page without having to do all the work yourself? If so, you're going to love working with templates.

A *template* is essentially a predesigned page that you can customize by replacing the images and text with your own content. Web site templates come in many forms, from basic HTML pages to more advanced template formats unique to the program in which they were created. For example, Macromedia Dreamweaver — a popular Web design program — offers a template format with special features that work in only that program. FrontPage boasts two kinds of template formats.

To help you create beautiful, professionally designed Web sites quickly and easily, I've included a collection of predesigned Web site templates on the CD that accompanies this book. In Chapters 11 through 14, you find instructions for personalizing these templates to create a variety of Web sites. The template pages on the CD are saved in basic HTML format so they can be opened and edited in any Web design program. If you want to take advantage of the special template features in FrontPage 2003, you can turn any of the predesigned template pages on the CD into FrontPage templates by using the instructions in this chapter.

If you want to use the templates provided on the CD but prefer to use Dreamweaver for your Web design, visit www.digitalfamily.com. On the site, you'll find a link to special bonus materials for readers of this book — instructions for using Dreamweaver MX 2004 to create the template sites featured in Chapters 11 through 14.

Understanding FrontPage Templates

Like other Web design programs, FrontPage 2003 enables you to open a pre-designed HTML page, such as the templates included on the CD, and edit the content as you would any other HTML page.

Because templates are so useful for creating Web sites, FrontPage features two special template formats. You can also open any basic HTML template in FrontPage. The following list will help you appreciate the differences between these two options.

- ✔ The simplest FrontPage template format uses the `.tem` extension. These templates are essentially basic HTML pages, but when you save a file in this template format in FrontPage, it becomes available in the New dialog box and can easily be used to create new pages.

- ✔ FrontPage also supports a more advanced format called dynamic Web templates. These files are designated by the `.dwt` extension and include locked regions, which can't be altered (a trick favored by professional designers who want to prevent novices from ruining their page layouts). Dynamic Web templates also enable you to make global changes to a Web site; any page created from a dynamic Web template can be automatically altered by changing the original template and applying those changes to all pages created from that template. Creating dynamic Web templates is much more technically complicated than creating basic FrontPage templates, and dynamic Web templates are generally used by professional designers on big Web sites with many contributors. If you want to get into these more advanced template features in FrontPage, I recommend *FrontPage 2003 For Dummies* by Asha Dornfest (Wiley Publishing).

Figure 9-1 shows an example of a simple HTML template designed for a baby Web site. Notice that the image area in the middle of the page is represented by a graphic with the words *Insert Photo* to make it easy to identify where to place your picture on the page. Similarly, the text area under the graphic reads, *Insert photo caption here.* No matter what format a template is in, you will often find images and text that include instructions like this to make it easier to see where you should personalize the content without altering the design. In a template such as this one, you can also edit the graphics, such as the Next and Previous buttons that appear to the right and left of the photo. However, image files have to be edited in a program such as Photoshop Elements 3 (covered in Chapter 6).

The template folders on the CD that correspond to Chapters 11 through 14 include the image files for the banners and buttons used in the page designs. That means you can customize the graphics as well as replace the images and text.

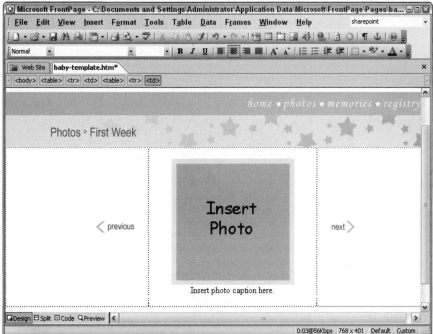

Figure 9-1:
Web page
templates,
such as the
one shown
here, often
include
images and
text with
instructions
like Insert
Image to
make it easy
to identify
the areas
that
should be
customized.

Finding Templates

You can get Web page templates from a variety of sources, starting with the CD that came with this book. In Part IV I walk you through the steps of using the templates on the CD to create four common Web sites: a baby site, a wedding site, a travel site, and a sports or hobby site. Although each template was designed for a specific kind of site, you can mix and match or alter these templates to create dramatically different site designs. For example, you can use the banner graphic and buttons from the baby site with the page layout for the wedding site to create a new design that combines your favorite elements of these two templates.

FrontPage comes with a variety of templates, and you can download more templates for free from the Microsoft Web site by visiting

```
office.microsoft.com/templates
```

These templates can also be used in their entirety or combined with any other templates to create new designs.

You'll find many services that sell templates designed especially for use in FrontPage. To locate sites that sell templates, type the words *FrontPage* and *template* in a search engine such as Google; you'll discover thousands of matches. The cost ranges from a few dollars to hundreds of dollars and the quality and designs vary dramatically.

No matter where you get your templates, the instructions in the following section will help you put them to use in FrontPage.

Creating New Pages and Sites

You can use templates to create one Web page or to create all the pages in a Web site. Often, you'll use one template for the main page of your site and a different template for each of the main subsections, such as the pages within a photo gallery. Microsoft has developed many Web site templates that provide a collection of page designs that combine to make up an entire site.

You can find the FrontPage templates in the New dialog box, which opens in the right side of the work area when you choose File⇨New. The New dialog box, shown in Figure 9-2, is divided into four sections: New page, New Web site, Templates, and Recently used templates.

The New dialog box, shown in Figure 9-3, is divided into four sections: New page, New Web site, Templates and Recently used templates.

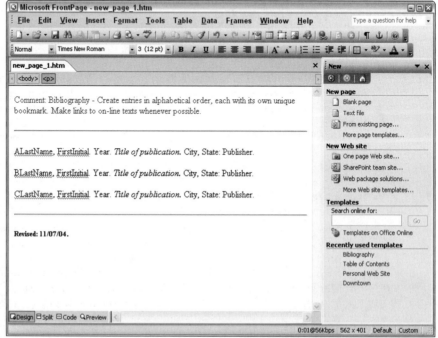

Figure 9-2: When you create a Web page with a template in FrontPage, such as the bibliography page shown here, the page is generated and opened in the main work area.

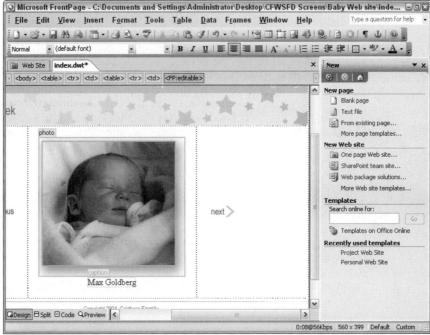

Figure 9-3:
The New dialog box (shown in the right side of this figure) provides access to templates for new pages, as well as complete Web sites.

I find the options in the New dialog box a little confusing, so let me try to help you make sense of your choices:

✔ **New page:** In this section, selecting the More Web site templates option opens the New Page Templates dialog box, where you'll find individual template pages, such as a single predesigned Photo Gallery page or the Bibliography page (refer to Figure 9-2). When you select one of these template options, FrontPage creates an individual HTML page from the template you selected and opens it in the main work area, where you can edit the new page as you would any other page in Front Page. You can create as many pages as you like from any of the New page templates. You can also save any of these individual page designs into an existing Web site. For example, you can add a bibliography page to a site you've created about the history of circus elephants. (You find step-by-step instructions for creating a page from a template in the exercise that follows.)

✔ **New Web site:** In this section, selecting the More Web site templates option opens the New Web Site Templates dialog box, where you'll find predesigned Web site templates. When you select a Web site template, such as the Corporate Presentation template, FrontPage creates multiple HTML pages from the site template and displays the names of the pages and folders in the site in the FrontPage Web Site window. In Figure 9-4, you see the files and folders generated when you select the Personal Web site template. Many of the FrontPage Web site templates include images, which are automatically copied to the `images` folder of the new site when it's created. To open a page in the new site, double-click the file name in the Web Site window. To edit the images, you need to use a program such as Photoshop Elements, covered in Chapter 6.

✔ **Templates:** This section of the New dialog box features a search field you can use to look for templates on the Microsoft site and a link labeled Templates on Office Online. If you click the link and are connected to the Internet, FrontPage launches Internet Explorer and opens the Office Templates page on the Microsoft Web site. Although both features can lead you to more templates that you can download and install in FrontPage, most of what you'll find on the Office site are templates designed for business use, not for personal or family sites.

✔ **Recently used templates:** As the name implies, this section of the New dialog box features shortcuts to the last few templates you've opened.

No matter which of these options you select, after you've created a page or a site from a template, you can edit the pages just as you would edit any page in FrontPage. To help you get the idea of how this all works, the following exercise shows you how to create a new HTML page from a template in the Page Templates dialog box.

Figure 9-4:
When you create a new Web site with a template in FrontPage, such as the Personal site shown here, the pages of the site are automatically generated and opened in the Web Site window.

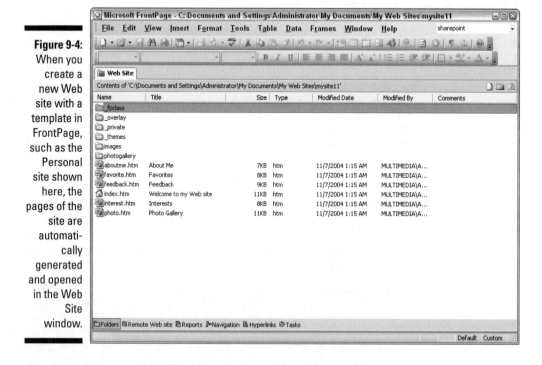

To use a FrontPage template to create a single new HTML page, follow these steps:

1. **Choose File⇨New.**

   The New page dialog box opens on the right side of the screen.

2. **In the New page section, select the More page templates option.**

   The Page Templates dialog box appears, as shown in Figure 9-5.

Figure 9-5:
FrontPage
features a
variety of
Web page
designs.

3. **Click to select the template you want to use to create your new page.**

   The Page Templates dialog box has four tabs across the top, each with a different set of options:

   - **General:** Displays templates that came with the program and can be used to create a single predesigned Web pages (open in Figure 9-5).

   - **My Templates:** Displays any templates you've added to FrontPage (adding a template is covered in the following section of this chapter).

   - **Frames Pages:** Displays templates for creating pages designed with HTML frames.

   - **Style Sheets:** Displays a list of predesigned Cascading Style Sheets (CSS). Style sheets in HTML, which work much like styles in a program such as Word, enable you to save a set of formatting options so that you can apply them all at once to text or other elements on a Web page. Style sheets are not templates, but they can be applied to pages created with templates just as they can be applied to any other page. Working with CSS is beyond the scope of this book, but you can find lots of information about CSS in *FrontPage 2003 For Dummies* by Asha Dornfest (Wiley Publishing).

4. Click OK.

FrontPage creates a page based on the selected template.

5. Choose File⇨Save to save and name the new page.

Always save any new page before you start setting links or inserting images. If you're adding the new page to an existing site, make sure to save the page in the main folder of that site. If you're using the new page to create a site, use the New folder icon at the top of the Save As dialog box to create a folder for the files of your site when you save the file.

You can name the new page anything you like; just remember not to use spaces or special characters.

You can edit a new page created from a template as you would any other file in FrontPage. To replace existing text, highlight the words you want to replace and type to enter new text. You can use the icons on the toolbars to format the text, align the text, and more. (Chapter 8 covers many basic page editing features in FrontPage, including inserting images and setting links.)

Adding Templates to FrontPage

You can save any page as a template in FrontPage to make it available from the New Templates dialog box. You have a few options for this task, depending on where your templates come from and how they were made.

If you downloaded templates from the Microsoft Web site, they're automatically added to the Page Templates or Web Site Templates dialog box. To download templates from the Microsoft site, visit

```
office.microsoft.com/templates
```

Browse the template section of the Office Template site until you find a template you want to download, as shown in Figure 9-6. When you click the Download Now button, the template is imported directly into FrontPage and becomes available in the list of Web site templates.

Several templates are in the `Author Files` section of the CD that came with this book. These templates are predesigned HTML pages. You can edit them as you would edit any HTML page in FrontPage, and you can save them as templates to make them available in the My Templates tab of the Page Templates dialog box. The templates on the CD are organized in folders based on the chapters to which they correspond. For example, the wedding site template pages are located in the `template-wedding-site` folder, which is in the `Ch12 Wedding Site` folder.

Figure 9-6:
When you download templates from the Microsoft Web site, they're added to the Templates dialog box in FrontPage.

Creating New Templates in FrontPage

You can save any HTML page as a template in FrontPage and add it to the options in the My Templates tab of New Page templates dialog box.

If you want to save an HTML page as a template in FrontPage (such as the templates on the CD that accompanies this book or templates you purchase from a Web site), follow these steps:

1. **Open the page you want to save as a template in FrontPage as you would open any other Web page.**

   Choose File➪Open and locate the file on your hard drive or other media, such as a CD.

2. **Choose File➪Save As.**

   The Save As dialog box appears.

3. **Click the arrow to the right of the Save as type box to reveal the file type options, and select FrontPage Template (see Figure 9-7).**

   The page is saved as a template and added to the My Templates section of the Page Templates dialog box.

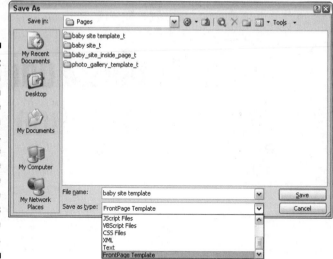

Figure 9-7:
To save a
page in
FrontPage
as a
template,
choose
FrontPage
Template
from the
Save as
type
options.

Using templates is a great way to create a well-designed Web site quickly and easily — even if you think you have the design talents of a toad. But don't stop with the predesigned pages of a template. You can alter templates as much as your imagination allows to create your own personalized Web site, while still benefiting from the original, professionally designed features of the template. You find instructions for editing Web pages in FrontPage in Chapter 8, and for creating and editing images in Chapter 6.

Chapter 10

Lights, Camera, Action: Adding Video, Audio, and Motion

A still photo is a great way to show off a baby's smile, but when you want to capture the sound of a child's laughter or the sight of a baby's first steps, you need audio, video, and other multimedia files on your Web pages.

This chapter provides an introduction to the many kinds of multimedia you can use on the Web, from video and audio to animations and interactive navigation features. Although I can't show you everything there is to know about editing video or creating animations — that gets complicated and would fill an entire book — you will find recommendations for easy-to-use video editing programs and other resources that can help you create multimedia yourself.

In the first section, I offer a few suggestions for creating digitized videos from your home movie collection and how to capture, with almost any digital camera, short clips that are ideal for the Web. Later in the chapter, I cover audio files and working with Macromedia Flash MX 2004 (the most popular program for creating animations and other interactive features for the Web) and offer some general information about the range of other multimedia software on the market.

One of the most important parts of this chapter is the series of step-by-step exercises in each section that show you how to use FrontPage 3 to insert multimedia files into your Web pages. Adding a video file or a Flash animation is similar to inserting an image into a Web page, with a few additional steps that control how the multimedia file will play.

If you have a video file ready and just want to find out how to add it to your Web site, skip ahead to the section on "Inserting video into a Web page." If you have an audio file, read "Inserting a background sound" and "Creating a link to a sound file." To add a Flash file to your pages, skip ahead to "Inserting Flash files."

If you're not sure where to begin, but you know that you want to spruce up your pages with multimedia, keep reading. Throughout this chapter, you find tips for creating and converting multimedia and an overview of the many options available.

Adding Video to Your Web Pages

Video is best for illustrating things that are hard to convey in words or still images, such as a gymnast's cartwheel or the trick or treat of a well-dressed goblin on Halloween. Use video as a complement to still photos and written stories. For example, in a Web site about your daughter's ballet class, you might describe the teacher's best lessons, share your daughter's aspirations to be a professional ballerina, and then offer a link to a short video clip where she shows off a few dance steps.

A little video goes a long way on the Web, where seconds of video may require minutes to download on a slow dial-up connection. Unless you're very experienced with video and know that your visitors have fast connections and fast computers, it's best to stick with short video clips of no more than 30 seconds to 2 minutes. That may not seem like much, but remember that most television commercials are only 15- to 30-second spots. If you're clever about editing your video, you can say a lot in a few seconds.

One of the greatest challenges of working with video is that you have so many choices. You can shoot video with a digital video camera or on videocassette and then convert it to a digital format. (You find tips about digitizing in the next section, "Preparing video for the Web.") If you want to edit your video, you can choose from a wide range of video editing programs, covered in the "Comparing video editing programs" sidebar. Then you have to decide which video format you want to use — Windows Media, QuickTime, RealMedia, or any of at least a half dozen options covered in the "Comparing video formats" section, later in this chapter.

After you've made those choices, you still have to think about how you want to link the video to your pages (covered in "Inserting video into a Web page"). And, finally, I recommend that you include at least a few words describing what visitors will see on the video, how long it is, and the type of program needed to view it. You want your visitors to know what to expect so that they don't get frustrated because they have to wait longer than they thought for your video to load or they can't play it because they don't have the right software.

Comparing video editing programs

Anyone who's had to sit through someone else's amateur home movies knows why video editing software is so crucial. Too many blurry, shaky images, stomach-wrenching zooms, and abrupt pans, and you find yourself clutching the arms of your chair and hoping you don't have to sit through much more.

Even professionals fall prey to these common mistakes, which is why even pros shoot at about a 20:1 ratio — that is, they expect to have to shoot 20 minutes of tape to capture 1 usable minute of video. Be kind to your audience and do what the pros do — *ruthlessly* cut your video down to only the very best moments, and arrange segments so that they have a logical beginning, middle, and end.

Every program listed in this section lets you perform basic editing and cutting as well as create fade-ins. The programs also support the addition of special features, such as opening titles, voice-overs, and music tracks. As you go up the price scale, you add features for creating special effects, slow motion, fast motion, and even filters that can make your video look like a scratchy sepia-toned 1920s era silent movie.

The following are some of the most popular video editing programs on the market today:

- **Adobe Premiere:** This high-end video editing program is comparable to the Hollywood standard, Final Cut Pro, but it's not quite as expensive and it works on a PC. To use this program effectively, you need a very fast computer, gigabytes of available hard drive space, and a lot of free time.

- **Adobe Premiere Elements:** This new "lite" version of Adobe Premier is much better suited to a home user. It costs about $600 less (retailing for about $100) and the menus and options are much simpler to master. Unless you've managed to get your mitts on a $30,000 high-definition video camera,

Premiere Elements is more than enough for your needs.

- **Pinnacle Studio Plus 9.0:** This program is aimed at the "prosumer" market, meaning it's designed for people who have some familiarity with shooting and editing video and want a lot of features but aren't professionals and don't have a company expense account to cover their costs. Studio Plus does the basics, capturing video and allowing you to cut and paste scenes, dub audio, and create titles. It also includes some special effects (such as slow motion, burring, and stretching an image) and even a bluescreen feature, which lets you film against a blue background and then combine video files to create movies of things that aren't possible, like making it appear as though your hamster can dunk a basketball as well as Michael Jordan can.

- **Ulead MediaStudio:** This program includes both VideoStudio and a useful audio editing program. "Lite" versions of Ulead's products are often bundled with capture cards or other hardware and provide basic video editing features. MediaStudio is designed for people who want to make their own versions of music videos on a tight budget. You can also add plug-ins that enable MediaStudio to work with high-definition video and do basic retouching of the images.

- **iMovie:** Part of Apple's iStudio suite and an excellent video editing program, iMovie is available only for the Macintosh. Many Macs now come with iStudio already installed, so if you have a newer Mac you probably already have this editing program. Acclaimed for its intuitive interface, iMovie is fully integrated with the rest of iStudio, which includes iPhoto, and works seamlessly with Mac's DVD and CD creation software.

Preparing video for the Web

Before you can add video to your Web pages, it must be in a *digitized* format so that it can be read by a digital device, such as a computer or a DVD player. If you use a digital camera, your video is already digitized. If you're using a camera that records to tape, however, you'll have to digitize the contents of the cassettes before you can put the video online.

Digitizing your home video collection and old family movies can yield great material for your family Web site. And the good news is that you don't have to digitize, optimize, or edit your own video — you can have someone do it for you. Many companies offer these video services for a reasonable fee. To find a service in your area, check your yellow pages under video editing services or ask about digitizing video wherever you can get film developed — many of these stores now offer video digitizing services as well.

After the video is digitized, it should be optimized, before you add it to your Web pages. *Optimizing* video involves stripping out excess information and using compression technologies to make the file download faster without compromising too much on quality. Unfortunately, the limits of bandwidth won't let you put motion-picture quality video on your Web site, but you can still produce video that looks good and works well on the Web if you have the right tools and know a little about video editing.

Video editing is more complex than working with still images. But if you have a video editing program, such as Adobe Premier Elements, optimizing video and doing simple editing and cutting is something most people who are comfortable with computers can master in a matter of hours or days.

Comparing video formats

Video can be saved for the Web in several video formats and compression options. Unfortunately, no one video option works for everyone on the Web. To make sure video works best for your visitors, you may want to include multiple choices. For example, you could have one link to a video file at the highest quality for visitors with fast connections, and another link to a file at a lower quality for those who are still limited to dial-up accounts. You may also want to save video in different formats. In this section, I describe the most common video formats and give you a few suggestions for choosing the one that will work best for your audience.

To view video, your Web site visitors need a video player, sometimes referred to as *plug-in* because it plugs in to the browser to extend its functionality. These days, most computers come with preinstalled video and audio players that will play the most common video formats, including Windows Media and

MPEG. If you use a Windows computer, you probably have Windows Media Player on your computer. If you use a Mac, you probably have QuickTime. Both video players can handle multiple video formats and can be used on both the Mac and the PC.

If you don't have the player you want, you can download most of them for free. Video players are relatively easy to install, even for novices, which is why I recommend that you include instructions for downloading the best player for the video on your Web pages. For tips on how to word these instructions, see the "Creating warnings for multimedia files" sidebar. (In the list of video formats that follows, I've included Web addresses for the most popular players.)

What happens when you click a link to a video depends on many factors, including the software available on your computer. Even if you use one of the most popular formats, video may not work the same on someone else's system. For example, your computer may be set to open any video format with Windows Media Player, but your cousin may watch the same video in another program, such as the RealPlayer, because her office computer is set up with different software.

Choosing the right video format

How do you know which format to use? One option is to ask your family and friends which format they prefer and use their favorite option. If your friends and family can't agree, or you're trying to reach a broad audience, your best bet is to choose the most popular formats and provide instructions on your Web page to help visitors download and install the corresponding player. (You find a description of video formats in the sidebar called "Popular video formats.")

According to many Web designers, the most widely supported option for video these days is Windows Media. Most PC computers now come with the Windows Media player, and a version is available for Mac users as well. Other Web designers prefer RealMedia and RealAudio formats from RealNetworks because they say these formats provide better streaming and quality options. The biggest challenge with RealMedia is that it requires special software on the Web server. (Check with your Internet hosting service for rates and support.) QuickTime is another popular format, especially among Mac users.

Windows Media, RealMedia, and QuickTime are most popular formats, in large part because they support streaming. To *stream* multimedia means to make it possible to play a file while its downloading from the server. This is valuable because video and audio files can take a long time to download.

Here's how streaming works. When you click a link to a video file, your computer begins to download it from the server. If you're using a player that supports streaming, the video or audio file begins to play as soon as the first part of it is successfully downloaded. If you don't use streaming, the entire file must be downloaded before play can start. Although it can take the same amount of time to download the entire file, streaming can greatly reduce the time it takes to *view* a video online.

You can convert video from one file format to another relatively easily with most video editing programs. For example, you can open a video in AVI format in a program such as Adobe Premier Elements (a great video editor for beginners) and then choose File⇨Export to convert it to any of a dozen formatting and compression options. For example, you could convert an AVI file to the Windows Media format with the compression setting for a 56K modem or into the QuickTime format with the compression setting for a cable modem. Editing video can get complicated, but converting a video file is easy after you understand the conversion options. (For more video software options, see the "Comparing video editing programs" sidebar.)

To help you appreciate the differences in quality and playback speed of some of the video formats covered in this chapter, I included a sample video on the CD and saved it in MPEG, Windows Media, and QuickTime formats with different compression options. For example, `karate-demo-QT-56k.qt` is a QuickTime file saved at a relatively low-quality setting so that it won't take as long to download over a modem. You'll find the same video clip saved in QuickTime at a higher-quality compression level better suited for those with a cable modem. That file is `karate-demo-QT-high.qt`. The files in Windows Media format and MPEG are named similarly. All were created from the same AVI file by using the Adobe Premier Elements Export option. I also included that original AVI file on the CD for comparison.

If you view these clips, you can quickly appreciate the variations in video quality when you use different compression options. For example, the version I saved in Windows Media at the 56K compression setting is only 146K, which should take about 20 seconds to download over a 56K modem, but the video looks very fuzzy because it has been compressed so much. In contrast, the version saved in Windows Media at the higher quality level is nearly 2MB, which takes about 4 ½ minutes to download over a 56K modem, but it looks a lot better. That's why many designers offer both options on their Web sites. Those who are willing to wait or have higher bandwidth are rewarded with better quality video.

To view these video clips and see some of the differences for yourself, insert the CD that came with this book into your computer's CD player. The sample files are in the `video-clips` folder, which is in the `Ch10 Multimedia` folder in the `Author Files` section of the CD.

You can copy the videos to your hard drive or just play them from the CD. But note that you need more than 50MB of free space on your computer for all the video files on the CD.

Popular video formats

The following list provides a brief description of the most common digital video formats:

✔ **Windows Media Video:** Defined by Microsoft and popular on the PC., this video format supports streaming and can be played with Windows Media Player as well as many other popular players. Beware that Windows Media is especially restrictive when it comes to copyrighted content and may restrict your ability to copy and play commercial content, such as a clip copied from a DVD.

File extension: `.wmv`

Web site: `www.microsoft.com/windows/windowsmedia`

✔ **RealVideo:** This streaming file format was designed by RealNetworks to play in RealPlayer (available for Mac and PC). RealMedia provides optimization well suited to low-speed and high-speed connections, but requires special software on your Web server.

File extension: `.rm`

Web site: `www.real.com`

✔ **MPEG:** Pronounced "m-peg." Video in the MPEG (Moving Picture Experts Group) format can be optimized to download much faster than formats with similar quality, such as AVI. MPEGs can be played on most video players, including Windows Media Player, RealPlayer, and dedicated MPEG players.

File extension: `.mpeg`

Web site: `www.mpeg.org`

✔ **QuickTime:** Based on the MPEG standard, QuickTime was developed by Apple. The QuickTime player is built into the Macintosh operating system and is used by most Mac programs that include video or animation. QuickTime is a great format for video on the Web and supports streaming, but it's used primarily by those who favor Macs (although QuickTime files can be viewed with the Windows version of the QuickTime plug-in).

File extension: `.qt`

Web site: `www.quicktime.com`

✔ **AVI:** Created by Microsoft, AVI (Audio Video Interleave) is one the most common video formats on Windows computers and can be played on most common video players. AVI is fine if you're viewing video on your own computer, where the file doesn't have to download, but these files are generally too big to use on the Internet. If your files are in AVI, you should convert them to one of the other formats in this list before adding them to your Web site. Otherwise, you force your visitors to download unnecessarily large video files.

File extension: `.avi`

Web site: No one site about AVI exists, but you can find information if you search for AVI at `www.microsoft.com`.

Inserting video into a Web page

You can insert a video file on your Web page so that the file plays when a visitor opens the page. However, I recommend that you create a special page for each video file and give your viewers an idea of what to expect before they click the link. You don't want to surprise your visitors with video. You want to coax them into it, setting the stage and making sure they know it's worth the wait to download your Academy-Award caliber production.

You insert video on a Web page much like you insert an image file, as you see in the following exercise, except you have more settings. For example, you can set video to play when someone opens a link, or you can require that visitors roll their cursor over an image to make it play.

You can also choose to *loop,* or repeat, the video. Why would you want to make a video file play over and over again? Playing a short video clip repeatedly is a clever way to make the clip seem longer than it is. For example, a 30-second clip of a child laughing may be highly entertaining when played over and over again because it can sound like ongoing laughter.

Creating warnings for multimedia files

Because multimedia files require special players, it's a good idea to include a warning message anytime you add video, audio, or other multimedia files to your Web site. The message should include an explanation of the type of file you're using, the size of the file, how long it may take to download, and what kind of player is required to view it.

The following is an example of a warning you might include just below a video file:

To play this video file, roll your cursor over the image above. The video clip is 30 seconds long and shows our daughter in her karate class. If you're using a modem connection, it may take a minute or two for the video to download and play. If the video does not appear to be playing or if you receive an error message, you may not have the necessary software to play the video.

You can download a free multimedia player for a Windows computer by visiting www.microsoft.com/windows/windowsmedia and clicking the link for Microsoft's Windows Media Player. Make sure to download the player that's right for your operating system. If you have an Apple computer, you'll want the Mac version. If you use a PC, choose the Windows version.

You may want to recommend another player or shorten the message. If you're sure your visitors have the necessary software to play your multimedia files, you may want to include only a description of the video or audio file and information about its length or file size. If you include more than one version of the file in different formats or sizes, make sure to explain the options so your visitors know which is best for their system.

Looping is easily overdone on the Web, so use it judiciously. If you've ever arrived at a page and been frustrated because you couldn't turn off a flashing animation or sound file, you understand the risk. Motion on a Web page can get distracting and even annoying. Used prudently, looping is a good trick for making a video clip seem longer than it is, but repeat a clip no more than three times and then turn it off automatically. You find out how to specify looping and other options in FrontPage in the "Setting video options" section, later in this chapter.

The steps in this section will work for video files in any of the formats covered earlier in this chapter, such as RealMedia, QuickTime, and Windows Media formats. The "Comparing video formats" section, presented earlier, describes the most common video options.

If you don't have a video file but want to follow this exercise, you can use the karate class video file, located in the `Ch10 Multimedia` folder in the `Author Files` section of the CD. (In Figure 10-1, you can see what the file looks like when inserted on a Web page.) I've included several versions of this video, but I suggest you use `karate-demo-WMV-high.wmv` or, if you prefer QuickTime, `karate-demo-QT-high.mov`.

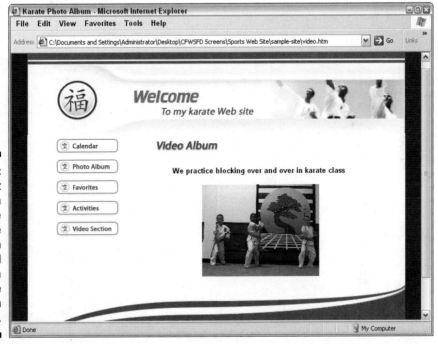

Figure 10-1: The short video file in this karate Web site adds motion and sound to bring a practice session to life.

To use FrontPage to insert a video file, follow these steps:

1. **Before you start, make sure the video file you want to insert is saved in the** `multimedia` **subfolder in your main Web site folder.**

   You should keep all the files in your Web site in one main folder on your hard drive. I suggest you create a subfolder for multimedia so you can keep videos and other files organized.

2. **In FrontPage, open the Web page, and click the cursor where you want the file to be displayed on your Web page.**

   Make sure you're in Design view in FrontPage by clicking the Design icon at the bottom left of the page.

3. **Choose Insert⇨Picture⇨Video, as shown in Figure 10-2.**

   (Video is the last option on the list, and you may need to use the down-pointing arrow at the bottom of the menu to make all options visible.) The Select Video dialog box appears.

4. **Browse your drive to locate the video file you want to insert on your page, and click to select it.**

   In the example I'm creating for this exercise, I selected a file called `karate-demo-WMV-high.wmv`, which is in the `Ch10 Multimedia` folder in the `Author Files` section of the CD.

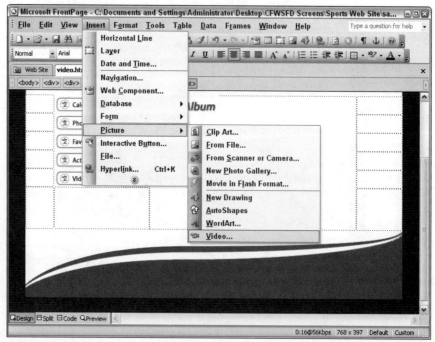

Figure 10-2:
Adding
video to a
Web page is
almost as
easy as
inserting an
image in
FrontPage.

5. **Click Open.**

   The dialog box closes and the file is inserted on the page. The first frame of the video appears on the page, representing the video.

6. **Double-click the video image.**

   The Picture Properties dialog box appears.

7. **Click the various tabs and specify the options you want:**

   - Click the Appearance tab and specify alignment, spacing, and size.

   - Click the General tab and specify link options.

   - Click the Video tab and specify loop, loop delay, and start options.

   For detailed descriptions of the different options, see the "Setting video options" section, which follows.

8. **Click OK.**

   The Picture Properties dialog box closes.

9. **To play the video, click the Preview button at the bottom of the FrontPage work area.**

   If you prefer, choose File➪Preview in Browser to see the video as it will appear when viewed with a browser on the Web.

It's always a good idea to save your work in FrontPage regularly. You can do so by choosing File➪Save, or using the key command, Ctrl+S (on a PC) or ⌘-S (on a Mac). If you haven't already saved your changes before you choose the preview option, FrontPage will prompt you to save your work before opening your page in a browser. If you haven't saved the page you're working on, FrontPage displays an asterisk in front of the file name in the tab at the top of the work area.

Setting video options

Inserting a video into a Web page is a simple process, but specifying all the options can get complicated. In this section, you find descriptions of FrontPage video options, divided into sections based on the tabs in the Picture Properties dialog box.

The Appearance tab

The Appearance tab in the Picture Properties dialog box, shown in Figure 10-3, offers the following options:

   ✓ **Wrapping Style:** Use this option to control how text wraps around your video file. If you choose None, the video appears centered on the page with nothing on either side. If you choose Left, the video appears on the left and the text wraps around the right side of the video. If you choose Right, text wraps around the left side of the video.

✔ **Alignment:** The option enables you to specify how the video is aligned on the page. Alignment works just as it does for images. Left, Right, and Center align the video file to the left, right, or center, respectively, as you would expect. The other options — Top, Middle, and Baseline — control how the text next to the video aligns in relation to the video file. For example, if you choose Middle, any text next to the video will align so that it starts at the same level on the page as the middle of the video file on the page. You can't align text to appear on top of a video file. (You'd have to do that in a video editing program before inserting the video on your page.)

✔ **Border Thickness:** This option specifies the width of the border around the file. If you don't want a border, enter 0 in this field.

✔ **Horizontal Spacing:** If you want to insert a blank space on either side of the video, enter the number of pixels you want to add. That amount of space will be inserted on the left and right sides of the video. Adding a little space around an image or video is a good practice because it provides some separation between the video and other features on the page and helps keep your design from looking too busy.

✔ **Vertical Spacing:** If you want to insert blank space above and below the video, enter the number of pixels you want to add. That amount of space will be inserted on the top and bottom of the video.

✔ **Specify Size:** If you want to specify the size of the area in which the video file will be displayed on the page, select this option. Otherwise, the video will appear in its actual size. To control the actual size of the video, you must use a video editor, such as Adobe Premier Elements. If you choose Specify Size, you can enter the width and height separately or you can choose Keep Aspect Ratio and when you change the width or the height the other will adjust automatically.

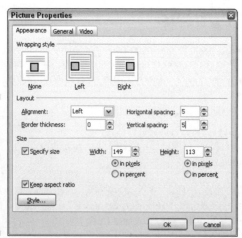

Figure 10-3:
The Appearance tab contains alignment, spacing, and size options.

- **Width:** You can specify the width of the video in pixels or as a percentage of the browser window's width.

- **Height:** You can specify the height in pixels or as a percentage of the browser window's height.

- **Keep Aspect Ratio:** Click this box if you want to ensure that the height and width remain relative to the actual size of the video. For example, suppose the video is 800 pixels wide by 600 pixels high. If you check this box, you can change the width to 400 and the height automatically changes to 200 to maintain the original ratio.

The General tab

Most of the options in the General tab, shown in Figure 10-4, don't apply to video, because FrontPage uses this dialog box for a variety of file types. The following options, however, *do* apply to video:

✓ **Text:** Check this option if you want to associate text with your video. The text appears on the page only if the video is not visible. It's important to use this option to provide a description so that anyone using a browser that can't view the video will know what the video contains. This text is used also by special browsers for the blind that "read" Web pages to their users.

✓ **Long Description:** Use this option if you want to provide a more detailed description of your video. You can use this option in addition to the Text option.

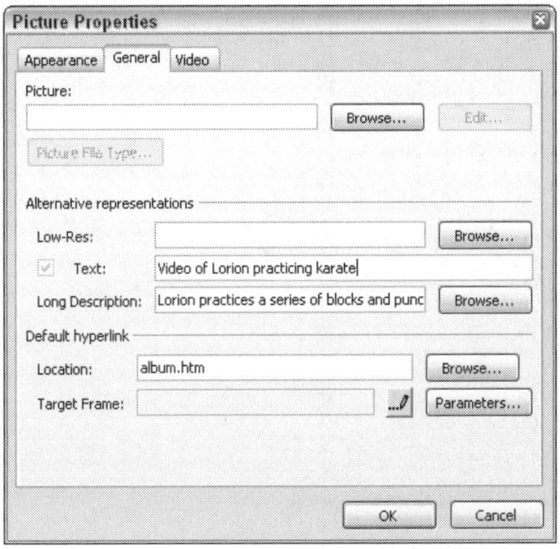

Figure 10-4: Use the Location option if you want to create a link from a video file to another page or Web site.

✔ **Location:** This option creates a link from the video clip on your Web page to another page or Web site. Although it's not common to link a video file like this, you may want to use a link on the video to lead your visitors to a related page or to more video. Use the Browse button to set a link to another page or file on your site. If you want to link to another Web site, enter the URL.

✔ **Target Frame:** If you use frames in your Web site, use this option to specify the target frame you want the linked page to open into. If your Web site uses frames and you don't specify a target, the link will open in the same frame as the link. A frames is an advanced Web design feature that makes it possible to display multiple Web pages on one screen. (I don't cover frames in this book, and I don't generally recommend that you use them.)

The Video tab

The options under the Video tab, shown in Figure 10-5, apply only to video files:

✔ **Video Source:** This option contains the link information that tells the browser the location of the video file on your Web site. If you've already linked your video to your page, the name of the video file and any folders that it resides in should appear in this area. Do not change this information unless you have moved the video file or want to reset the link.

✔ **Loop:** If you set the video to loop more than once, the video will replay the number of times specified.

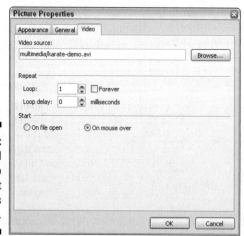

Figure 10-5:
You'll find the Loop and Start options here.

- **Forever:** Check this option if you want your video to play continuously, but beware that your visitors will have no way to stop your video short of closing the page.

- **Loop Delay:** Use this option to specify how long you want the browser to wait after playing the video before starting it again.

- **Start:** This area of the dialog box contains two options relating to when the video begins to play:

  - **On File Open:** As soon as the page is opened, the video begins to download and then plays.

  - **On Mouse Over:** After a user moves the cursor over the image that represents the video file on the page, the video begins to download and then plays.

Shooting video with a digital camera

If you're in the market for a new video camera, go digital. You'll be able to use the video for your Web site much more easily and you can still save the video to a DVD to play on your home entertainment system.

You may also be pleased to discover that you can create short videos with many of the still digital cameras on the market. For example, most consumer-level digital cameras from Canon, Nikon, and others can be used to record video (they even capture sound). You may be limited to shooting only 30 seconds of video at a time, but the quality is remarkably good. Many people don't even realize their digital camera will capture video as well as still images. Most cameras with this feature have a setting option that looks like a small, old-fashioned movie camera. With a digital camera in this mode, pushing the shutter starts video recording, pushing it again stops it. If you don't press the shutter again before the 30-second limit, the video stops recording automatically. You can take multiple video clips and edit them together or cut them into even smaller segments. Set the camera back on the auto setting to take still pictures.

The example of the karate video featured in this chapter and included on the CD was taken with this technique. Using a Canon PowerShot digital camera, I captured a 30-second video of a karate class and edited it to an even shorter 20-second clip — plenty long enough to give viewers an idea of what the kids look like in a practice session. (You find the clip in the `video-clips` subfolder in the `Ch10 Multimedia` folder on the CD.)

Remember, video fills up a camera's memory card much faster than still images (because video files are much larger). The average 30-second AVI format video from a digital camera is at least 25MB. If you don't already have a memory card that holds at least 128MB, invest in one before you start shooting video.

Adding Audio to Your Web Pages

FrontPage provides two choices for adding sound to your Web pages. The first choice is to insert the sound file as a background sound so that the file plays as soon as a visitor opens the page. The second choice is to create a link to the sound file. When a user clicks the link, a multimedia player, such as Windows Media Player, opens and plays the sound file.

Inserting a background sound

You can use FrontPage to insert a sound file into the background of a Web page. The sound plays when a visitor opens the page. You can get many kinds of sound files on CDs and Web sites, or you can record your own by plugging a microphone into your computer and using any common sound recording program, such as Sound Recorder.

In case you don't already have an audio file and want to use one to follow this exercise, I included a WAV file on the CD called `jungle-animals.wav`. You can find this file in the `Ch10 Multimedia` folder in the `Author Files` section of the CD.

Follow these steps to insert a sound file:

1. **Before you start, make sure the audio file you want to insert is saved in the main folder for your Web site.**

   I recommend creating a `multimedia` folder in your main Web site folder for audio and other multimedia files, just as you should create an `image` folder for your image files.

2. **In FrontPage's Design view, open the Web page to which you want to add the audio file.**

   Make sure you're in Design view by clicking the Design icon at the bottom left of the page.

3. **Choose File⇨Properties.**

   The Page Properties dialog box appears. This dialog box contains many settings that affect the entire page.

4. **Click the General tab.**

5. **In the Background Sound area at the bottom of the page, click the Browse button next to the Location option.**

   The Background Sound dialog box appears.

6. **Browse to locate the sound file you want to insert in your page.**

7. **Click the file name to select it, and then click the Open button (or double-click the file name).**

   The sound file is inserted into the background of the page, and the file name and path appear in the Location box in the Background Sound dialog box. In the example I'm creating in this exercise, I selected a file called `jungle-animals.wav`, which was saved in the `multimedia` folder for my sample Web site, as shown in Figure 10-6.

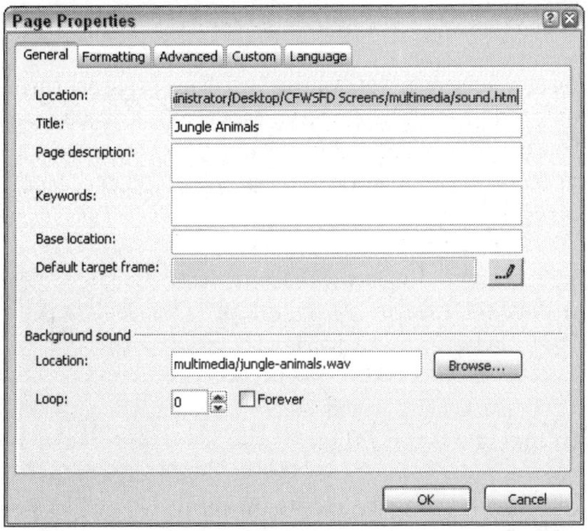

Figure 10-6:
If you insert an audio file into the background of a page, it will play when a visitor opens the page.

8. **Specify the loop options in the Page Properties dialog box.**

   The loop options are at the bottom of the dialog box. You can choose to *loop*, or repeat, the sound file a set number of times, or you can click to select the Forever box and the sound file will play continuously. If you set the Loop option to 0, the file will play once.

9. **Click OK.**

   Your audio file options are saved and the Page Properties dialog box closes.

Creating a link to a sound file

The second way to add audio to your Web page is to link to a sound file. When a user clicks the link, it launches a sound player, such as Windows Media Player, and plays the file.

Popular audio formats

The following list provides a brief description of each of the most common digital audio formats:

✔ **MP3:** By far the most successful audio compression format, MP3 comes from the same family as MPEG and supports streaming audio. Most music you can download from the Internet is in MP3 format, and it is clearly the first choice of most Web developers. This format includes technology to add watermarks, identification marks that are invisible to most viewers but identify the creator of the original music file when analyzed more carefully.

File extension: .mp3

Web site: www.mp3.com

✔ **Windows Audio:** Microsoft's Windows Audio format supports streaming and can be played with Windows Media Player as well as many other popular players. Windows Audio is especially restrictive when it comes to copyrighted content, which makes it popular among big recording studios but may prevent your ability to copy and play commercial music, such as songs copied from a CD, even for legal personal use.

File extension: .wma

Web site: www.microsoft.com/windows/windowsmedia

✔ **RealAudio:** This streaming file format was designed for the Internet by RealNetworks and can be played in RealPlayer (available for Mac and PC). RealAudio is especially popular among radio stations and entertainment sites because it provides optimization well suited to low-speed and high-speed connections.

File extension: .ra

Web site: www.real.com

✔ **Ogg Vorbis:** The newest audio format on the Web, Ogg Vorbis is open source that is not patented. As a result, it is constantly being improved by programmers who volunteer to work on it, but you may not get much direct support for this file type. Ogg Vorbis is the only audio format for the Web that offers surround sound for those who have multiple speakers.

File extension: .ogg

Web site: www.vorbis.com

✔ **WAV:** This file format is popular in digital media because it offers the highest sound quality possible. But audio files in this format are often too big for use on the Web, averaging 10MB for a minute of audio (in comparison, an MP3 file that is five times longer can be less than one third the size). Although WAV files are commonly used on the Internet because of their nearly universal compatibility, I recommend that you convert WAV files (especially for long audio clips) to one of the other audio formats described in this sidebar and compress them before linking them to your Web site.

File extension: .wav

Web site: No official Web site exists for WAV files, but you can find some documentation at www.microsoft.com if you search for WAV.

To create a link to a sound file, follow these steps:

1. **Before you start, make sure the audio file you want to insert is saved in the** `multimedia` **folder in your Web site folder.**

   I suggest that you create a `multimedia` folder in your main Web site folder for your multimedia files.

2. **In FrontPage, create a new page or open the page on which you want to create a link.**

   Remember, always save the page you're working on before you set links.

3. **Select the text or image that you want to serve as the link.**

   That is, select the text or image that, when clicked, will open the sound file.

4. **Click the Insert Hyperlink icon on the standard toolbar.**

   (The icon looks like a globe with a link of chain next to it.) The Insert Hyperlink dialog box appears.

5. **Select the name of the sound file that you want your image or text to link to, and then click OK.**

   The link is set and the dialog box closes. If you selected text, the words appear underlined and in a different color. If you selected an image and have not added a border, you will not see any change in the way the image appears.

When a user clicks a link to a sound file, the browser must open a multimedia player capable of reading the sound file format. If no such program is available on the user's computer, the audio file will not play. Because of this, include a description of the audio file on your Web page with instructions for downloading the media player. For details of this process, see the "Creating warnings for multimedia files" sidebar, earlier in this chapter.

Adding Animations with Flash

Macromedia Flash is by far the most widely used technology on the Web for creating animations as well as many other interactive features, such as games and interactive quizzes. Flash is ideally suited for use on the Web because you can use it to create highly complex images and interactive features that download quickly and adjust to fit any size screen.

Flash is so popular on the Internet because it utilizes *vector graphics,* a technology in which the graphics are based on mathematical descriptions that take up far less space than bitmapped graphics. Vector graphics can be scaled up or down to fill a browser window of any size without affecting the image quality or the size of the file that's downloaded.

Flash files can be recognized by their file extension, .swf. As a format designed specifically for the Web, Flash continues to win acclaim and widespread adoption, and the program needed to view Flash files is now built into most browsers. You can even synchronize sound in Flash.

Inserting a Flash file into your Web site is easy, but creating Flash files gets complicated and requires Macromedia's Flash creation program. If you want to find out how to create Flash files, I recommend *Flash MX 2004 For Dummies* by Gurdy Leete and Ellen Finkelstein (published by Wiley).

The good news is that Flash is so popular you can find Flash animations almost as easily as you can find clip art. A number of Web sites offer free Flash animations, and you can buy Flash files if you want something more sophisticated or original. Just type the word *Flash* in any search engine and you'll find many great resources.

Inserting Flash files

If you don't already have a Flash file, use the sample Flash file on the CD accompanying this book. Just look for any file with the .swf extension, such as logo-animation.swf in the Ch10 Multimedia folder in the Author Files section.

To add a Flash file to a Web page with FrontPage, follow these steps:

1. **Before you start, make sure the Flash file you want to insert is saved in the** multimedia **folder in your Web site folder.**

   I suggest that you create a multimedia folder in your main Web site folder for Flash files and other multimedia files.

2. **Create a page, or open an existing Web page in FrontPage.**

3. **Click to insert the cursor where you want the Flash file to be displayed on your Web page.**

   Make sure you're in Design view in FrontPage by clicking the Design icon at the bottom left of the page.

4. **Choose Insert➪Picture➪Movie in Flash Format, as shown in Figure 10-7.**

   The Select File dialog box appears. Note that you may need to use the expansion arrow to make the Picture option visible, as shown in Figure 10-7.

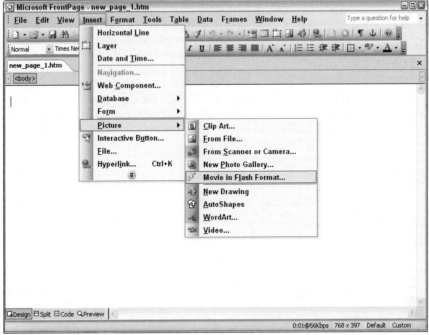

Figure 10-7:
The Insert
Movie in
Flash
Format
option in
FrontPage is
located
under the
Insert
Picture
option.

5. **Browse your drive to locate the Flash file you want inserted on your page, and click to select it.**

   In the example I'm creating for this exercise, I selected a file called `logo-animation.swf`.

6. **Click Insert.**

   The dialog box closes and the Flash file is inserted on the page. In Design view, the Flash file is represented by a large grey box with the name of the file, as shown in Figure 10-8.

7. **Double-click the grey box that represents the Flash file.**

   The Movie in Flash Format Properties dialog box opens.

8. **Click the Appearance tab and specify options such as background color, alignment, spacing, and size.**

   You find detailed descriptions of these options in the "Setting Flash options" section that follows.

9. **Click the General tab and specify options such as Auto play and loop.**

   Again, refer to the "Setting Flash options" section for more information on these options.

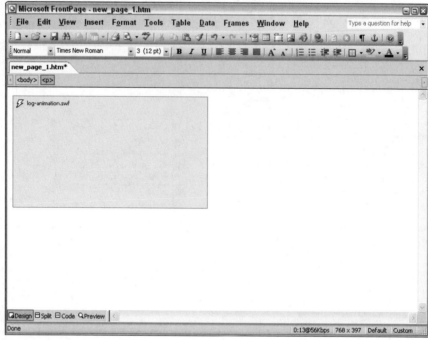

10. Click OK.

The Movie in Flash Format Properties dialog box closes.

11. Click the Preview button at the bottom of the FrontPage work area to play the Flash file.

FrontPage doesn't display Flash files in Design view, but it will play them in Preview mode. If you prefer to check your work in a browser, choose File➪Preview in Browser and the page will be displayed in a Web browser, where the Flash file should function as it would on a Web page.

Flash files require a special Flash plug-in, which is built into most browsers. If your visitors don't have such program on their computers, the file will not play. Because of this, make sure you include a description of the multimedia file and instructions for downloading the player. See the sidebar on "Creating warnings for multimedia files" for an example of such a warning.

The Flash plug-in, which you can get at www.flash.com, is free and downloads very quickly.

Setting Flash options

Like other multimedia formats, Flash, has many options. These options, called *attributes* in HTML, are especially important for Flash files because many of them — such as height and width — are required for the files to work properly in a browser. FrontPage takes care of setting the height and width automatically, but you may want to change some other settings.

The Appearance tab

The Flash options shown in Figure 10-9 are available under the Appearance tab in the Movie in Flash Format Properties dialog box in FrontPage.

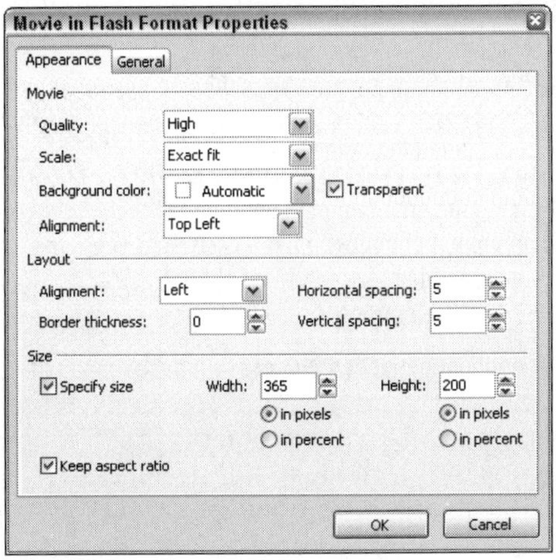

Figure 10-9: Double-click a Flash file and you'll find most of these settings.

The following is a brief description of each setting:

- ✔ **Quality:** This option enables you to prioritize the antialiasing options of your images versus the speed of playback. *Antialiasing,* which makes your files appear smoother, can slow down the rendering of each frame because the computer must first smooth any rough edges. The Quality parameter enables you to regulate how much the process is slowed down by letting you set priorities based on the importance of appearance versus playback speed. You can choose from these Quality options:

  - **Low:** Antialiasing is never used. Playback speed has priority over appearance.

- **Auto Low:** Playback begins with antialiasing turned off. If the Flash player detects that the processor can handle it, antialiasing is turned on. Use this option to emphasize speed at first but improve appearance whenever possible.

- **Auto High:** With this more sophisticated option, playback is set to begin with antialiasing turned on. However, if the frame rate supported by the user's computer drops too low, antialiasing turns off to improve playback speed. This option emphasizes playback speed and appearance equally at first but sacrifices appearance for the sake of playback speed if necessary.

- **Medium:** Antialiasing is used only when needed. Appearance and playback speed are balanced.

- **High:** Antialiasing is always used. Appearance has priority over playback speed.

- **Best:** Antialiasing is always used. Appearance has priority over playback speed. Not noticeably different from the High option

✔ **Scale:** Specify this option only if you change the file's original Height and Width settings. The Scale parameter enables you to define how the Flash movie displays within those settings. The following options in the Scale drop-down list enable you to set preferences for how a scaled Flash movie is displayed in the window:

- **Default (Show All):** This option displays the entire movie in the specified area. The width and height proportions of the original movie are maintained and no distortion occurs, but borders may appear on two sides of the movie to fill the space.

- **No Border:** This option enables you to scale a Flash movie to fill a specified area. No border appears, and the original aspect ratio is maintained.

- **Exact Fit:** The Flash movie is shown with the set width and height, but the original aspect ratio may not be maintained.

✔ **Background Color:** This option sets a background color that fills the area of the file. This color appears if the specified height and width are larger than the file and during periods when the movie isn't playing because it's loading or has finished playing.

✔ **Alignment (under Movie):** This alignment option controls how the Flash file is aligned within the Flash display area on the page (as specified by the selected height and width options). Unless you've changed the display area of the Flash file so that it's larger than the actual size of the Flash file (which I don't recommend), you should keep this set to the default, Center.

✔ **Alignment (under Layout):** This alignment option enables you to specify how the Flash file is aligned on the Web page. Layout alignment for a

Flash file works just as it does for images. Left, Right, and Center align the video file to the left, right, or center, respectively, as you would expect. The other options — Top, Middle, and Baseline — control how the text next to the video aligns in relation to the video file. For example, if you choose Middle, any text next to the video will align so that it starts at the same level on the page as the middle of the video file on the page. You can't align text to appear on top of a video file. (You have to do that in a video editing program before inserting the video on your page.)

✔ **Border Thickness:** This option specifies the width of the border around the file. If you don't want a border, enter 0 in this field.

✔ **Horizontal Spacing:** If you want a blank space on the left and right sides of the Flash file, enter the amount of space in pixels.

✔ **Vertical Spacing:** If you want a blank space above and below the Flash file, enter the amount of space in pixels.

✔ **Specify Size:** To specify the size of the area in which the Flash file will appear on the page, select this option. Otherwise, the Flash file will appear in its actual size.

  • **Width:** You can specify the width of the Flash file in pixels or as a percentage of the browser window's width.

  • **Height:** You can specify the height in pixels or as a percentage of the browser window's height.

  • **Keep Aspect Ratio:** Check this box if you want to ensure that the height and width remain relative to the size of the Flash file. For example, if the Flash file is 400 pixels wide by 200 pixels high and you check this box, you can change the width to 200 and the height automatically changes to 100 to maintain the original ratio.

The General tab

The Flash options shown in Figure 10-10 are available under the General tab in the Movie in Flash Format Properties dialog box in FrontPage. The following is a brief description of the most important settings:

✔ **Name field:** This name is not the same as the file name. You need to provide a name for the Flash file only if you're using a programming or scripting language to control the file. The name is used by the script to identify the file. You can leave this field blank or name the file whatever you want (just don't use spaces or special characters). FrontPage applies a name if you leave the field blank.

✔ **Source URL:** This text field specifies the location of the .swf file. When you create a link to a URL, this field is filled in by FrontPage. Although you can change it manually, I recommend you do so only if you are very experienced with creating links.

✔ **Base URL:** You can use this attribute to specify the directory where your Flash files are stored. If your visitors have trouble displaying your Flash files, this setting can help their browsers identify the location of Flash files. Unless your visitors use older browser version, this setting should not be necessary.

✔ **Playback:** The following options control how the Flash file will play.

- **Auto Play:** This option controls the Play parameter, enabling you to determine whether a Flash movie starts as soon as it downloads to the viewer's computer or a user must click the Flash file to play it. A check mark in this box causes the Flash file to start playing as soon as the page finishes loading. If you don't check this box, whatever option is set in the Flash file itself will be used to start the movie.

- **Loop:** Checking this box causes the Flash file to repeat (or *loop*). If you don't check this box, the Flash movie will play once and then stop after it reaches the last frame.

- **Show Menu:** This option enables you to display a menu of options if you've created a menu to go with the file.

- **SWLiveConnect:** Checking this box will insert the value "true." This attribute is used only by Netscape. Checking the box can help ensure that your files play properly for visitors who use the Netscape browser.

✔ **Network Location:** These settings identify the Class ID for Flash files and the location of the Flash Player in case a visitor doesn't have the plug-in needed to display a Flash file. Microsoft automatically inserts the Class ID and Netscape and Internet Explorer plug-in URLs in these boxes. You should not to change these settings unless you know that you want to specify a different location.

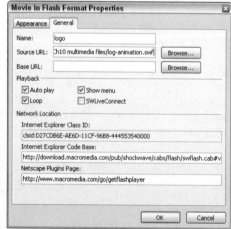

Figure 10-10:
This is where you specify loop and auto play options.

Working with Other Multimedia Formats

So many plug-ins, so little bandwidth. You can find hundreds of technologies that use plug-ins to add special features to Web pages. Some of them give you fabulous results, such as special sound effects, 360-degree images, and even three-dimensional worlds. But with plug-ins — perhaps more than with any other technology on the Web — you have to be careful. Web page visitors aren't usually excited about having to download a new plug-in, even if you as a Web site creator are excited about deploying it. Indeed, many visitors are scared by the idea, others are just plain annoyed, and still others lack the hardware or software requirements to run the plug-in. Don't risk doing that to your viewers, especially when they're family, unless you have a compelling reason.

If you send visitors off to get a plug-in just so they can see a logo spinning around in all its three-dimensional splendor, they aren't going to be happy. On the other hand, if your site features interactive games or a three-dimensional environment with chat capability targeted for visitors with those interests, they may be quite happy to go get a plug-in. Make sure that you let your users know what they're in for before you send them off on a plug-in adventure.

The best place to find out about multimedia formats is the Web itself. Any technology that's worth using should have a sophisticated Web site that explains how the program works and where to find the necessary software to create and watch it.

Part IV

Creating Special Project Sites

The 5th Wave   By Rich Tennant

"YOU KNOW KIDS — YOU CAN'T BUY THEM JUST ANY WEB AUTHORING SOFTWARE."

In this part . . .

The project-specific chapters in this part are designed to tell you everything you need to get a Web site up and running quickly for special events. Whether you want to create a site for your new baby, for your wedding, or to show off family vacation photos, you'll find everything you need in Chapters 11, 12, and 13. In Chapter 14, find out how to create a site for your hobbies, clubs, or sporting events, complete with instructions for including video. On the CD that accompanies this book are predesigned template pages and graphics that make it easy to personalize the designs featured in each of these chapters. In Chapter 15, you discover how one of the fastest growing trends on the Internet — blogging — is a great way to post frequent messages and family stories online.

Chapter 11

It's a Baby! Web Site

*N*othing compares to a baby's first photos or the eagerness of friends and family who want to see them right away. That's why this chapter shows you how to get photos online in the quickest and easiest way possible, and then goes on to cover creating a more elaborate Web site where you can chronicle a child's growth and development over time.

In the first section of this chapter you find out about online photo album services, which provide an immediate solution to getting your photos online and accessible to anyone with a connection to the Web. Then I introduce you to online services that provide one-stop Web site solutions. Finally, you find out how to use the templates included on the CD to create your own custom baby Web site. You can use all three options or go directly to the section that covers the option you like best.

Creating an Online Photo Album

If you want to get a few digital images online as fast as possible, the simplest and least expensive option is a free photo album site, such as Shutterfly or Ofoto. Here's how they work. You log on with a Web browser, fill out a registration form, and then click a button to select the images you want to upload from your hard drive. The images become instantly available on the site (to anyone to whom you've given your user ID and password).

You don't even have to optimize your pictures to make them download faster. These sites want you to upload high-resolution images because those are better for printing — and that's how they make their money, selling prints for 20 to 30 cents each. (Just beware that on a dial-up connection, it can take several minutes to upload a big image file.)

The most popular free online photo album sites are Shutterfly (`www.shutterfly.com`), Kodak's Ofoto (`www.ofoto.com`), Yahoo Photos (`photos.yahoo.com`), and You've Got Pictures (available only to AOL members).

The downside of these sites is that they don't give you any choice about the design for your photo album pages and little room for text to go with your images. If you like the simplicity of an online service but want to create a Web site that's more advanced than an online photo album, consider using a service such as `family.myevent.com`. For more on these and other services, see Chapter 1.

If you want to create a custom Web site for your baby, read on. The rest of this chapter is filled with instructions for creating your own baby site by personalizing the template pages and graphics on the CD.

Using the Templates on the CD

To make it easier for you to create a Web site, I've designed a template Web site with graphics of a stork, a sun, and a baby bottle, in soft pastel blues and yellows. A *template* is essentially a predesigned Web page that you can customize by replacing the images and text with your own content. As the owner of this book you are welcome to use the templates on the CD in any way you like. You can make minor changes to insert your child's pictures and name, or you can make more dramatic changes, altering the graphics and page layout. To keep things simple, I saved the page templates on the CD as basic HTML files so you can edit them with any Web design program.

In this chapter, you find out how to customize the templates in Microsoft FrontPage 2003 and edit the images in Photoshop Elements 3.

If you prefer to use the Macromedia Dreamweaver MX 2004 program, visit `www.digitalfamily.com`, where you'll find step-by-step instructions for using Dreamweaver to customize the baby Web site template.

All the template pages and images you need to create the design featured in this chapter are on the CD that came with this book. To use them, insert the CD into your computer and copy the contents of the `Ch11 Baby Site` folder (located in the `Author Files` section of the CD) to your hard drive. Inside that folder you'll find three subfolders:

> ✔ `sample-baby-site` contains a completed Web site you can use as a model.
>
> ✔ `template-baby-site` contains the pages you should work with as you create your own site.
>
> ✔ `photoshop-files` contains all the graphics for the site in their original PSD format, which makes them easy to edit in Photoshop Elements.

When you copy images from a CD to your hard drive, you may find that the files are locked, meaning you can't save changes to them. To correct this on a PC, right-click the `Ch11 Baby Site` folder and choose Properties. In the Attributes area of the Properties dialog box, deselect the Read Only option. Click Apply and then click OK. If you're using a Mac, ⌘-click the folder name, choose Get Info, and deselect the Locked option.

Touring Baby Sites

As you see in Figure 11-1, the photos are the focus of the sample Web site, which begins with a picture of Max the day he was born. The photo album begins on the front page, but you can choose to create the photo album as a subsection and include more text or multiple images on the front page. Either way, the Next and Previous buttons help your visitors navigate through your pages, and the buttons on the left can make it easy to jump to any of the main sections. Using the template pages on the CD, you can add as many pages as you want to your baby's Web site and create new buttons for as many sections as you want.

If you have a large collection of images you want to add to your Web site, you'll appreciate the creation tools in Photoshop Elements 3.0. These tools automate the process of resizing images and creating the pages and links. You find instructions for creating Web photo galleries in Chapter 7.

Most baby Web sites feature lots of photos, as well as other relevant information about a newborn — time and date of birth, weight, height, and other details. In the template site for this chapter, I called that section Details, but you can change the text on that button (as well as any of the other graphics in this site) by following the instructions in the following section, "Editing the Graphics for Your Baby Site."

Another popular feature of a baby site is a gift registry (like the one shown in Figure 11-2), where you can include links to online stores that offer gift registry services. Shops such as Baby Gap and Pottery Barn Kids have everything you need to create a registry and identify all the goodies you'd like for your child. If you search Google with the words *baby gift registry,* you'll find dozens of Web sites that provide these services. Adding links to these sites is easy, as you'll see in the "Creating a Gift Registry" section later in this chapter.

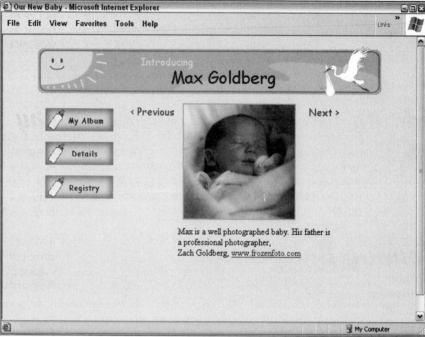

Figure 11-1:
A photo
album is a
great way to
showcase
baby
pictures,
like this
photo
taken by
professional
photog-
rapher Zach
Goldberg
(`www.
frozen
foto.com`).

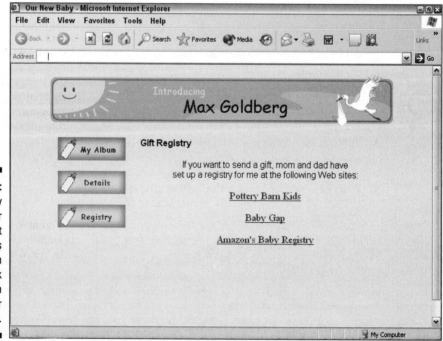

Figure 11-2:
Many
stores offer
online gift
registries
and you can
easily link
to them
from your
Web site.

Before you build your own baby Web site, I encourage you to visit other baby Web sites for ideas. One of the most impressive baby sites I've ever seen is The Trixie Update at `www.trixieupdate.com`. Mori Central at `www.mori central.com` is another great example of a site that showcases baby photos, stories, and more.

Editing the Graphics for Your Baby Site

The button and banner graphics for this baby site use generic words, so you don't have to edit them. However, I encourage you to personalize the graphics and make them your own. For example, the banner in the template folder includes the text *Introducing Our New Baby,* but I changed the text in the sample site (refer to Figure 11-2) to *Introducing Max Goldberg*.

In this section, I show you how to personalize the banner and buttons in the template site. In the next section, you find out how to optimize photographs and insert them into the photo frame included in the site's design. You'll find that it's easier to put your site together if you prepare all the graphics (photos, buttons, and so on) before you start building your pages.

If you haven't already copied the graphic files for this chapter from the CD, insert the CD into your computer and copy the `Author Files` in the `Ch11 Baby Site` folder to your hard drive. Inside that folder, you'll find a subfolder called `photoshop-files` that contains all the graphics in their original Photoshop Elements format (indicated by the `.psd` extension). These image files are saved in a high-resolution format and include layers, which makes them easier to edit than the optimized graphics in the `images` folder in the `template-baby-site` folder.

If you don't already have a graphics program that supports layers, I recommend Photoshop Elements 3.0. If you use another image program, such as Photoshop CS or Dreamweaver Fireworks, the editing techniques described in this chapter will be similar but not identical.

Editing the banner graphic

At the top of the main page of the baby template Web site, I created a graphic that features a sun and a stork and the words *Introducing Our New Baby*. In this section, you personalize the graphic by replacing the words *Our New Baby* with your baby's name.

To add your baby's name to the banner graphic, follow these steps:

1. **Launch Photoshop Elements 3 (or any image design program that supports layers).**

2. **Open the** `banner.psd` **graphic in the** `photoshop-files` **folder.**

   Choose File➪Open and locate the file on your hard drive.

3. **If the Layer's palette is not already open, choose Window➪Layers to open it.**

   The Layers palette opens on the right side of the screen, as shown in Figure 11-3. Note that this graphic has four layers, called Stork, Baby Name, Introducing, and Background. Before you can edit any part of this graphic, you must first select the layer that corresponds to the section you want to change.

4. **In the Layers palette, click the Baby Name layer.**

   The Baby Name layer becomes shaded in a darker grey, indicating that it's the active layer, as shown in Figure 11-3.

5. **Click the text tool (represented by a T) in the Tools palette on the left side of the work area.**

   If the Tools palette is not open, choose Window➪Tools to open it.

Figure 11-3: To add your baby's name to the banner graphic, you need to select the corresponding layer.

6. **Click and drag to highlight the words *Our New Baby,* and then type your baby's name.**

   The words *Our New Baby* disappear and your baby's name appears in their place. You can also use the Backspace and Delete keys to remove the original text.

7. **Use the text formatting options at the top of the work area to change the font face, color, and font size.**

   In the banner image included on the CD, I used a 30-point, bold Comic Sans MS font for the words *Our New Baby.* If you don't have Comic Sans or you want to change it, you can use any font you want.

8. **Change other parts of the banner, as desired.**

   If you want to change the word *Introducing,* for example, click to select the Introducing layer and repeat Steps 5 through 7. I used the same Comic Sans MS font for the word *Introducing,* but reduced the point size to 18. For more information on editing text in graphics and adjusting font options, see Chapter 6.

9. **To save your changes, choose File⇨Save For Web.**

   The Save for Web dialog box opens.

10. **In the Optimized File Format list, choose GIF, as shown in Figure 11-4.**

    The GIF format is the preferred file format for line art, such as cartoons and logos, on the Web. (You find more on image formats for the Web in Chapter 6.)

11. **In the Colors box, set the number to 64.**

    Limiting the number of colors reduces the file size and makes the image download more quickly. For an even smaller file size, reduce this number, but don't go too far or you'll adversely affect the appearance of the image. For more information on Web graphics options, see Chapter 6.

12. **Click OK to save the new banner.**

    The Save Optimized As dialog box opens.

13. **Save the file in the `images` folder in your Web site folder, and give it a new name.**

    You can name the new banner anything you like as long as you don't use spaces or special characters.

Your new customized banner is now ready to be inserted in your Web page. You'll find instructions for doing so later in this chapter in the "Editing a template page" section.

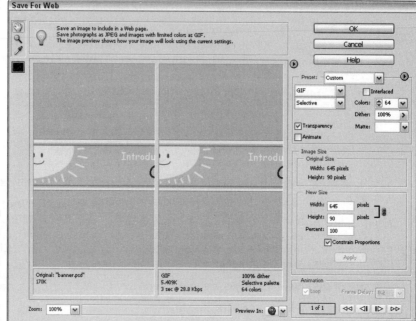

Figure 11-4:
Choose the
GIF format
for the
banner
graphic.

If you make changes to the banner that you're not happy with and want to start over again, you can always go back to the .psd file you were working on before you saved the image as a GIF. If you really mess up and want to start over, open the banner2.psd file. It's the same as banner.psd. I added it to the folder as a backup because I know how easy it is to make mistakes when you're just starting out in a program like Photoshop Elements. Similarly, I've included button.psd and button2.psd graphics to give you a second chance with that design as well. As a general rule, save a backup copy of any photo or graphic before you start editing it.

Editing the button graphics

The buttons on this site are labeled My Album, Details, and Registry. Optimized versions of all three are saved in the images folder, which is in the template-baby-site folder, with the names button-album.gif, button-details.gif, and button-registry.gif, respectively.

You can change the words on these buttons and you can create additional buttons with new text, or you can skip this exercise and use any or all the predesigned buttons just as they are. (They're already linked to their respective pages.) If you don't want to use a particular button, simply delete it from the template pages.

To keep text readable on buttons and banners, you need to be concise. The fewer words the better and the shorter the words the better. For example, don't try to provide a long explanation like "Baby's height, weight, and time of birth" in a button. Instead, limit yourself to a simple word that conveys a more general meaning, like "Details."

To edit the text on the `button.psd` graphic, follow these steps.

1. **Launch Photoshop Elements 3.**

2. **Open the `button.psd` graphic in the `photoshop-files` folder.**

   Choose File⇨Open and locate the file on your hard drive.

3. **If the Layers palette is not already open, choose Window⇨Layers to open it.**

   The button graphic has three layers, called Text, Bottle, and Background, as shown in the Layers palette in Figure 11-5.

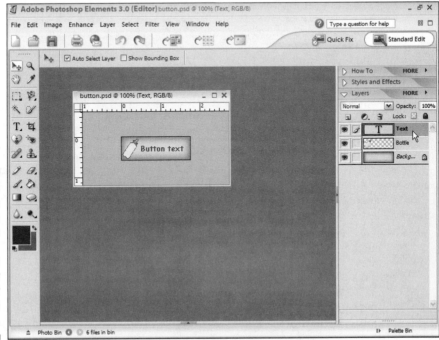

Figure 11-5: You can change the text in the `button.psd` file to create new buttons for your Web page.

4. **In the Layers palette, select the Text layer.**

The Text layer becomes shaded a darker grey, indicating it is the active layer.

5. **Select the text tool (the T in the Tools palette).**

If the Tools palette is not open, choose Window⇨Tools to open it.

6. **Highlight the words *Button Text* on the sample button, and then type the text you want to use.**

Your text replaces the words *Button Text.*

If you have trouble changing the text, try the following. Delete the Text layer by dragging it to the small trash icon at the top of the page, click to insert your cursor on the button, and type new text by using the text tool.

7. **Use the text formatting options on the toolbar at the top of the work area to change the font face, color, and font size, as shown in Figure 11-6.**

I used a 13-point, bold, Comic Sans MS font for the buttons in this template. If you change the font in one button, I recommend that you change the font in all the buttons so that they look the same. For more information on changing text in graphics, font options, and colors, see Chapter 6.

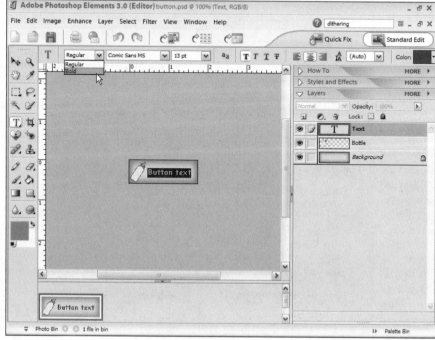

Figure 11-6: You can format the text in a graphic with the font, size, style, and other options available from the toolbar at the top of the work area.

8. **When you finish editing the button, choose File⇨Save for Web.**

   The Save For Web dialog box opens.

9. **In the Optimized File Format pull-down, choose GIF.**

10. **In the Colors box, set the number to 32.**

    Limiting the number of colors reduces the file size and makes the image download more quickly. I'm using fewer colors in this image than I did in the banner because the design is less complex and has less color variation.

11. **Click OK to save the new button.**

    The Save Optimized As dialog box opens.

12. **Save the file in the** images **folder in your Web site folder and give it a new name.**

Repeat these steps for each button you want to create. After you edit all the button graphics, you'll be ready to create the navigation area for your Web site.

Preparing Photos for Your Baby Site

In most families, new babies are a favorite photo subject. But before you put those cute pictures on your Web site, you need to optimize them so they download as quickly as possible for your visitors. You find more detailed information about editing and optimizing images in Chapter 6, but to help you get your baby site online as quickly as possible, the following steps walk you through the basic process of resizing and converting photos to prepare them for the Web so you can add photos to your baby site right away.

To resize and optimize a photo and insert it into the photo frame used in the templates for the baby site featured in this chapter, follow these steps.

1. **Launch Photoshop Elements 3.**

2. **Open one of the photo frame graphics in the** photoshop-files **folder in the** Ch11 Baby Site **folder from the CD.**

   Choose File⇨Open and locate the photo-frame graphic. For this template, I've created three photo frames, one for tall photos (photo-frame-tall. psd), one for wide photos (photo-frame-wide.psd), and one for photos you've cropped into a square (photo-frame-square.psd).

3. **In the Layers palette, click to select the Photo layer.**

   If the Layers palette isn't open, choose Window⇨Layers. All three photo frame graphics have two layers called Photo Layer and Background, as shown in Figure 11-7.

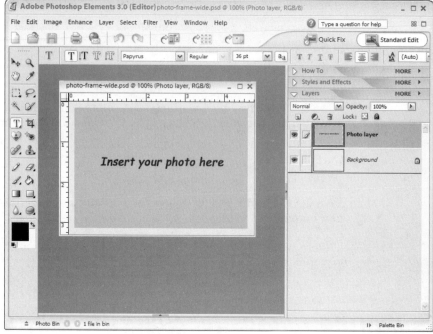

Figure 11-7:
Insert your
resized
photos into
a photo
frame to
create a
more
finished look
for your
photo
album.

4. **Open the photograph you want to use on your Web site.**

   Choose File➪Open, locate the photo on your hard drive, and double-click to open the file.

5. **Resize the photo to fit in the photo frame.**

   Choose Image➪Resize and specify the height and width you want in the Image Size dialog box. For your images to fit into the photo frames for this template, wide photos should be no larger than 320 x 215 pixels, tall photos should be no larger than 180 x 275 pixels, and square photos should be no larger than 210 x 210.

6. **Copy the photo and paste it into the picture frame.**

   a. **Click to select the move tool in the Tools palette.**

   b. **Click to place your cursor anywhere in your photo file, and then choose Select➪All.**

   c. **Choose Edit➪Copy.**

   d. **Click to place your cursor in the middle of the picture frame image, and then choose Edit➪Paste.**

   Your photo appears in the picture frame and a new layer is created. You can adjust the position of your photo by dragging it within the picture frame image or by using the arrow keys on your keyboard.

      e. Delete the original Photo layer.

         To do so, click to select the original Photo layer (the tan box) and then drag it to the small trash can icon at the top of the Layers palette.

      f. Delete the Text layer.

  7. Choose File➪Save For Web.

    The Save For Web dialog box appears.

  8. In the Optimized File Format list, choose JPEG.

  9. Set the Quality to 80 percent.

    Lowering the quality helps reduce the file size and makes the image download more quickly. For an even smaller file size, reduce this number more, but don't go too far or you'll adversely affect the appearance of the image.

  10. Save the new photo in your Web site folder with a new name.

Repeat these steps for each photo you want to prepare for your site. Then follow the steps in the next section to insert the images into your pages.

Creating a Baby Web Site by Using the Templates

The templates in this chapter were designed to make it easy to create a simple Web site for a baby. Remember, though, that you can always add more pages and even new sections to your site later.

To help you get started and make it easy for you to build a complete site quickly, I created five template pages for your baby site:

- ✔ `index.html` is the main page.
- ✔ `registry.html` is the gift registry.
- ✔ `details.html` is where you list the baby's height, weight, and other information.
- ✔ `album.html` and `album2.html` are two photo album pages.

You can use any of these template pages. And you can create new pages based on any of these page designs by choosing File➪Save As and giving the page a new name.

If you want to edit the banner, buttons, or other graphics for this site, I suggest you work on the images before you start building your pages. For instructions on editing the image files in this site, see the "Editing the Graphics for Your Baby Site" section, earlier in this chapter.

Opening the template site in FrontPage

Before you edit any pages of a Web site in FrontPage, you should first use the Open Site command in FrontPage to identify your main Web site folder. Keep all the files that you will use in your Web site in one main folder and then use sub-folders to organize files within your site. Doing so makes it easier to upload the files correctly to your server and helps FrontPage set the links properly. In the following exercises you work with the files in the `template-baby-site` folder.

Follow these steps to open the main folder for your baby Web site in FrontPage:

1. **If you haven't done so already, insert the CD that came with this book into your computer's CD drive and copy the folder called `template-baby-site` from the `Ch11 Baby Site` folder onto your hard drive.**

   I also suggest you rename the folder something that has more meaning for you, like Baby Jessica's Web site. Also make sure that any new image files you created in the earlier exercises are saved in the `images` folder inside the main site folder before you continue with these steps.

2. **Open the template site in FrontPage 2003 as you would open any other Web site.**

   Choose File➪Open Site and locate the `template-baby-site` folder (or whatever you named it) on your hard drive. Click to select the folder and click Open to open the site in FrontPage. The Web site opens in FrontPage and the files and subfolders are displayed in the Web Site window, as shown in Figure 11-8.

Editing a template page

After you open the template site, you can begin to work on the individual pages of the site. To edit the text in any of the template pages, follow these steps:

1. **With the Web site open in FrontPage, as shown in Figure 11-8, double-click the name of the file you want to edit.**

   If you choose `index.html`, the front page of the site opens.

   The first page of any Web site must be named `index.html`, but the other pages can be named anything you like, as long as you don't use any spaces or special characters.

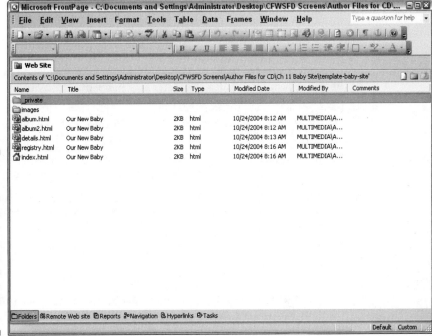

Figure 11-8:
Use the
Open Site
feature in
FrontPage
to load the
files and
subfolders
into the
workspace
area.

2. **Highlight any text you want to replace on the page and type your own words in its place.**

   This works much like replacing text in any word processing program. Simply click and drag to select a word or words, use the Delete key to delete the existing text, and then type to enter your own text. You can also use the copy and paste function to copy text from another document, such as a Word file, into a page in FrontPage.

3. **Click File⇨Save.**

   Any changes you made to the page are saved.

4. **Choose File⇨Preview in Browser.**

   The page is displayed in a Web browser. If you have more than one browser on your computer, you may see multiple browser options, such as Netscape and Internet Explorer. Choose the one that you prefer.

To edit the text on any of the pages in the site, follow the preceding instructions. For more information on FrontPage's editing features, such as formatting text and setting links, see Chapter 8.

To replace the images in any of the template pages, follow these steps:

1. **Copy your photo files into the** `template-baby-site\images` **folder.**

   Before you link new photos into a Web site, it's important that you first copy all the image files to the `images` folder in the Web site folder. Copy or move your image files the same way you would copy or move any files from one folder to another on your computer's hard drive.

2. **With the Web site open in FrontPage, double-click the name of the file you want to edit.**

   The page opens in the FrontPage work area. For example, if you choose `album.html`, the first photo album page of the baby site opens.

3. **With the Web page open in FrontPage, click to select the image you want to replace. Then use the Delete key on your keyboard to delete the image.**

   The image disappears from the page. Be careful not to move your cursor's location on the page before the next step because you want to insert the new image in exactly the same place as the old one.

4. **Choose Insert➪Picture➪From File, locate the image you want to use on your hard drive, and click to select the image.**

   The new image appears in place of the old one. In the example in Figure 11-9, I replaced the photo-frame image in the photo album page with a photograph of Max and his mother.

5. **Repeat Steps 2 through 4 to replace any other images on the page.**

6. **Choose File➪Save.**

   Any changes you made to the page are saved.

7. **Choose File➪Preview in Browser.**

   The page is displayed in a Web browser.

To replace images in any other pages in the site, follow the same instructions. For more information on working with images in FrontPage, see Chapter 8.

Creating and changing links

The Next and Previous buttons in the photo album pages are already set to link from one to the next, with the third page linking back to the first page. If you add photo album pages, you need to adjust these links accordingly.

Figure 11-9:
Replace the graphics in the template pages with your own photos.

To change or create a link from one page on your site to another, follow these steps:

1. **With the Web site open in FrontPage, double-click the name of the file you want to edit.**

   If you choose `album2.html`, the second album page of the baby template site opens. The template page contains a blank image that you should replace with your own picture. In Figure 11-10, you see the page after I've inserted a photograph of Max and his father, Zach, who is playing monster for the camera.

2. **Click to select any image or text you want to use to create a link.**

   The selected image or text is highlighted. In the example, I selected the Next button.

3. **With the image or text area still selected, click the Insert Hyperlink icon on the standard toolbar.**

   (The icon is labeled with a tooltip in Figure 11-10.) The Edit Hyperlink dialog box appears, as shown in Figure 11-11.

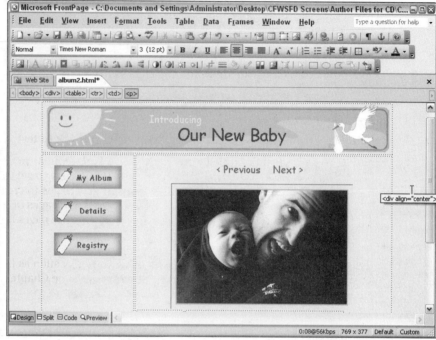

Figure 11-10:
If you add new photo album pages, make sure to adjust the Next and Previous links accordingly.

Figure 11-11:
You can easily create or edit links in the Edit Hyperlink dialog.

4. **Browse to find the page you want to link to, and click the file name to select it.**

In the example, I created a link to a new photo album page, which I called `album3.html`. I encourage you to use numbers in file names for photo album pages because it makes it easier to keep track of the sequence as you create links.

5. **Click OK to close the dialog box.**

   The link is set.

6. **Choose File➪Save.**

   Any changes you made to the page are saved.

7. **Choose File➪Preview in Browser.**

   The page is displayed in a Web browser.

8. **Click the image or text where you created the link to test your work.**

   If you set the link properly, the page you linked to opens in the browser. It's a good idea to test your links because it's so easy to set them incorrectly (especially when you're linking a series of pages to create a photo album). Although you're using the browser to view pages on your hard drive, the links should work just as they will when the pages are published on the Internet.

For more information about creating links in FrontPage, such as how to create links to other Web sites or to e-mail addresses, see Chapter 8.

Creating or deleting pages

To further customize your baby Web site, you can add or delete pages. To delete a page, simply click to select the file name of the page in the Web Site window in FrontPage and press the Delete key on your keyboard.

If you remove a page or section, make sure that you also delete any navigation buttons that link to that page. For example, if you decide not to include a gift registry on your site, you should delete the `registry.html` page and delete the Registry button on each page in which it appears. (To delete the button, simply click to select it and press Delete.) When you delete the button, the link is removed automatically. If you add or remove photo album pages, you may need to adjust the Next and Back button links accordingly. Use the instructions in the preceding section to create new links.

To add new pages, choose the template page that is most like the page you want to add, and then choose File➪Save As to create a copy. Give the new page a new name so that you don't overwrite the existing page. After you save a copy of the page, you can make changes to it in FrontPage without affecting the original page.

Creating a gift registry

The links in the gift registry page are special because instead of linking to another page on your Web site, they link directly to your personalized gift registry page within the store's Web site.

To create a link to another Web site, such as an online store with a gift registry section, follow these steps:

1. **Open the file in FrontPage where you want to create a link to another Web site.**

   To create your gift registry links, open `registry.html`.

2. **Click to select the image or text you want to use to create the link, and then click the Insert Hyperlink icon on the standard toolbar.**

   You can create your gift registry links with text, such as the name of each store (refer to the sample site in Figure 11-2).

3. **In the Address box of the Insert Hyperlink dialog box, insert the URL of the page you want to link to.**

   If you're not sure of the URL or you don't want to type it, you can use the Browse the Web option (you have to be connected to the Internet for this to work). To use this feature, click the Browse the Web icon (it looks like a globe with a magnifying glass) at the top of the Insert Hyperlink dialog box. FrontPage launches Internet Explorer. Navigate in IE to find the page you want to link to. Then, leave that page displayed in the browser and switch back to FrontPage. The URL is automatically inserted into the Address box.

   If you prefer to enter the URL by copying and pasting (perhaps because you already have the page displayed in a browser and don't want to have to go through all the steps of logging into your registry to open it again), see the instructions on copying a URL into the Insert Hyperlink dialog box in Chapter 12.

4. **Click OK to close the dialog box.**

   The link is set.

5. **Choose File➪Save.**

   Any changes you made to the page are saved.

6. **Choose File➪Preview in Browser.**

   The page is displayed in a Web browser.

7. **To test your work, click the link.**

Repeat these instructions to link to additional gift registries and other Web sites.

Publishing Your Web Site

You should always test your work before you put it up for all the world to see on the Internet. Before you publish your site to a server, preview it in a browser and test the links and images to make sure they look good and work properly. Ideally, you should have someone else test it as well because a fresh eye often catches things we miss in our own work. If you know someone with a good eye for detail, have that person read your text, too. To preview your site with a browser, open the first page of the site in FrontPage and choose File➪Preview in Browser.

To publish your Web site on the Internet, you need a Web server, such as those offered by commercial service providers (you find suggestions for choosing a service provider in Chapter 4). After you set up an account with a service provider, you simply transfer the files you created from your hard drive to the server. You find instructions for using FrontPage to send your site to your server at the end of Chapter 8.

If you want more instructions for editing your pages than I've provided in this chapter, check out Chapter 8, which provides a basic FrontPage tutorial. If you want to get into more advanced editing and design with FrontPage, I recommend *FrontPage 2003 For Dummies* by Asha Dornfest (Wiley Publishing).

Chapter 12

Happily Ever After: Creating a Wedding Site

In This Chapter

▶ Visiting other wedding sites for ideas

▶ Creating wedding graphics

▶ Editing the template pages

▶ Publishing your wedding site

Something old, something new, something borrowed, and now you better have something on the Internet too. Wedding Web sites have become an important part of the planning process and a vital place for guests to find everything from maps to your online gift registry.

The instructions in this chapter combine with the templates and images provided on the CD to help you create the important sections of your Web site — from the invitation to the wedding photo album. I know you have plenty of details to worry about, so my goal is to make building your wedding Web site as easy as possible.

With that in mind, if you want the easiest, fastest one-stop-shopping kind of solution for your wedding Web site needs, consider using a service such as the one at family.myevent.com. Although your design options are limited to their templates and they charge a monthly fee, MyEvent.com provides everything you need for your Web site in one place; you don't even have to install any software on your computer. For more on this and other similar services, see Chapter 1 or visit family.myevent.com.

The instructions in this chapter show you how to edit the graphics in this site in Photoshop Elements 3, and how to edit template pages in Microsoft FrontPage 2003. If you prefer to use the Macromedia Dreamweaver MX 2004 program, visit www.digitalfamily.com, where you'll find instructions for using Dreamweaver to customize this wedding Web site template.

Touring Wedding Sites

I've created a sample wedding site based on the template for this chapter and included the sample pages on the CD as a model. As you see in Figure 12-1, this site features a photo of the bride and groom on the first page, as well as a place to list the people in the wedding party.

The sample site in this chapter features pictures from Scott and Kelly's wedding. Before the wedding, the most important information to have on the site is directions and a gift registry. After the wedding, you may want to go back and add images taken during the ceremony. (Special thanks to photographer Zach Goldberg of www.frozenfoto.com for letting me use his beautiful images in this chapter and others.)

Many people like to keep the gift registry on their site even after the wedding date, to give guests a chance to send late gifts.

The templates for this chapter are designed to help you create the most common pages in a wedding site — the invitation, directions, and registry pages. You can always add or remove pages and change the design as much as you like.

Figure 12-1:
Introduce the happy couple with a photo of the bride and groom on the front page of a wedding site.

Maps and instructions for finding your wedding and reception locations are probably the most valuable resources you can include on a wedding site. In addition to writing out the directions, you may want to link directly to a map at Yahoo Maps (`maps.yahoo.com`) or Mapquest (`www.mapquest.com`).

You can also make it easier for your friends and family to buy you presents (and what's better for them may also be better for you.) Most wedding Web sites include a page with links to online stores and other Web sites that offer gift registry services. Shops such as Williams Sonoma and Macy's make it easy to create your own gift registry and identify the place settings and home furnishings you'd like as you start your new life together. If you search Google. com with the words *wedding gift registry*, you'll find dozens of Web sites that provide gift registry services. Adding links to these sites is easy, as you'll see in the "Creating a link to another Web site" section later in this chapter.

Even before the wedding, you can create a wedding album section, like the one shown in Figure 12-2, and feature photos of the engaged couple and even the bachelor party (if you're not too embarrassed). Creating a section for the photo album now lets your visitors know that this is the place to come back to later to see the wedding photos — and saves you time later when you're anxious to put those wedding photos online.

Figure 12-2: After the wedding, you can transform your site into a showcase for your best pictures with an online photo album.

Ready to dive in and create your own wedding Web site? Before you get started on your own site, spend some time looking at other Web sites. You can find lots of great ones at www.topweddingsites.com.

Preparing Photos for Your Wedding Site

Unlike most of the other template Web sites in this part of the book, this site was designed so that you don't have to edit the buttons or headings as graphics. Instead, these elements were created as text, which you can edit in a Web design program. (You find instructions for doing that in the "Creating Your Wedding Site" section, later in this chapter.)

In this section, you find out how to optimize photographs and insert them into the photo frame included in the site's design. I encourage you to do this before you start building your pages because it's easier to create your site when the images are prepared.

If you don't have a graphics program that supports layers, I recommend Photoshop Elements, which I used for the exercises in this chapter. You can also use another image program, such as Photoshop CS or Dreamweaver Fireworks. The process will be similar, but you may need to make minor adjustments to the steps in this section.

Before you get started, insert the CD that came with this book into your computer's CD drive and copy the author files from the Ch12 Wedding Site folder onto your hard drive. To help you design your site, I've included three folders in the Ch12 Wedding Site folder:

- ✔ photoshop-files has the graphics in a format that makes them easy to edit.

- ✔ sample-wedding-site features the site shown in Figures 12-1 and 12-2.

- ✔ template-wedding-site has the pages and graphics you should use as you build your site.

When you copy images from a CD to your hard drive, you may find that the files are locked, meaning you can't save changes to them. To correct this on a PC, right-click the Ch12 Wedding Site folder and choose Properties. In the Attributes area of the Properties dialog box, uncheck the Read Only option. Click Apply and then click OK. If you're using a Mac, ⌘-click the folder name, choose Get Info, and uncheck the Locked option.

Before you put any photos on your Web site, you need to optimize them so they will download as quickly as possible for your visitors. (If you're not sure what I mean by that, you find more detailed information about editing and optimizing images in Chapter 6.) The steps in this section walk you through the basic process of resizing and optimizing photos so you can add them to the templates and create a photo album for this site right away.

To resize and optimize a photo and insert it into the photo frame used in the wedding site templates, follow these steps.

1. **Launch Photoshop Elements 3.**

2. **Open one of the photo frame graphics in the** `photoshop-files` **folder, which is in the** `Ch12 Wedding Site` **folder on the CD.**

   Choose File➪Open and locate the file on your hard drive. For this template, I created three photo frames, one for tall photos (`photo-frame-tall.psd`), one for wide photos (`photo-frame-wide.psd`), and one for photos you've cropped into a square (`photo-frame-square.psd`).

3. **If the Layers palette isn't open, choose Window➪Layers.**

   The Layers palette opens in the right side of the screen. Each of the photo frame images has two layers, called Photo layer and Background. In Figure 12-3 you see the `photo-frame-wide.psd` file open in Elements. Before you can change a part of any graphic, you must first select the layer that corresponds to it.

4. **In the Layers palette, select the Photo layer.**

   The Photo layer becomes shaded in a darker grey, indicating it is the active layer.

5. **Open the photograph you want to use on your Web site.**

   Choose File➪Open, locate the photo on your hard drive, and double-click to open it. In Figure 12-3 you see both the photo frame image and a photograph open at the same time in Photoshop Elements. You can open multiple images in Photoshop Elements, making it easy to copy the contents of one graphic into another.

6. **Resize the photo so that it fits in the photo frame.**

   Choose Image➪Resize and specify the height and width you want in the Image Size dialog box. If you want to insert your photo into the photo frame designed for this template, you need to make it the same size or smaller than the tan or purple area that appears in the sample image. Wide photos should be no larger than 325 by 240 pixels, and tall photos should be no larger than 240 by 315 pixels. The smaller frame used on the front page requires a photo no larger than 260 by 165.

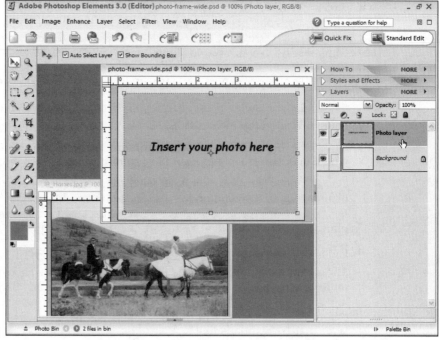

Figure 12-3:
To use the
photo
frames
designed
for this
template,
you first
resize your
photo and
then copy
and paste it
into the
frame.

7. **Copy and paste the photo into the picture frame image.**

   a. **Select the move tool from the Tools palette.**

   b. **Click to place your cursor anywhere in your photo file and then choose Select➪All.**

   c. **Choose Edit➪Copy.**

   d. **Click to place your cursor in the middle of the picture frame image and then choose Edit➪Paste.**

      Your photo appears in the picture frame and a new layer is created. You can adjust the position of your photo by clicking and dragging it within the picture frame image or by using the arrow keys on your keyboard.

   e. **Delete the original Photo layer.**

      To do so, select the original Photo layer (the tan box) and drag it to the small trash can at the top of the Layers palette.

   f. **Delete the original Photo layer.**

      For more information about resizing an image or using copy and paste to copy an image from one file to another, see Chapter 6.

8. **Choose File⇨Save For Web.**

   The Save for Web dialog box opens.

9. **In the Optimized File Format pull-down list, choose JPEG.**

10. **Set the Quality to 80 percent.**

    Lowering the quality helps reduce the file size and make the image download more quickly. For an even smaller file size, reduce this number further, but don't go too far or you'll adversely affect the appearance of the image.

11. **Save the new photo in your Web site folder with a new name.**

    You can name the photo anything you like as long as you don't use spaces or special characters.

Repeat these steps for each photo you want to prepare for your site. Then follow the steps in the next section to insert these images into your pages.

Creating Your Wedding Site

I designed the templates for this chapter to include the kinds of common features you're likely to want on a wedding site. In the `template-wedding-site` folder, you find a predesigned page for the front page, which includes a place for a photo and the names of those in the wedding party. You also find separate template page designs for the ceremony, directions, and a gift registry, as well as pages designed for a photo album.

The templates are predesigned Web pages that you can customize by simply replacing the images and text with your own content. (FrontPage offers two special template formats, which you can find out about in Chapter 9.) To keep things simple, I've saved the templates as basic HTML files so you can edit them with any Web design program and quickly turn them into your own Web site. If you're planning to build a larger, more complicated Web site and want to create lots of new pages with these same designs, you may want to save the page designs as FrontPage templates. For more information, see the instructions in Chapter 9.

To help you get started and make it easy for you to build a complete site quickly, I created eight template pages for your wedding site:

✔ `index.html` is the front page.

✔ `invitation.html` is the invitation.

✔ `directions.html` is the directions page.

  ✔ ceremony.html is the ceremony page.

  ✔ album1.html, album2.html, and album3.html are the photo album.

  ✔ registry.html is the gift registry.

By naming these files so that they correspond to their contents, it makes it easier to identify the pages later when you want to work on them.

The main page of any Web site must be named index.html, but the rest of the pages can be named anything you like, as long as you don't use spaces or special characters and you use the .html extension at the end of every page.

You can create new or additional pages for your site from any of the templates on the CD by choosing File⇨Save As and using a new name to the new file (just make sure you keep the .html extension).

Starting with the Open Site process

FrontPage works best when you use the program's Open Site feature to identify your Web site folder before you edit any pages. Keep the files for your Web site in one folder — doing so makes it easier to upload the files to your server later and helps FrontPage set the links properly.

You'll be working with the files in the template-wedding-site folder. You may want to begin by renaming that folder something else, such as Our Wedding Site, so you can identify it more easily on your hard drive.

Follow these steps to use the FrontPage Open Site command to open the template folder for the wedding Web site:

1. **If you haven't done so already, insert the CD that came with this book into your computer's CD drive and copy the folder called** template-wedding-site **from the** Ch12 Wedding Site **folder to your hard drive.**

2. **Open the template site in FrontPage as you would open any other Web site.**

   Choose File⇨Open Site and locate the template-wedding-site folder (or whatever you named it) on your hard drive. Click to select the folder and then click Open in the Open Site dialog box. The Web site opens in FrontPage and the files and subfolders are displayed, as shown in Figure 12-4.

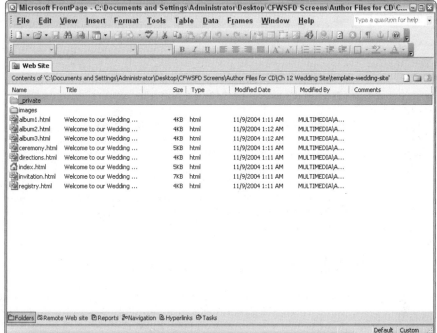

Editing a template page

After you open the template site, you can begin to work on the individual pages of the site.

To edit the text in any of the template pages, follow these steps:

1. **With the Web site open in FrontPage, as shown in Figure 12-4, double-click the name of the file you want to edit.**

   For example, if you choose `directions.html`, the directions page of the wedding template site opens.

2. **Highlight any text you want to replace on the page and type your own words in its place.**

   The process is similar to replacing text in any word processing program. Simply click and drag to select a word or words, use the Delete key to delete the existing text, and then type to enter your own text. You can also use the copy and paste function to copy text from another document, such as a Word file, into a page in FrontPage.

Be careful when you delete text in these predesigned pages because it's easy to delete more than you intend, altering other aspects of the page. If that happens, choose Edit➪Undo to reverse the step. If you really mess up the design (which is easy to do, especially when you're new at this), you can always copy the page from the CD to your hard drive again and start over.

3. **Choose File➪Save.**

Any changes you made to the page are saved.

4. **Choose File➪Preview in Browser.**

The page is displayed in a Web browser.

Follow these instructions to edit the text on any of the other pages in the site. For more information on editing pages with FrontPage, see Chapter 8.

Adding images to your pages

Adding and replacing images on a Web pages is almost as easy as editing the text. To replace an image in any of the template pages, follow these steps:

1. **Copy your photo files into the** `images` **folder in your main wedding Web site folder.**

   The main folder is called `template-wedding-site` unless you've renamed it.

Before you link new photos into a Web site, it's important that you first copy all the image files into the `images` folder in the Web site folder so that the links to the images will be set properly. If you don't do this, your images may not display properly when you transfer the site to a Web server. Copy or move your image files the same way you copy or move any files from one folder to another on your computer's hard drive.

2. **With the Web site open in FrontPage, double-click the name of the template or other HTML page you want to edit.**

   The page opens in the FrontPage work area. In the example, shown in Figure 12-5, I've opened the template page called `ceremony.html`.

3. **Click to select the image you want to replace.**

   The image is selected in the work area.

4. **Press the Delete key on your keyboard to delete the image.**

   The image disappears. Be careful not to move your cursor — in the next step, you insert the new image in the same place as the old one.

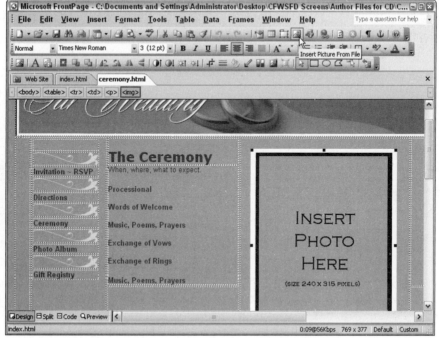

Figure 12-5:
To insert an image into one of the template pages, delete the placeholder image (the words *Insert Photo Here*) and replace it with your picture.

5. **Choose Insert⇨Picture⇨From File, locate the image you want to use on your hard drive, and click to select the image.**

The new image appears in place of the old one.

6. **Repeat Steps 3 through 5 to replace any other images on the page.**

7. **Choose File⇨Save.**

Any changes you made to the page are saved.

8. **Choose File⇨Preview in Browser.**

The page is displayed in a Web browser.

To replace images in any other pages on the site, open the page you want to edit and follow these same instructions. For more information on working with images in FrontPage, see Chapter 8.

Changing and adding links

Creating links from one page on your site to another, especially in a program like FrontPage, is much easier than most new Web designers imagine. In the following exercise, I show you how to create a link from the photo album page (`album.html`) to another photo album page called `album2`. You can use these same instructions to create a link from any page on your site to another, such as a new page with the bride and groom's vows linked to the ceremony page.

To change or create a link, follow these steps:

1. **With the Web site open in FrontPage, double-click the name of the file in which you want to create or change a link.**

   In the example shown in Figure 12-6, I chose `album.html`.

   It's a good idea to create the pages you want to link to before you create the links. In this example, I opened the `album.html` file, and chose File➪ Save As to create a new page that I named `album2.html`. Then I used File➪Save As again and created `album3.html`. Next, I opened each file separately and inserted a different image in each file.

2. **Click to select the image or text that you want to use to create a link, and then click the Insert Hyperlink icon on the standard toolbar.**

   In Figure 12-6, I selected the Next button.

3. **In the Insert Hyperlink dialog box, browse to find the page you want to link to, and then click the page's file name to select it.**

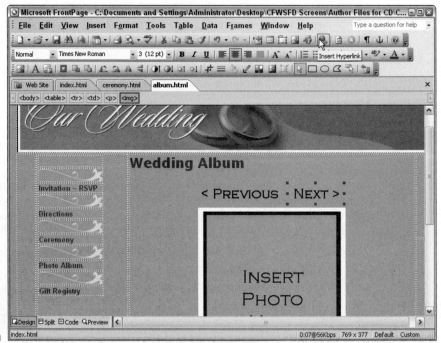

Figure 12-6:
When you add new pages to the photo album, you need to change the Next and Previous links accordingly.

4. **Click OK to close the dialog box.**

   The link is set. In the example, I created a link to a new photo album page, which I named `album2.html`. Using numbers in file names for photo album pages makes it easier to keep track of the sequence as you create links.

5. **Click File⇨Save.**

   Any changes you made to the page are saved.

6. **Choose File⇨Preview in Browser.**

   The page is displayed in a Web browser. It's always a good idea to test your links because it's so easy to set them incorrectly (especially when you're linking a series of pages to create a photo album).

7. **Test your work by clicking the new link.**

   If you set the link properly, the page you linked to opens in the browser. Although you're using the browser to view pages on your hard drive, the links should work just as they will when the pages are published to the Internet as long as you keep all your pages in the same folder when you transfer them to the server.

For more information on creating links with FrontPage, such as how to create links to other Web sites or to e-mail addresses, see Chapter 8.

Deleting pages from your site

If you decide that you don't want to use a page in the template wedding site, just delete it. To delete a page, click to select the page's file name in the Web Site window in FrontPage (refer to Figure 12-4), and press the Delete key.

If you remove a page or section, make sure that you also delete any navigation buttons that link to that page. For example, if you want to delete the invitation page, you need to open each of the pages in the site with a link to the invitation page, click to select the button or text that links to that page, and delete it. When you delete the graphic or text that is linked, you automatically remove the link as well.

Creating a link to another Web site

Linking to a page in another Web site is similar to linking to a page within your own site. But instead of using the Insert Hyperlink dialog box to browse for a page on your hard drive, you insert the URL of the site you want to link to.

Two places where you're likely to want to create links to other Web sites are the directions page, where you may want to link to a map on a site such as

Mapquest.com, and the gift registry page, where you'll want to link directly to your gift registry sites. When you create the link, it's easier to use copy and paste to insert the URL rather than type a long, complicated address. You find instructions for using copy and paste to create a link in the following exercise.

To create a link to another Web site, follow these steps:

1. **Open the file in FrontPage where you want to create a link to another Web site.**

   I chose directions.html because I want to add a link to a Mapquest. com map to the reception.

2. **Click to select the image or text you want to use to create the link and then click the Insert Hyperlink icon on the standard toolbar.**

   I selected the words *map to the reception.*

3. **In the Address area of the Insert Hyperlink dialog box, insert the URL of the page you want to link to.**

   If you're not sure of the URL or you don't want to type it, you can use the Browse the Web option (you have to be connected to the Internet for this to work). To use this feature, click the Browse the Web icon (it looks like a globe with a magnifying glass) at the top of the Insert Hyperlink dialog box. FrontPage launches Internet Explorer. Navigate in IE to find the page you want to link to. Then leave that page displayed in the browser and switch back to FrontPage. The URL is automatically inserted into the Address box.

   If you prefer to enter the URL by copying and pasting (perhaps because you already have the page displayed in a browser and don't want to have to go through the steps of logging into your registry to open it again), see the instructions on copying a URL into the Insert Hyperlink dialog box in the following section, "Copying a URL to create a link."

4. **Click OK to close the dialog box.**

5. **Choose File⇨Save.**

   Any changes you made to the page are saved.

6. **Choose File⇨Preview in Browser.**

   The page is displayed in a Web browser.

7. **To test your work, click the link.**

   If you set the link properly and are connected to the Internet, the site you linked to will open in the browser, even though the page you're working on is on your computer and not yet published on the Web. That's because a link to a URL simple instructs a browser to open the address of the Web site, irrespective of where the page with the link is located.

For more information about creating links with FrontPage, such as how to create links to other Web sites or to email addresses, see Chapter 8.

Copying a URL to create a link

You can save a lot of time and tedious typing by using the copy and paste functions to insert a URL in the Insert Hyperlink dialog box when creating a link to another Web site.

This is an especially valuable trick when you're linking to a gift registry page or to a specific map, because these links are long, complicated addresses designed to take a visitor directly to a customized page on the site.

To use copy and paste instead of trying to retype the address, follow these steps:

1. **Open a browser, such as Internet Explorer, and enter the URL of the Web site you want to visit.**

   For example, enter `www.mapquest.com` to visit the map site.

2. **Place your cursor at the beginning of the address line in your browser.**

   Make sure you're at the very beginning of the address so you don't miss any of it. You can use the arrow keys on your keyboard to adjust the location of your cursor.

3. **Click and drag to select the entire URL (make sure you don't miss any part of it), and then choose Edit⇨Copy.**

   Although you won't see anything happen, the URL is copied and saved to your computer's clipboard.

4. **Open the page where you want to create the link in FrontPage.**

   You can have multiple computer programs open at once on your computer so you can more easily switch from a page in FrontPage to your browser and back.

5. **With the text or image that you want to link selected in FrontPage, click the Edit Hyperlink icon.**

6. **In the Insert Hyperlink dialog box, click to place your cursor in the Address area, and choose Edit⇨Paste.**

   The URL you copied from the browser appears in the address line.

7. **Click OK to close the Insert Hyperlink dialog box.**

   The link is created.

8. Choose File⇨Preview in Browser.

The page is displayed in a Web browser.

9. Click the image or text where you created the link to test your work.

Publishing Your Web Site

You should always test your work before you put it up for all the world to see on the Internet. To preview your site with a browser, open the first page of your site in FrontPage, choose File⇨Preview in Browser, and then systematically click the links to make sure they go where you intended. If you find a broken or misdirected link, open the page with the bad link in FrontPage and recreate the link correctly. (You find instructions in the "Changing and adding links" section, earlier in this chapter.) Check the images as well, to make sure they look good and work properly.

If you know someone with a good eye for detail, ask that person to test your site too — and to check the text for typos, misspellings, or other errors that can make your pages more difficult to understand. I suggest you publish your Web site online and then send the address to a few close friends or family so that they can check the site for you. After you get their feedback, make any necessary changes to the site, and then send out a broad announcement.

To publish your Web site on the Internet, you need a Web server, such as those offered by commercial service providers (you find suggestions for choosing a service provider in Chapter 4). After you have set up an account with a service provider, you simply transfer the files you created from your hard drive to the server. You find instructions for using FrontPage to send your site to your server at the end of Chapter 8.

If you want more instructions for editing your pages than I provide in this chapter, Chapter 8 provides a basic FrontPage tutorial. If you want to get into advanced editing and design with FrontPage, I recommend *FrontPage 2003 For Dummies* by Asha Dornfest (published by Wiley).

Chapter 13

Wish You Were Here: Vacation Sites

*I*f your family is anything like mine, you've had to sit through your share of family vacation slide shows and spend hours looking through snapshots from camping trips, cruises, and other adventures.

Sharing travel photos is nothing new, but the modern computer is replacing the old slide projector and more and more families are now using travel Web sites to share their stories. Equipped with a digital camera and a laptop, adventure travelers, especially those on extended trips, are creating detailed sites — often before they even return home.

In this chapter, I introduce you to the world of travel Web sites with a sample site created by my friend Ken Riddick to show off his amazing underwater photography from a scuba diving adventure. Ken graciously agreed to let me share his photos and Web site in the book. I used his site as a model for the templates that go with this chapter, so you can create a similar site with your travel photos — even if you take them on land. The templates and graphics shown in this chapter are on the CD, in the Ch13 Travel Site folder in the Author Files section.

Inside that folder you'll find three subfolders:

- ✔ `sample-travel-site` contains a complete Web site you can use as a model.
- ✔ `template-travel-site` contains the pages you should work with as you create your own site.
- ✔ `photoshop-files` has all the graphics for the site in their original .psd format, which makes them easy to edit in Photoshop Elements.

In the following pages, you create an image montage to showcase many photos on one page. You also find out how to optimize images so they download quickly on the Web and how to create a virtual slide show against a black background so your pictures really stand out on your pages. You use Microsoft FrontPage 2003 to customize the pages of this template site and Photoshop Elements 3 to edit the graphics.

If you prefer to use Macromedia Dreamweaver MX 2004, visit `www.digital family.com`, where you'll find instructions for using Dreamweaver to customize the travel Web site.

When you copy images from a CD to your hard drive, you may find that the files are locked, so you can't save changes to them. To correct this on a PC, right-click the `Ch13 Travel Site` folder and choose Properties. In the Attributes area of the Properties dialog box, deselect he Read Only option. Click Apply and then click OK. If you're using a Mac, ⌘-click the folder name, choose Get Info, and deselect the Locked option.

Putting photos online the easy way

I've tried to make it as easy as possible for you to create a travel Web site in this chapter. But if all you want to do is show off your photos, here are a couple of alternatives that are much faster and easier.

If you're not concerned about the design and just want to make your photos accessible over the Internet, consider using an online photo site, such as `Ofoto.com` or `Shutterfly.com`. These sites make it easy to upload your photos, and they automatically create a simple online photo album. They provide this service for free and make their money by trying to convince you and your visitors to use their services to print the photos (20 to 30 cents each).

If you want to create something more advanced than an online photo album but not as complicated as creating your own custom site like the one described in this chapter, consider using a service such as `family.myevent.com`. For more on this and other similar services, see Chapter 1.

Taking Your Visitors with You

Before you start building your own Web travel site, I encourage you to visit a few others for ideas. For a look at a site by a family of true adventure travelers, visit `www.rfleming.net` and discover how mom, dad, and two little girls spent two years circling the globe.

To get a glimpse of the deep and an idea of the kind of Web site you can create with the templates for this chapter, take a tour of Ken's scuba site at

`www.counsinswest.com/fpdiving`

Ken's Web site is made up of a colorful collection of underwater photos that come to life against the black background of his pages. No matter what the subject of your travel site, you can appreciate the simple but effective design principals he uses to invite you into his site and take you on your own underwater adventure.

As you see in Figure 13-1, Ken's front page features a photomontage made up of eight images. Notice how he's edited the images so that they're not the same size, a key factor in making the montage graphically interesting.

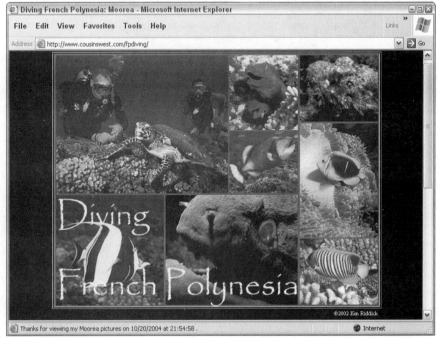

Figure 13-1: A photomontage is a great way to show off several photos on one page.

He's also used a large font and white letters for the words *Diving French Polynesia,* and he's carefully placed the letters against dark parts of the images so there's enough contrast for the text to be readable.

One of the challenges of placing text over an image is that the words can get lost when set against a busy background. The safest options are light-colored letters against a dark area in an image or dark letters against a light area. For example, you might use dark burgundy letters against a sandy stretch of beach, or bright yellow letters over the darkest part of a photo of a sunset.

Below the montage, as you can see in Figure 13-2, Ken has written a brief introduction to the site, which explains where French Polynesia is and what he saw there. Moreover, he tells visitors how many photos are in the slide show and how to navigate through the pages. In addition to the Next and Previous links on each page, each photo in the montage is linked to a larger version of the image.

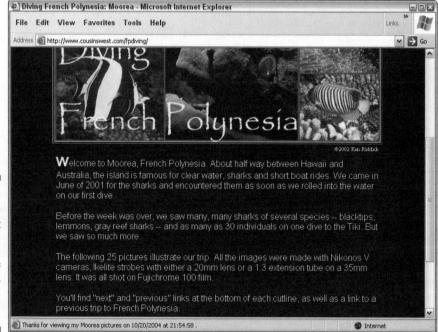

Figure 13-2:
The text on the front page should give readers an idea of what they will find inside.

Preparing the Photos for Your Web Site

Most travel Web sites feature lots of photos, and preparing those images should be the first step in creating a Web site. In the following exercise, you find out how to crop a photo, resize it to fit a design, and save it in the right format for the Web. Cropping is especially important on the Web because you generally have to reduce the size of an image for it to display well on a computer screen. Trimming the edges of an image enables you to focus your viewer's attention on the most important parts of a picture.

The following steps will walk you through the process of cropping, resizing, and optimizing a photograph for your travel site:

1. **Launch Photoshop Elements 3.**

2. **Open the photograph you want to prepare for your Web site.**

   Choose File⇨Open and locate the file on your hard drive.

3. **Crop out any unnecessary or distracting elements in the image.**

   a. **Click to select the cropping tool in the Tools palette.**

   b. **Click to place your cursor in your photo and drag to draw a box where you want to make the crop.**

   c. **Use the small squares at the corners of the box to adjust the cropping area, as shown in Figure 13-3.**

   d. **Double-click the center of the image to complete the crop.**

   The area outside the cropping square is removed.

4. **Resize the photo.**

   Choose Image⇨Resize⇨Image Size and specify the height and width you want in the Image Size dialog box. To fit the design in the sample site, make horizontal photos no more than 375 pixels wide, and vertical photos no more than 275 pixels wide. If you keep the Aspect Ratio option checked, the height of your images will automatically adjust to remain proportional to the width you specify.

5. **Choose File⇨Save For Web.**

   The Save for Web dialog box opens.

6. **In the Optimized File Format pull-down, choose JPEG.**

   JPEG is best for photographs on the Web, and GIF is best for images with limited colors, such as buttons and logos.

Figure 13-3:
Cropping
out any
unnec-
essary
background
can help
your images
look better
on the Web.

7. Set the Quality to 80 percent.

Lowering the quality reduces the file size and makes the image download more quickly. For an even smaller file size, reduce this number more; but don't go too far or you'll adversely affect the appearance of the image. For information on optimizing graphics for the Web, see Chapter 6.

8. Save the new photo into your Web site folder and give it a new name.

Repeat these steps for each photo you want to prepare for your site. Then follow the steps in the next section to create a photomontage. For more information about cropping, resizing, and retouching your images, see Chapter 6.

Creating a Photomontage

A photomontage is a great way to show off several photos at once and makes an ideal centerpiece for the front page of a travel site. The montage Ken uses on his front page is stunning, but it's also complicated and big. Ken can get away with that because he knows most of the people who visit his site have fast connections to the Internet and nice big monitors. I don't assume that's the case for everyone who will visit your site, so for this exercise, I created a much simpler design for a montage. I also built a color-coded frame (see Figure 13-4) to make it easy for you to follow along. You'll find the image in the `photoshop-files` folder. The file is called `montage-design.psd`.

In case creating a montage seems too complicated or you don't want to take the time to create a personalized banner, I've created a banner with a diverse collection of travel photos designed to go with any travel site. The banner is in the `images` folder of the `template-travel-site` folder. You can skip the following section and use the completed banner if you prefer. (You find out how to insert a banner into the main page of your travel site in the "Customizing the Sample Template Site" section, later in this chapter.)

Preparing images for the montage

To create this montage, you need to select four photos to feature in the design. In the following exercise, I show you how to resize your images and fit them into the montage:

1. **Launch Photoshop Elements 3.**

2. **Open all four of the photographs you want to include in your montage.**

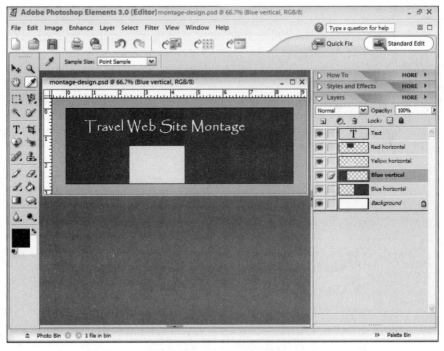

Figure 13-4:
The colored boxes in this image can be replaced with photos to create a simple montage as the banner for your travel Web site.

Choose File⇨Open and locate each file on your hard drive. You can have multiple image files open at once, but you can work on only one image at a time. You can switch from one image file to another by simply clicking to place your cursor anywhere on the image you want to work on. If the image you want is not visible, choose Window and select the name of the image from the open image file names displayed at bottom of the menu.

3. **Crop each image to the size and shape required for the montage.**

    The images in this montage will be small, so it's often best to use only a portion of the image. To crop an image, follow these steps:

    a. **Click to select the cropping tool in the Tools palette.**

    b. **Click to place your cursor in your photo, and then drag to draw a box where you want to make the crop.**

    c. **Use the small squares at the corners of the box to adjust the cropping area.**

    d. **Double-click in the center of the image to complete the crop.**

       The area outside the cropping square is removed.

4. **Resize the photos.**

    For each photo, choose Image⇨Resize⇨Image Size and specify the height and width you want in the Image Size dialog box. To fit the images in the montage, you need four images with these sizes:

    • The leftmost image should be 175 x 200 pixels

    • The two images in the middle area should be 150 x 100 pixels.

    • The image on the right should be 275 x 200 pixels.

5. **Choose File⇨Save As and save the resized image with a new name.**

    It's a good idea to save each of your resized and prepared images in case you need to go back and change anything in your montage image later. If you use the Save As option and give the edited images new names, you can keep your original images untouched.

Pasting images into the montage

Next, copy and paste each image into the montage by following these steps:

1. **Choose Window, and then choose the file name of the first image you want to copy into your montage.**

2. **Copy the image.**

    a. **Click to select the move tool in the Tools palette.**

    b. **Click to place your cursor somewhere in your prepared image, and then choose Select⇨All.**

    c. **Choose Edit⇨Copy.**

3. **Click to place your cursor in the montage image.**

4. **Click to select the first layer in the Layers palette (or any other area you want to replace with your image).**

   The selected layer turns to a darker grey, indicating that it's the active layer.

5. **Choose Edit➪Paste.**

   The photo appears in the montage. When you paste a photo into an existing image like this, a new layer is automatically created (see Figure 13-5). You can move the image you pasted by clicking and dragging it within the montage or by using the arrow keys on your keyboard (a great trick for making more precise adjustments to placement).

6. **Repeat Steps 1 through 6 for each image in the photomontage.**

   If you want to delete a layer, click to select it, and then drag it to the trash can at the top of the Layers palette. You can also click and drag to change the order of layers. This is useful if you want one layer to appear above another layer, for example a text layer on top of an image layer. When two or more layers overlap, the layer that is highest in the list in the Layers palette appears on top.

7. **Choose File➪Save For Web.**

   The Save for Web dialog box opens.

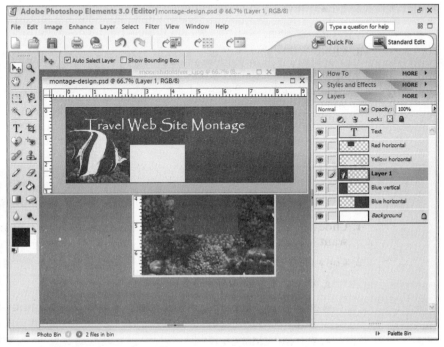

Figure 13-5: Copy and paste your prepared images into the montage and align them over the colored squares.

8. **In the Optimized File Format pull-down, choose JPEG.**

9. **Set the Quality to 80 percent.**

    Lowering the quality reduces the file size and makes the image download more quickly.

10. **Save the photomontage in your Web site folder and give it a new name.**

Customizing the Sample Template Site

You can use the travel site design for any kind of site and, conversely, you can use any of the templates featured in Part IV to create a travel site. (Although you may have to make more changes to the template that was intended for the wedding site before it will serve you well as a travel design, any template can be edited to fit any topic. You can even combine elements from different templates to create a new design. For example, you can create a photomontage by using the predesigned images and instructions from this travel site to create a montage of newborn photos for the front page of your baby site.)

You can edit template pages as you would any other file. For example, to format text, you use the standard Microsoft icons on the toolbar at the top of the FrontPage work area. You find instructions for customizing the travel site in the exercises that follow, but these instructions assume you have at least some general knowledge of FrontPage. (For more information on FrontPage 3, see Chapter 8.)

Opening the template site in FrontPage

FrontPage 3 works best when you use the program's Open Site feature to identify your Web site folder before you edit any pages. Make sure you keep the files for your Web site in one folder; doing so makes it easier to upload the files to your server later and helps FrontPage set the links properly.

In the following exercises, you'll be working with the files in the `template-travel-site` folder from the `Author Files` section of the CD. To help you get started and make it easy for you to build a complete site quickly, I created four template pages for your travel site:

  ✔ `index.html` is the main page.

  ✔ `album1.html`, `album2.html`, and `album3.html` are photo album pages that are already linked to one another.

After you copy the `template-travel-site` folder to your hard drive, I suggest you name it something else, such as Hawaii Vacation Site, so you can identify it more easily. You should also make sure that you've copied all your edited photos and graphics into the `images` folder before going through the steps that follow so that FrontPage can identify all your files during the Open site process.

Follow these steps to use the FrontPage Open Site command to open the template folder for the travel Web site:

1. **If you haven't done so already, insert the CD that accompanies this book into your computer's CD drive and copy onto your hard drive the** `travel-template-site` **folder, which is in the** `Ch13 Travel Site` **folder in the** `Author Files` **section.**

   See the warning at the beginning of the chapter if you have trouble saving these files after you edit them. I've named the template folder `template-travel-site`, but you may want to begin by renaming the folder something that has more meaning to you, such as Hawaii Vacation Site, so you can identify the folder more easily on your hard drive.

2. **Open the template site in FrontPage as you would open any other Web site.**

   Choose File➪Open Site and locate the Web site folder on your hard drive. Click to select the folder name, and then click Open. The Web site opens in FrontPage and the files and subfolders are displayed, as shown in Figure 13-6. You can open any files into the FrontPage editor by double-clicking the file name.

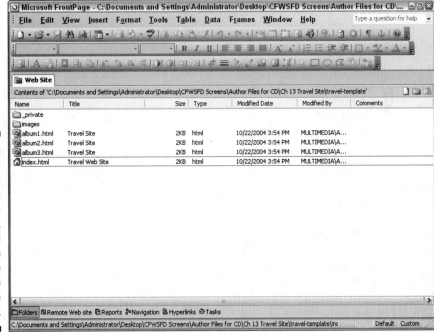

Figure 13-6:
When you open the template site in FrontPage, the files and subfolders become visible in the workspace area.

Replacing graphics in a template page

After you opened the template site, you can begin to work on the individual pages of the site. In the exercise that follows, I start by replacing the banner image in the first page of the template site, but you can use these same steps to replace any image in the site, such as the photos in the photo album pages.

To replace an image in any the template pages, follow these steps:

1. **With the Web site open in FrontPage (refer to Figure 13-6), double-click the file name of any page you want to edit.**

   If you choose index.html, the front page of the travel site template opens. The main page of any Web site must be named index.html, but the other pages can be named anything you like, as long as you don't use spaces or special characters.

2. **Click to select the image on the Web page that you want to replace.**

   In the example in Figure 13-7, I'm replacing the banner image in the main page of the site.

3. **Press the Delete key on your keyboard to delete the image.**

   The image disappears from the page. Be careful not to move your cursor before the next step — you want to insert the new image in the same place as the old one.

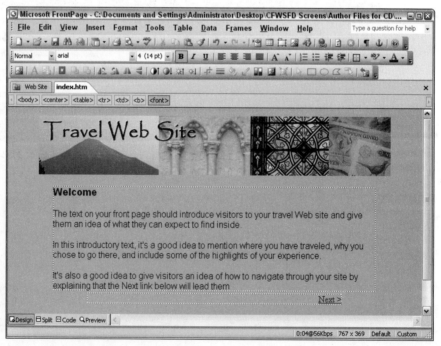

Figure 13-7:
Use the banner that's already linked to the template site or replace it with your own personalized banner or montage image.

4. **Choose Insert⇨Picture⇨From File, locate the image you want to use on your hard drive, and click to select the image.**

The new image appears in place of the old one.

5. **Repeat Steps 2 through 4 to replace any other images on the page.**

6. **Choose File⇨Save.**

Any changes you made to the page are saved.

7. **Choose File⇨Preview in Browser.**

The page is displayed in a Web browser.

To replace images on any other pages, follow the same instructions. For more information on working with images in FrontPage, see Chapter 8.

Editing text in a template page

In Ken's travel site, he wrote wonderful descriptions of the fish, sharks, and other critters he and his friends saw on their scuba diving trip. No matter what the topic of your travels, your images will have greater meaning if you include written descriptions.

To add or edit text in any of the template pages, follow these steps:

1. **With the Web site open in FrontPage (refer to Figure 13-6), double-click the name of the file you want to edit.**

If you choose `album1.html`, the first photo album page of the travel site opens.

2. **Highlight any text you want to replace on the page, and type your own words in its place.**

The process is similar to replacing text in any word processing program. Simply click and drag to select a word or words, use the Delete key to delete the existing text, and then type to enter your own text. You can also copy text from another document, such as a Word file, and paste it into your Web page in FrontPage.

3. **Choose File⇨Save.**

Any changes you made to the page are saved.

4. **Choose File⇨Preview in Browser.**

The page is displayed in a Web browser.

To edit the text on any of the other pages in the site, follow the same instructions. For more information on editing pages with FrontPage, see Chapter 8.

Changing background and text colors

In Ken's scuba site, he uses a black background, which provides a dramatic setting for his photos. In the sample template site, I chose a lighter background, using an image I created in Photoshop Elements, so that I could better control the color and make it match the banner image.

To change the background and text colors in a Web page, follow these steps:

1. **With the Web site open in FrontPage (refer to Figure 13-6), double-click the name of the file you want to edit.**

   For this example, I opened `album1.html`, the first photo album page of the travel site.

2. **Right-click anywhere on the page and choose Page Properties.**

   The Page Properties dialog box appears, as shown in Figure 13-8.

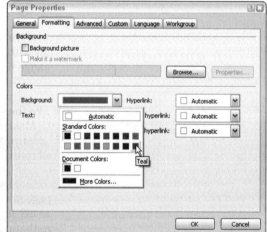

Figure 13-8: You can change background and text colors here.

3. **Click the Formatting tab.**

4. **In the Colors area, choose a background color.**

   Click the down arrow next to Background and choose any color you like from the displayed colors in the pull-down list, or choose More Colors to open the More Colors dialog box, where you can click to select any color from the color wheel. The color you select fills the color swatch box. The color does not fill the background of your page until you click OK, which also closes the dialog box. If you want to alter the text color or other options, don't click OK until you've made all your changes.

If you prefer to use a background image, as I did in the template site, select the Background picture option and use the Browse button to locate the image you want to use as a background. If you don't want to use the background color in the template page, deselect the Background picture option.

5. **In the Text pull-down list, choose a text color.**

The process is similar to setting the background color. Choose any color you like from the displayed colors in the pull-down list, or choose More Colors to open the More Colors dialog box and click to select any color from the color wheel. The color you select fills the color swatch box.

6. **Click OK.**

The Page Properties dialog box closes and any colors you selected are applied to the page. If you're not happy with the results or you want to make further changes, go back to Step 2.

Creating or deleting pages

The `template-travel-site` folder includes a main page and three photo album template pages that are already linked to one another with Next and Previous buttons. (If you want to find out how to add or change links, see Chapter 8.)

To add new pages, choose the template page that is most like the page you want to add and then choose File➪Save As to create a copy. Make sure to give the new page a new name so you don't overwrite the existing page. After you save a copy of the page, you can make changes to it in FrontPage without affecting the original page.

To delete a page, simply click to select the file name of the page in the Web Site window in FrontPage and press the Delete key on your keyboard. If you remove a page or section, make sure that you also delete any links to that page.

Publishing Your Web Site

Before you publish your site for all the world to see, make sure you preview it in a browser and test the links on your hard drive. To preview your page, choose File➪Preview in Browser.

To publish your Web site, you need access to a Web server, such as those offered by commercial service providers. (Suggestions for choosing a service provider are in Chapter 4.) After you set up an account with a service provider, you simply transfer the files you created from your hard drive to your Web server. You find instructions for using FrontPage to send your site to your server at the end of Chapter 8.

If you want more instructions for editing pages, see Chapter 8 for a basic tutorial in using FrontPage. If you want to get into more advanced editing and design with FrontPage, I recommend *FrontPage 2003 For Dummies* by Asha Dornfest (published by Wiley).

Chapter 14

In Your Spare Time: Creating Club, Sports, and Hobby Sites

. . . .

In This Chapter

▶ Identifying the sections of your site

▶ Customizing buttons, banners, and other graphics

▶ Editing template pages in FrontPage

▶ Adding video to your site

▶ Sending your site to a Web server

. . . .

Some of my favorite family Web sites were created for sports teams and clubs. I love these sites because they often feature action photos from sporting events as well as inspiring stories of unexpected victories.

If you're involved in a sport, club, or hobby, or have a child or other family member who is and you want to create a Web site to help organize a calendar of games or special events, explain the intricacies of the new rules, or show off photos or trophies, this chapter is for you.

In the following pages, you find a sample Web site I created for my friend Lorion LaRose Edwards. She and I both study karate at United Studios of Self Defense in Los Angeles. (You can find more about the karate classes they offer throughout the country at www.ussd.com). Although I use Lorion's karate Web site as a model in this chapter, you can create any kind of sports, hobby, or related Web site by using the templates designed for this chapter.

To make this as easy as possible for you, I've included everything you see in this chapter on the CD, including the full sample karate site, the templates for the Web pages in the exercises, and the buttons, banners, and other images. You'll find these files in the Author Files section of the CD in the Ch14 Sports Site folder.

Putting up a Web site the easy way

I've designed this chapter to make it as easy as possible for you to create a Web site for a sport, club, or hobby with FrontPage and Photoshop Elements. But even with the templates and graphics on the CD, you still have a multistep process to go through before your Web site can be published. If creating your own pages in FrontPage and setting up your own account with a service provider are more than you want to do, try a simpler alternative.

The fastest and easiest way I've found to create a Web site like this is to use an online service, such as the one at `family.myevent.com`. You won't have as much design control with a service such as MyEvent, and they charge more than a Web hosting provider, but they do make it as easy as possible for you to get your site online quickly.

This chapter walks you through the process of personalizing the pages and graphics in this site so you can quickly and easily create your own Web site. In the first section, you tour the sample karate Web site to get a better idea of the pages you'll want in your own site. Next, you edit the banner, the buttons, and other images by using Photoshop Elements 3. Finally, you put it all together in FrontPage 2003 and add a video file to really bring this site to life. I encourage you to focus on the sections most important to you and skip any that you don't need. For example, if you don't want to change the text in the buttons, you can skip that section and use them as they are. Similarly, if you don't plan to include video on your site, you don't need to read the video section at the end of the chapter.

If you prefer to use Macromedia Dreamweaver MX 2004 to edit these templates, visit `www.digitalfamily.com` for instructions.

Identifying the Key Sections of Your Site

Before you get into the details of creating pages and graphics, it's a good idea to step back and think about what you want to include on your Web site. To give you some ideas, this section takes you on a tour of Lorion's karate site.

Designing the main sections

The first page of your Web site is the most important. As the starting place for your visitors, the home page should welcome people into the site and provide easy access to the most relevant information for each visitor. More than anything, you want to give visitors lots of options and enough introductory information to help them make informed choices when they click a link to another page in the site.

In the front page of the sample karate site, shown in Figure 14-1, the navigation buttons on the left provide easy access to the main sections of the site. The introductory text on the right explains that this site is about Lorion's karate class and that visitors will find photos, a calendar, and even a video by following the links on the left. The challenge in writing text for the main page of a Web site is to keep it brief but still provide a good overview. If you put too much information on the front page, you risk creating confusion or overwhelming your visitors. But if you don't include enough information, your visitors may get lost or miss some of the best parts of your site.

At the top of the page, note the banner graphic. Most good Web sites include some kind of main heading like this to quickly identify what the Web site is about. In the sample site, the banner states, *Welcome to my karate Web site*. The template site has a more generic banner that states *Welcome to my Web site*, but you can personalize the banner later. (You find instructions for changing the text on the banner and other graphics in the "Customizing Your Web Site Graphics" section.)

Figure 14-1:
Your front page should invite visitors into your site and give them an idea of what they will find inside.

Defining the subsections

For each subsection of your Web site, you may want to create a different banner. For example, the front page banner might say *Welcome to my Karate Web Site*, and the front page of the photo section might say *Karate Photo Album*.

To keep things simple in the sample site, I used the same banner at the top of all the sections, and added a heading below the banner with the name of the section, such as the *Photo Album* heading you see in Figure 14-2. Whatever you choose, it's a good idea to use the same option throughout your site because it's easier for visitors to find their way around when navigation options and page headers are consistent.

Figure 14-2: The heading at the top of the photo album section helps visitors find their way around the site.

Customizing Your Web Site Graphics

Before you start building your Web pages in FrontPage, I suggest that you prepare the graphics in Photoshop Elements because it's easier to put your site together when you have all the pieces ready. I've broken the graphics section of the chapter into four parts, based on each type of image in the site: the banner, the buttons, the headings, and the photo frames. In the exercise that follows, you find instructions for customizing the banner graphic.

Before you get started, insert the CD that came with this book into your computer's CD drive and copy the Ch14 Sports Site folder from the Author Files section of the CD onto your hard drive. To help you design your site, I've included three folders in the Ch14 Sports Site folder:

- ✔ photoshop-files has the graphics in a format that makes them easy to edit. These are the images you should use for the exercise in the next few sections.
- ✔ sample-karate-site features the site shown in Figures 14-1 and 14-2.
- ✔ template-sports-site has the template pages and graphics you should use as the basis of your site.

When you copy images from a CD to your hard drive, you may find that the files are locked, so you can't save changes to them. To correct this on a PC, right-click the Ch14 Sports Site folder and choose Properties. In the Attributes area of the Properties dialog box, uncheck the Read Only option. Click Apply and then click OK. If you're using a Mac, ⌘-click the folder name, choose Get Info, and uncheck the Locked option.

Editing the banner graphic

At the top of the main page of the sample karate Web site, I created a graphic that features images symbolizing karate. I designed this banner image to make it easy for you to replace each part with your own content. Take a look at the banner at the top of the page in Figure 14-2 and think about changes that you want to make to your banner graphic. You can replace the text, add your own logo or team emblem on the left, and insert an image on the right.

To edit the banner graphic, follow these steps.

1. **Launch Photoshop Elements (or any image design program that supports layers).**

2. **Open the** banner.psd **graphic, which is in the** photoshop-files **folder.**

   Choose File➪Open and locate the file on your hard drive.

3. **If the Layers palette is not already open, choose Window➪Layers.**

   The Layers palette opens on the right side of the screen, as shown in Figure 14-3. This graphic has the following layers: Welcome, Text, Logo, Graphic, and Background. Before you can change any part of this graphic, you must first select the layer that corresponds to it.

4. **To change the words *To my Web site,* which are on the Text layer, do the following:**

   a. **In the Layers palette, click to select the Text layer.**

      The Text layer becomes shaded in a darker grey indicating that it's the active layer.

b. Click to select the text tool in the Tools palette.

If the Tools palette is not open, choose Window⇨Tools to open it.

c. Click to highlight the words *To my Web site* and then type to replace the words with the text you want in your banner.

In the sample site, I simply added the word *karate*, so the text reads *Welcome to my karate Web site.*

d. Use the text formatting options at the top of the work area to change the font face, color, and size.

In the sample site, I used 16-point, bold, italic Myriad Pro for the words *To my Web site.* You can use any font you want; just click and drag to select the text before you change the text formatting options. If you change the font, however, I recommend that you also change the font in the other graphics on this site so that they all look the same. For more information on editing text in graphics and adjusting font options, see Chapter 6.

5. If you want to change the word *Welcome*, click to select the Welcome layer, click and drag to select the word *Welcome,* and repeat Steps 4b through 4d.

I used 30-point bold, italic Myriad Pro for the word *Welcome.*

Figure 14-3:
To edit the banner graphic, you first select the layer with the feature you want to change.

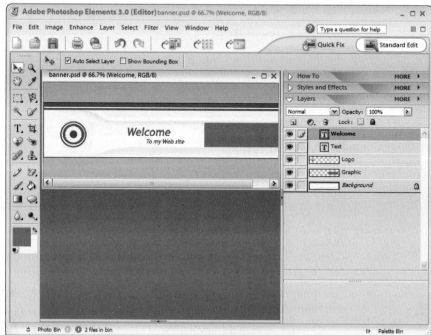

Now that you've replaced the text, it's time to turn your attention to the logo. I used a generic graphic in this banner (a series of colored circles instead of the Chinese text you see in the karate sample site). You should replace this graphic with your own logo or another image that better represents the topic of your Web site. Continuing where you just left off, follow these steps:

1. **Open the image file that you want to add to the banner.**

   Choose File⇨Open, locate the image file on your hard drive, and double-click to open it.

2. **Resize the image.**

   Choose Image⇨Resize and specify the height and width in the Image Size dialog box. If you want to integrate your logo into the existing banner design, make it approximately the same size as the circle in the sample image, about 1 inch, or 72 pixels, square.

3. **Copy and paste the logo into the banner image.**

   a. **Click to select the move tool in the Tools palette.**

   b. **Click to place your cursor somewhere in your logo image, and then choose Select⇨All.**

   c. **Choose Edit⇨Copy.**

   d. **Click to place your cursor on the left side of the banner image.**

   e. **Click to select the Logo layer in the Layers palette.**

   The Logo layer turns to a darker grey, indicating that it's the active layer.

   f. **Choose Edit⇨Paste.**

   The new graphic appears in the banner and a new layer is created. You can adjust the position of the graphic by clicking and dragging it within the banner image or by using the arrow keys on your keyboard. For more information about resizing an image or using copy and paste to copy an image from one file to another, see Chapter 6.

4. **Delete the original Logo layer.**

   To do so, click to select the original Logo layer and then drag it to the small trash can icon at the top of the Layer palette.

5. **Add your own image to the right side of the banner.**

   If you don't have an image you want to insert in the right side of the banner, you can simply leave it blank and skip ahead to Step 6.

   The blue rectangle in the sample image is there to make it easy for you to replace it with your own image, as follows:

   a. **Delete the Graphic layer by selecting it and dragging it to the small trash can icon at the top of the Layers palette.**

    b. **Choose File➪Open, locate on your hard drive the image file you want to use, and double-click to open it.**

    c. **Resize or crop the image.**

        Because this is a long, narrow, small area, you may want to crop a small part of a graphic or photo, as I did with the banner for the karate site shown in Figure 14-1. To fit your image in the area of the blue image, resize or crop it to about 250 by 65 pixels. For more information on cropping or resizing, see Chapter 6.

6. **Choose File➪Save For Web.**

   The Save for Web dialog box opens.

7. **In the Optimized File Format pull-down, choose GIF, as shown in Figure 14-4.**

8. **Set the number in the Colors box to 64.**

   Limiting the number of colors reduces the file size and makes the image download more quickly. For an even smaller file size, reduce this number further, but don't go too far or you'll adversely affect the appearance of the image. For more information on Web graphics options, see Chapter 6.

9. **Save the new banner in your Web site folder and give it a new name.**

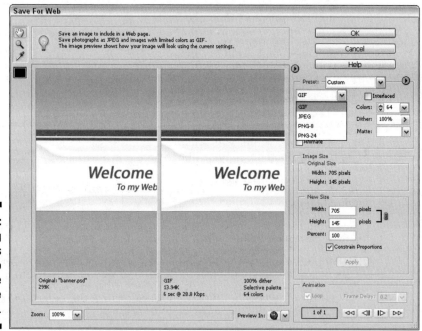

Figure 14-4:
This dialog box makes it easy to optimize your image for the Web.

Your new, customized banner is now ready to be inserted into your Web pages. You find instructions for doing so later in this chapter in the "Customizing the Template Site" section.

Editing the button graphics

The buttons in the sample Web site are labeled Calendar, Photo Album, Activities, Favorites, and Video Section. All five predesigned buttons are in the `images` folder in the `template-sports-site` folder, and are already linked to their respective pages. You can use these buttons just as they are in your site, or you can edit them to change the text, image, and links. If you don't want to use one of the predesigned buttons in the template site, simply delete it (just make sure you delete it from every page where it appears).

In the following exercise, you find instructions for editing the `button.psd` file included in the `photoshop-files` folder in the `Ch14 Sports Site` folder. This image was created with layers, to make it easy to change any one element without affecting the others. For example, you can replace the text but keep the blue circle if you don't have a logo you want to use in its place.

I've included a `.psd` file for each button, labeled `button-calendar.psd`, `button-activities.psd`, and so on. You can edit any of these buttons or you can use the generic `button.psd` file to create a new button, as you do in the following exercise.

 When you add text to buttons and headings, the trick is to be concise. The fewer and the shorter the words, the better. For example, don't try to provide a long explanation like *My favorite Web sites* in a button. Instead, limit yourself to the most important word, *Favorites*.

To edit any button graphic in the `photoshop-files` folder or to create a new one based on the `button.psd` file, follow these steps.

1. **Launch Photoshop Elements.**

2. **In the `photoshop-files` folder, open the button graphic that you want to edit.**

   Choose File⇨Open and locate the file on your hard drive. To create a new button, I suggest you use `button.psd`.

3. **If the Layers palette is not already open, choose Window⇨Layers.**

   The Layers palette opens on the right side of the screen. The `button.psd` file has three layers: Text, Logo, and Background. Before you can change any part of this graphic, you must first select the layer that corresponds to it.

4. **In the Layers palette, click to select the Text layer.**

The Text layer becomes shaded in a darker grey, indicating that it's the active layer.

5. **Click to select the text tool in the Tools palette.**

If the Tools palette is not open, choose Window➪Tools to open it.

6. **Click to highlight the words on the button, and then type to replace the words with the text you want to use.**

In the `button.psd` file, you want to replace the words, *Your Text Here.*

If you have trouble changing the text, you can delete the Text layer by dragging it to the small trash icon at the top of the page, click to select the Text tool from the toolbox, insert your cursor on the button, and type new text.

7. **Use the text formatting options at the top of the work area to change the font face, color, and font size.**

Remember, you have to click and drag to select the text before you can change the formatting options. In the buttons for this template, I used 12-point, bold Myriad Pro. If you don't have Myriad Pro or you prefer to change it, you can use any font you want. If you change the font, however, I recommend that you also change the font in the other graphics in this site so that they all look the same.

8. **To replace the logo on the button, first open the image file that you want to add to the button.**

Choose File➪Open, locate the image file on your hard drive, and double-click to open the file.

You can enlarge the display of an image to make it easier to work on the details. To do so, click the zoom tool (which looks like a magnifying glass) from the Tools palette and then click the image where you want to enlarge it. To reduce the image display size, press Alt+Click (on a PC) or ⌘+Click (on a Mac). To return the image to its actual size, double-click the zoom tool.

9. **Resize the image.**

Choose Image➪Resize and specify the height and width in the Image Size dialog box. If you want to integrate the image into the existing button design, make it approximately the same size as the circles in the sample image, about 20 pixels square.

10. **Copy and paste the image.**

a. **Click to select the move tool in the Tools palette.**

b. **Click to place your cursor somewhere in your logo image, and then choose Select➪All.**

c. **Choose Edit➪Copy.**

   d. **Click to place your cursor on the left side of the button image.**

   e. **Click to select the Logo layer in the Layers palette.**

   The Logo layer turns to a darker grey, indicating it's the active layer.

   f. **Choose Edit⇨Paste.**

   The new graphic appears in the button and a new layer is created. You can adjust the position of the graphic by clicking and dragging it within the button image or by using the arrow keys on your keyboard.

11. **Delete the original Logo layer.**

    To do so, click to select the original Logo layer and drag it to the small trash can at the top of the Layer palette.

12. **Choose File⇨Save For Web.**

    The Save For Web dialog box opens.

13. **In the Optimized File Format pull-down, choose GIF.**

14. **Set the number in the Colors box to 32, as shown in Figure 14-5.**

    Limiting the number of colors reduces the file size and makes the image download more quickly, but if you reduce the number too far, you risk degrading the image quality. (For more information on optimizing images for the Web, see Chapter 6.)

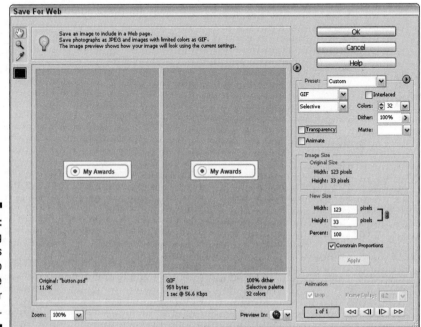

Figure 14-5:
This dialog box makes it easy to optimize images for the Web.

15. Save the new button in your Web site folder and give it a new name.

In the example in Figure 14-5, I created a button with the words *My Awards* but I didn't change the logo image, so the image retains the generic round circle you'll find in the `button.psd` file.

Repeat these steps for each button you want to create or change. The next task is to edit the heading graphics for your Web site.

Editing the heading graphics

The heading graphics are the easiest to edit because they have only two layers, one for the background and one for the words, as you see in Figure 14-6. To edit a heading graphic, open it and follow Steps 1 through 7 in the preceding exercise. The file names for the heading graphics are the same as the button labels — Calendar, Photo Album, Activities, Favorites, and Video Section — preceded by the word *heading* (for example, `heading-activities.psd`). I've also included a generic `heading.psd` file that you can use to create new heading graphics.

It's a good idea to use the same words for heading graphics and their corresponding navigation buttons. That way, it's easier for visitors to find their away around the pages of your Web site.

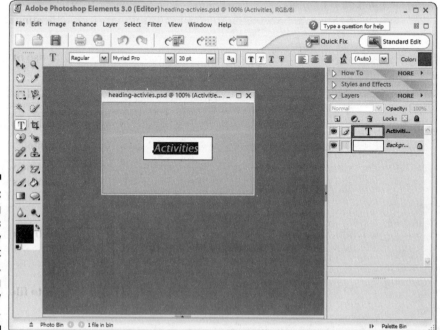

Figure 14-6:
The heading graphics have only one text layer, making them easy to edit.

Preparing the photos for your Web site

Before you add photos to your Web site, you should optimize them so that they will download as quickly as possible. If you're not sure what I mean by optimizing an image, read Chapter 6.

The following steps walk you through the process of resizing and optimizing a photo and inserting it in the photo frame used in the template:

1. **Launch Photoshop Elements.**

2. **Open the** `picture-frame-tall.psd` **graphic in the** `photoshop-files` **folder.**

   Choose File⇨Open and locate the file on your hard drive. You can open it from the CD if you prefer.

   I created two photo frames, one for a tall image and one for a wide image. On the front page, the design calls for a tall image, but in the photo album pages you can use both tall and wide images.

3. **If the Layers palette is not already open, choose Window⇨Layers.**

   The Layers palette opens on the right side of the screen. This graphic has three layers, called Text, Photo, and Background. Before you can change any part of this graphic, you must first select the layer that corresponds to it.

4. **In the Layers palette, click to select the Photo layer.**

   The Photo layer becomes shaded in a darker grey, indicating that it's the active layer.

5. **Open the file containing the photograph you want to use on your Web site.**

   Choose File⇨Open, locate a photo on your hard drive, and double-click to open it. If you're using the tall photo frame, you need to use a vertically oriented photo or crop a wide photo into a vertical shape.

6. **Resize the photo you want to insert into the photo frame.**

   Choose Image⇨Resize and specify the height and width you want in the Image Size dialog box, as shown in Figure 14-7. Wide photos should be no larger than 315 by 210 pixels, and tall photos should be no larger than 180 by 275 pixels.

7. **Copy the photo and paste your photo into the picture frame image as follows:**

   a. **Click to select the move tool in the Tools palette.**

   b. **Click to place your cursor anywhere in your photo file, and then choose Select⇨All.**

   c. **Choose Edit⇨Copy.**

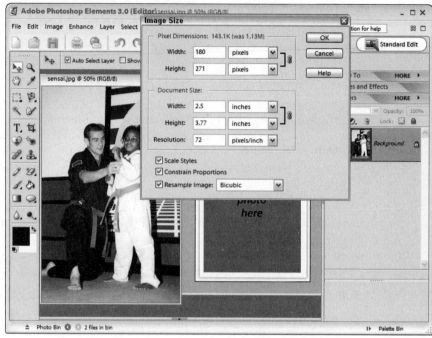

Figure 14-7:
Resize your
photos and
insert them
into the
photo frame
graphic to
give them a
finished
look.

   **d. Click to place your cursor in the middle of the picture frame
   image, and then choose Edit⇨Paste.**

   Your photo appears in the picture frame and a new layer is created. You can adjust the position of your photo by clicking and
   dragging it within the picture frame image or by using the arrow
   keys on your keyboard.

   e. Delete the original Photo layer.

   To do so, click to select the original Photo layer (the blue box) and
   drag it to the small trash can icon at the top of the Layers palette.

   f. Delete the Text layer.

 8. **Choose File⇨Save For Web.**

   The Save For Web dialog box opens.

 9. **In the Optimized File Format pull-down, choose JPEG.**

 10. **Set the Quality to 80 percent.**

   Lowering the quality helps reduce the file size and make the image
   download more quickly. For more information on optimizing graphics
   for the Web, see Chapter 6.

 11. **Save the new photo in your Web site folder with a new name.**

Repeat these steps for each photo you want to prepare for your site. Then follow the steps in the next section to insert these images into your pages.

Customizing the Template Site

I've created the templates for this chapter with a sports, hobby, or club site in mind. If you don't plan to edit any of the graphics on the Web site, you can jump right in and start building your pages by following the steps in this section. If you want to edit the banner, buttons, or other graphics, I suggest you work on the images first so that you have all the pieces of your site ready before you begin working on the page designs.

I include a template for each of the sections of the site, but you can use the same template for all the pages. In the exercises in this section, I start with the first page of the site because it's the starting point for everything else and the most complicated page to create.

Opening the template site in FrontPage

You can edit template pages as you would edit any other file in FrontPage. For example, to add text, you simply place your cursor on the page where you want the text to appear and type. FrontPage is a relatively easy Web design program, especially if you already use a program like Microsoft Word. For example, FrontPage has the same standard Microsoft icons on the toolbar for aligning and formatting text.

FrontPage works best when you use the program's Open Site feature to identify your Web site folder before you edit any pages. You should also keep all the files for your Web site in one folder — doing so makes it easier to upload the files to your server later and helps FrontPage set the links properly. You'll be working with the files in the `template-sports-site` folder, but I suggest you begin by renaming that folder something else, such as My Karate Site, so you can identify it more easily on your hard drive.

Follow these steps to use the FrontPage Open Site command to open the template folder for the sports Web site:

1. **If you haven't done so already, insert the CD that came with this book into your computer's CD drive and copy the** `template sports-site` **folder from the** `Ch14 Sports Site` **folder onto your hard drive.**

2. **Open the template site in FrontPage as you'd open any other Web site.**

   Choose File➪Open Site, locate the Web site folder on your hard drive, click to select the folder, and then click Open. The Web site opens in FrontPage and the files and subfolders are displayed, as shown in Figure 14-8.

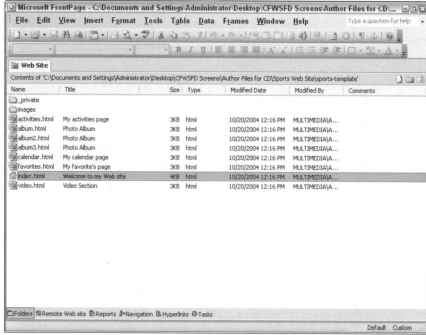

Figure 14-8:
When you
open a Web
site folder in
FrontPage,
the files and
subfolders
become
visible in the
workspace
area.

Editing text in a template page

After you open the template site, you can begin to work on the individual pages of the site. To edit the text in any of the template pages, follow these steps:

1. **With the Web site open in FrontPage (refer to Figure 14-8), double-click the name of the file you want to edit.**

   If you choose `index.html`, the front page of the sports site template opens. The main page of any Web site must be named `index.html`, but the other pages can be named anything you like. I named the files in this site with the same names as the buttons and heading graphics to make it easy for you to identify them. For example, the activities page is called `activities.html`. In the example (see Figure 14-9), I opened `album3.html`.

2. **Highlight any text you want to replace on the page and type your own words.**

   Simply click and drag to select a word or words, press the Delete key to delete the existing text, and then type to enter your own text. You can also use the copy and paste function to copy text from another document, such as a Word file, into your Web page in FrontPage.

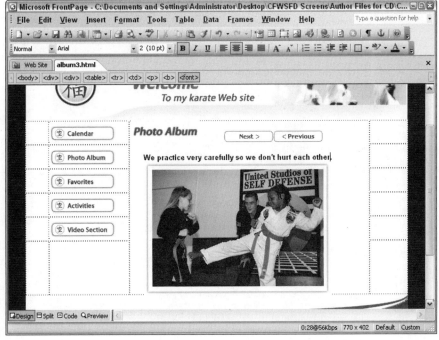

Figure 14-9:
You can add and edit text in FrontPage much like you would in Microsoft Word.

3. Choose File⇨Save.

Any changes you made to the page are saved.

4. Choose File⇨Preview in Browser.

The page is displayed in a Web browser.

To edit the text on any of the other pages in the site, follow the same instructions. For more information on editing pages with FrontPage, see Chapter 8, which covers many basic page editing features.

Replacing images in a template page

The following instructions show you how to replace or add an image to a page. Before you do, however, make sure all your image files are in the images folder in the main Web site folder so that the links will be set properly.

To replace the images in any of the template pages, follow these steps:

1. With the Web site open in FrontPage (refer to Figure 14-8), double-click the name of the file you want to edit.

The page opens in the FrontPage workspace.

2. **Click to select the image you want to replace.**

   In the example in Figure 14-10, I'm replacing the banner image, which is called `banner.gif`, in the main page of the site, which is called `index.html`.

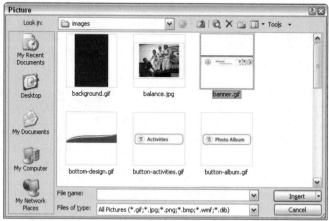

Figure 14-10: To customize the template, replace the generic graphics with your images.

3. **Press the Delete key on your keyboard to delete the image.**

   The image disappears from the page. Be careful not to move your cursor or to delete more than the image, because you want to insert the new image in the same place as the old one.

4. **Choose Insert⇨Picture⇨From File, and locate and select the image you want to use on your hard drive, as shown in Figure 14-10.**

   The new image appears in place of the old one.

5. **Repeat Steps 2 through 4 to replace any other images on the page.**

6. **Click File⇨Save.**

   Any changes you made to the page are saved.

7. **Choose File⇨Preview in Browser.**

   The page is displayed in a Web browser.

To replace images in any other pages in the site, follow the same instructions. For more information on working with images in FrontPage, see Chapter 8.

Creating or deleting pages

The `sports-template` folder includes a template page for each of the main pages in the sample site. You can add pages or remove pages to further customize the site to your own liking.

To add pages, choose the template page that is most like the page you want to add and choose File⇨Save As to create a copy. Give the new page a new name so you don't overwrite the existing page. After you save a copy of the page, you can make changes to it in FrontPage without affecting the original page.

If you remove a page or a section, make sure that you also delete the navigation buttons that link to that page. To do that, you need to open each page in the site, click to select the button that links to that page, and delete the graphic that represents the button. When you delete the button, you automatically remove the link.

One of the best ways to develop a Web site is to experiment. Don't be afraid to add more text and images to the pages or to add new sections. If you need more instruction than I've provided in this chapter, see Chapter 8 for a basic tutorial in using FrontPage. If you want to get into more advanced editing and design with FrontPage, I recommend *FrontPage 2003 For Dummies* by Asha Dornfest (published by Wiley).

If you want to add an interactive calendar to your site to keep track of games, meetings, and other events, check out Yahoo! Calendar (`yahoo.calendar.com`), one of the most widely used calendar programs. This free service is powerful and adaptable. You can choose from a gallery of images so that each month (or week or whatever) will have a different picture. You can even specify who to share your calendar with — which is useful if you're trying to keep track of dance recitals or soccer practices and you want multiple people to have access to the dates. Yahoo! also has a handy feature that enables you to sync their online calendar with a Palm or Outlook program. You can also choose which holidays you want to have listed, and even set reminders for special dates.

Editing the Video Pages

Sports and club sites are especially well served by adding video files because you have so much great motion to show off. Only video can capture the swing of a bat, the twirl of a skirt in a dance class, the laughter and play in a clubhouse, or the blocks and kicks featured in the video in the sample karate site.

If you don't want to add video to your site, I suggest you simply delete the `video.html` page and the Video Section button on each of the remaining pages. If you do want to add video, read on.

In case you don't have a video file and want to follow this exercise to see how it works, I included on the CD a video file used in the sample karate site. This `.wmv` file is in the `multimedia` folder of the `sample-karate-site` folder, which is in the `Ch14 Sports Site` folder.

Adding a video file to your Web page is similar to adding an image file. To use FrontPage to insert a video file, follow these steps:

1. **Make sure the video file you want to insert is saved in the main folder of your Web site.**

   I suggest you create a `multimedia` folder inside your main Web site folder so you can keep your video files separate from the other files in your site. This helps with the organization of your site and makes it easy to find the video if you want to edit or remove it later.

2. **Open the Web page in FrontPage, and click to insert the cursor where you want the file to be displayed on the page.**

   Make sure you're in Design view in FrontPage by clicking the Design icon at the bottom left of the page.

3. **Choose Insert⇨Picture⇨Video.**

   Note that Video is the last option at the bottom of the list, and you may need to use the expansion arrow to make it visible. The Select Video dialog box appears.

4. **Browse your drive to locate the video file you want to insert, and click to select it.**

   In the example for this exercise, I selected the `karate-demo.wmv` file.

5. **Click Open.**

   The dialog box closes, the video file is inserted on the page, and the first frame of the video appears on the page.

6. **Double-click the video image to open the Picture Properties dialog box.**

   You can set many options in the Picture Properties dialog box, as shown in Figure 14-11.

7. **Click the Appearance tab and specify alignment, spacing, and size options.**

   Alignment works much like it does with images. If you align the video to the left or right, you can wrap text around it. The settings in the Size area are inserted automatically, but you may want to change this setting to display the video in a smaller area, which can improve the quality and help the video fit better on smaller monitors. You find detailed descriptions of Picture Properties options in Chapter 10.

8. **If you want to create a link from the video file to any other Web page, video, or other file, click the General tab.**

   Most of the options in the General tab don't apply to video. (FrontPage uses this same dialog box for a variety of file types.) However, at the bottom is the Link box, where you can set your video to link to another page or Web site. Just enter the URL of the site you want to link to or use the Browse button to locate a page within your Web site.

Figure 14-11:
The Picture
Properties
dialog box
contains
the video
options.

9. **Click the Video tab and specify loop, loop delay, and start options.**

   If you choose to not loop your video, it will play once and stop. If you want your video file to play over and over, set the number of times you want it to repeat in the Loop box. The Loop Delay option will cause the video to pause for the specified time before it repeats.

10. **Click OK.**

   The Picture Properties dialog box closes.

11. **To play the video, click the Preview button at the bottom of the FrontPage work area.**

   FrontPage doesn't display video files in Design view, so you have to switch to Preview. If you prefer to view the page in a browser, choose File➪Preview in Browser. You'll see the video as it will appear when viewed with a browser on the Web.

Publishing Your Web Site

Congratulations, you made it to the end of the chapter. You should be well on your way to completing your club, hobby, or sports Web site. Your final step is to publish your site to a Web server to make it accessible to other people on the Internet.

Most family sites are hosted by commercial service providers. (You can find suggestions for choosing a service provider in Chapter 4.) After you set up an account with a service provider, you simply transfer the files from your hard drive to the Web server. To use FrontPage to send your site to the server, see Chapter 8.

Even after you've published your Web site to a server, you're not really finished. All good Web sites grow, and you can always add more pages and graphics to your site in the future. Updating seems to work best when you develop a regular schedule. For example, you could add new photos every Sunday or update team stats the day after each game. This works well for your visitors, too, because they know what to expect and when to return to the site to see updates.

If you want more instructions for editing and updating your pages, see Chapter 8, which provides a basic FrontPage tutorial. If you want to get into advanced editing and design with FrontPage, I recommend *FrontPage 2003 For Dummies* by Asha Dornfest (published by Wiley).

Chapter 15

The Family Blog: Sharing Stories with an Online Journal

*B*logs are increasingly in the news. You may have heard about blogs on the radio or read about them in a newspaper or magazine, but if these strangely named Web sites are new to you, don't worry, this chapter is designed to help you appreciate this dynamic part of the Internet.

Blogs, or Web logs, are online journals that are updated frequently, sometimes even daily. An update, (also called an *entry* or a *post*) is usually quite short, perhaps just a few sentences, and readers can often respond to an entry online. People who write blogs are commonly called *bloggers*. Bloggers, tongue in cheek, call themselves and their blogs the *blogosphere*.

Many early blogs focused on technology, news, and politics, but that has changed dramatically in the last few years. Today, blogs are written by people who are chronicling their lives, keeping track of a particular interest, or just writing for themselves. Increasingly, mothers, fathers, teenagers, even entire families are writing blogs. Their informal, engaging style and interactive format make them attractive for families looking to continue conversations they begin in e-mail messages, letters, or phone calls. For families spread across the state, country, or globe, a blogcan be an instant "family fix" when time differences make a phone call impossible.

Blogs are a great way to keep everyone in a family abreast of the latest family news without running up the phone bill — you can simply read back over important updates to find out the latest news. In addition, many blogs are being used to host photographs, and their chronological structure can be a great way to keep track of a baby's growth, a trip, or the process of planning a wedding.

But what makes a blog different from any other family Web site? A blog is designed around a particular form of publishing: frequent, short updates, often using links and accompanied by a corresponding set of comments from readers. Blogs are meant to be written and read regularly — even daily. Their tone is usually informal, almost stream of consciousness. Although the writing may be free form, a blog has some common organizational structures that make understanding and participating in the conversation easy for readers.

Reading a Typical Blog

Most people name their blogs and display the name prominently at the top of the page. Some names are simple and descriptive, such as the blog shown in Figure 15-1 called Suman Kumar's Wedding Blog. Others are clever twists of a phrase, or personal, funny word combinations.

Figure 15-1: Suman Kumar's Wedding Blog is a good example of standard blog layout practices.

Below the name, you usually find the most recent update or blog entry. The date and sometimes the time are displayed so that you can tell when the last entry was created. Previous entries appear in reverse chronological order down the page. Blogs are often long pages that scroll on and on with a series of dated entries and invitations to readers to comment. (You find more about comments in the "Invite comments" section, later in this chapter).

On the right or left side of the browser window, a blog often includes a collection of links and related resources, such as an invitation to subscribe to an e-mail list, explanatory or biographical information, links to archived entries, or links to recommended Web sites.

To blog or not to blog

Most of the blogs in this chapter are focused on a specific topic, such as a new baby, a wedding, or the life of a busy mom. Blogs can be created as stand-alone Web sites or you can choose to create a blog as a part of a bigger Web site. For the most part, you have more options and greater design control if you create a site yourself in a program such as FrontPage (covered in Chapters 8 and 9) than if you use one of the blogging software programs featured at the end of this chapter. If your main goal is to update your site regularly with written text, a blog may be your best and simplest choice. If you're more interested in sharing lots of photos, video, and other information and you want to be able to create a more complex design or use the templates included with this book, you're better off using one of the design options covered in Chapters 11 to 14. If you really want both, consider creating your own custom site and then linking to a blog.

How Families Are Using Blogs

Families are making use of blogs to share a wide range of information with family and friends. The examples in this section will provide you with ideas for how you might use this technology to create your own online journal.

Communicating with friends and family

At heart, a blog is a communication tool. Whatever else it does, a blog is first and foremost about establishing dialogue. With a family blog, the dialogue is usually with family members and friends near and far.

Busymom.net, shown in Figure 15-2, is a good example of a blog that keeps friends and family up-to-date on all the family news, from first days at school to the different grocery shopping strategies of Busy Mom and Busy Dad. Busy Mom's blog, at Busymom.net, goes back to April 2003. She posts frequently, usually multiple times a day. On August 24, 2004, for example, she wrote three entries. The longest was only 63 words.

Busy Mom's audience is very vocal, often posting a dozen or so comments on each entry (see Figure 15-3). In response to an entry about trying to plan a week's worth of meals, for example, her audience responded with favorite recipes, shopping strategies, and sympathetic anecdotes.

Readers of Busymom.net can keep track of big and little events in Busy Mom's life. Sometimes that means a lot of posts about errands that need running and back-to-school shopping, but sometimes things take a serious turn. In June

2003, Busy Mom's mom was diagnosed with lung cancer, and many of her blog posts talked about her mom's treatments and experiences, as well as Busy Mom's sadness about her mom's illness.

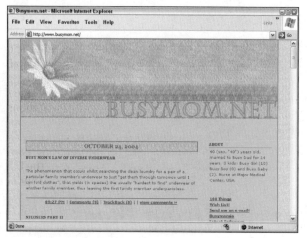

Figure 15-2: Here's a blog one mother uses to communicate with her friends and family.

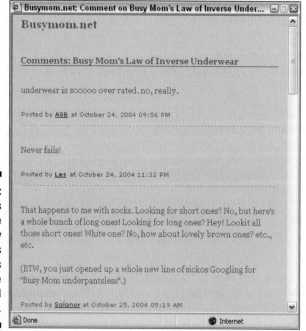

Figure 15-3: Comments in response to Busy Mom's postings offer advice and suggestions.

Busy Mom also uses her blog to share pictures of her children and link to Web sites and sound clips she finds interesting. At the top of the home page, Busy Mom has a countdown to her next birthday, when she will turn 40.

Sharing wedding stories

Many a blog is devoted to chronicling wedding planning and the ceremony itself. Blogs make the complicated organization and endless details involved in wedding planning a little easier, because the bride and groom can post information to the blog instead of making phone call after phone call. Some wedding blogs are also used to advise guests on accommodations and wedding activities.

One of the best wedding blogs I've seen was created by Jonathan and Joanne, who created `wedding.studio2f.com` for their wedding in the U.S. Virgin Islands. Their Web site, shown in Figure 15-4, keeps guests apprised of the arrangements they're making for the ceremony and reception, such as hotel accommodations, ferry schedules, and a trip to a nearby island.

Figure 15-4: This beautiful blog is designed to keep wedding guests up-to-date on weather, accommodations, and other pre- and post-wedding activities.

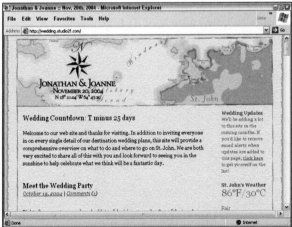

The site also includes links to Jonathan and Joanne's gift registries, a countdown to the wedding day, and current weather information for St. John. Although there are many ways to design a wedding Web site (see Chapter 13 for alternatives), many people use blogging software because it's quick and easy to set up and requires little technical experience. (You find more about blogging software later in this chapter.)

Babbling about babies

Everyone loves a new baby, and grandparents who don't live nearby can never get enough information and pictures. A baby blog makes it easy to share the trials and tribulations of a new baby's life with friends and family. A variety of software programs and technologies are available for designing baby sites and blogs. Use any of the blogging software programs featured at the end of this chapter, and see Chapter 11 for some other alternatives for creating a baby Web site.

One of the most impressive baby blogs on the Internet is The Trixie Update, at www.trixieupdate.com/, which chronicles the life and times of Beatrix MacNeill, born July 31, 2003. The site is astonishing in its detail, seemingly covering every moment of Trixie's daily routine. When you arrive, you find out whether Trixie is awake or asleep, find out about her daily actives, and can even keep track of changes in the Diaper Log (2,611 as of 7:45 p.m. August 26, 2004). The Trixie Update is maintained by her dad, Ben. He started the blog because Trixie's mom, Jennifer, had to go back to work and wanted to stay connected during the day.

An important component of The Trixie Update is the TPOD (Trixie Picture of the Day), as shown in Figure 15-5. You can follow Trixie's growth from day one by tracking back through more than a year of photos. The Trixie Update also has postings sorted into categories such as Behavior, Day-to-Day Minutiae, Inner Workings, Milestones, and Site News.

Figure 15-5:
The Trixie Update is a meticulously detailed chronicle of Trixie MacNeill's infant life, right down to the last diaper.

New stories are added to Trixie Update every couple of weeks or so and the site's comments often include advice and commiserations from other parents, as well as responses from a growing list of people who have become fans of Trixie and her well-reported activities.

The data-tracking features of The Trixie Update (numbers of diaper changes, feedings, naps, and so on) have been spun off into software called Trixie Tracker, a subscription-based program built by Trixie's father Ben, who sells it in three-month subscriptions for $10. You can visit `www.trixietracker.com/` to get more information.

Traipsing the travel logs

When family members travel, individually or together, an extended group of people usually want to know all about the trip. If you're a college student preparing for a semester abroad, a young couple going around the world, or a family taking an unusual vacation, consider starting a blog so your friends and family can track your progress. It's cheaper than postcards and your messages are sure to get home before you do!

The Fleming family, Sarah and Ray and their two young daughters, left home, career, and school behind in the U.K. to pursue a trip around the world in July 2003. The Flemings decided to chronicle their trip with a blog, as shown in Figure 15-6. To produce their travel site, called The Fleming Family Travel Tales, they brought along a computer, two digital cameras, and a digital video camera.

Figure 15-6: When the Fleming family left their home and work behind to travel, they stayed in touch with regular journal postings, photos and videos.

Visit the site at `www.rfleming.net` to read about their stops in places like Canada, the United States, Fiji, Australia, New Zealand, Singapore, Malaysia, Thailand, Laos, Cambodia, Vietnam, and France.

Writing a Good Blog

Professional writers often look down on bloggers, because their informal online writing rarely benefits from a good editor. Blogs are known for their casual writing and unpredictable subject material, but the best blogs have proven that — regardless of punctuation and spelling — even "novice" writers can be entertaining enough to attract a broad audience.

Bloggers with an especially engaging subject, such as chronicling a trip around the world, have the advantage of inherently interesting material, but even mundane material can attract an audience if you have an engaging style and voice.

Here are three guiding principles to writing a successful blog:

 ✔ Develop a writing style and tone appropriate to your subject material.

 ✔ Post often, even if your posts are short.

 ✔ Allow your readers to comment on your posts.

Develop a writing style and voice

A great site design and technical gimmicks are no replacement for developing an interesting, readable writing style. Most of us don't do much personal writing in our everyday lives or even keep a diary. Writing about yourself is never easy, and you may find yourself freezing up in front of the computer screen or becoming stilted and unnecessarily verbose.

A number of great books about writing are available in your local bookstore, and they may be good resources if you're having trouble and are determined to improve. Some of my favorite books on writing include the following:

 ✔ *Woe Is I: The Grammarphobe's Guide to Better English in Plain English,* 2nd Edition, by Patricia O'Connor (Riverhead Books): An unexpectedly entertaining and cleverly written book on grammar that will help you correct some of the most common mistakes in English.

 ✔ *Bird by Bird: Some Instructions on Writing and Life,* by Anne Lamott (Anchor Publishing): In her humorous and self-deprecating style, Lamott shares her secrets for staying sane as a single mom while struggling to become a successful writer. Lamott's other best-selling books include *Traveling Mercies* and *Operation Instructions,* based on the first year of her son's life.

 ✔ *On Writing,* by Stephen King (Pocket Books): With an honest account of the many rejection letters and other setbacks he suffered in his early days as a writer, King shares his best advice for other aspiring authors.

> ✔ *On Writing Well*, by William Zinsser (Harper Resource): Celebrating its 25th anniversary, this book is a classic guide on writing clearly and concisely.

Here are a few suggestions you can use to develop your own voice and style for your blog. First, remember that a blog is a conversation. Try to write the way you speak. Avoid jargon and clichés and don't overuse the thesaurus. It may be helpful to speak your entry out loud before trying to type it or to read it aloud after you've written it. If you find yourself struggling as you read aloud or speaking unnaturally, think about what you might have said if you were talking to a friend rather than writing.

Second, write your blog with a specific friend or family member in mind. Thinking of someone you know well and who might want to read your blog will help you relax your writing style. That's why it's become popular for many people to start personal journal entries with *Dear Diary*. The goal is to get your writing to sound more like you and less like a lofty essay.

Always consider your audience. If you're writing for only close friends and family, you don't need to explain that Sarah is your 8-year-old daughter every time you mention her. But if your blog attracts a wider audience, you may want to create references or glossaries to help new readers follow along.

Finally, before you start blogging, spend some time visiting other blogs that are like the one you're thinking of starting. Read one or two for a few weeks and pay attention to things like the length of posts, frequency, writing style, and subject material. You can get some great ideas for your own blog by noting what you find interesting and compelling in other people's blogs.

Update, update, update

The blogs that attract the most readers are the ones with frequent updates. If you start a blog, be prepared to spend some time working on it every day or two. If you're going to be a blogger, you have to blog! It takes discipline for most of us to write, even conversationally, every day. If you find yourself dreading posting to your blog, maybe a blog isn't for you.

As you go about your day, keep the blog in the back of your mind. You may even want to carry a notebook where you can jot down reminders for topics you want to blog about later. Start paying attention to the parts of your life that are most interesting to you; those will likely be the areas your friends and family are most interested in as well. Don't be afraid to write about everyday activities — parking tickets and car repairs — but don't neglect to talk about what you're thinking and feeling. All these areas will make it possible for you to update frequently.

Having a co-blogger can take some of the pressure off, especially if all authors contribute regularly. If you're going to be working with several people on one blog, talk over how often you expect each other to post so that you can keep some focus and cohesion to your blog.

If you will be updating your blog on a weekly, biweekly, or monthly basis, try to be consistent about when you add new posts so that your readers know when to catch up. For example, you may choose to update your site every Sunday evening.

Invite comments

One of the most important aspects of blogs is that they feature the writing of the blogger as well as the comments of readers. When you visit a blog, you often find a comment link under the text of each blog posting. Clicking that link enables you to read comments from other people and submit your own. Usually bloggers make their own comments in the posts on their site, but sometimes a blogger adds a response in the comment section because it's a more direct way to address someone else's comment.

Not all bloggers choose to implement the comment feature, but if you want to develop a dialogue with your audience, comments are the best way to do so. The comment feature is an easy way to involve your audience and get valuable feedback about what you're doing with your blog.

If you do decide to allow comments on your blog, be sure to keep an eye on them. The comment feature makes it possible for anyone to add comments to your blog and you may not always like what they have to say. For example, spammers sometimes take advantage of inattentive bloggers to do some marketing that you may not want on your blog. All good blogging software makes it easy for the author to remove comments. (You find more about software options at the end of this chapter.)

Before You Blog

Blogs are a lot of fun for bloggers and readers, but you should consider some issues before you get started. I've already mentioned the time and commitment a blog requires. If your life is already busy and you don't absolutely love writing your blog, the likelihood is that you'll put off posting and eventually let your blog die. Guilt over infrequent posts can definitely increase your stress load, so consider yourself warned.

If I haven't scared you off yet, the next thing you should consider is whether to use your own name and those of your friends and family. Some bloggers choose to remain anonymous to the general public to maintain some personal privacy; others have decided that keeping an online journal is already so public that they may as well use their name. This is a personal decision that may be affected by the kinds of subjects you plan to discuss in your blog.

You should consider some legal and professional issues as well. You may be tempted to talk about specific situations that made you angry — be careful about identifying people you are upset with and making statements that might be construed as libelous. Any written material that is untrue and harmful can be the basis for legal action. For example, if you write about a current or former employer in a way that you can't prove to be true and that could be construed as harmful to their business, you may risk legal action. Your family may read with sympathy and support; others may not.

Even if you don't write anything directly negative about your work, your employer may become concerned about your blog (especially if they see that you're posting to it on company time). If you plan to talk about your professional life, think hard about how much you should reveal about life at the office and be especially careful about what you say.

Finally, be aware that someone may become unhealthily interested in you or your family. This has not been a common experience on the Net, but don't take unnecessary risks by providing your home address or phone number. Some bloggers choose not to even identify the city they live in or the company they work for.

Bleeding-edge blogs

The snazziest blogs today are using some of the most cutting-edge Internet technology available. Here's a quick list of what's hot and what you can expect to see on more blogs in the future:

✔ **Moblogging:** Blogging with photos, often taken on-the-go with your mobile phone and sent via your phone to your blog.

✔ **RSS/XML feeds:** RSS (Rich Site Summary) is an Internet technology that can deliver your posts to your reader's computers or notify them whenever you update your blog.

✔ **Audblogging:** Posting audio entries to your blog by recording messages from your phone (mobile or otherwise).

Comparing Blogging Software and Services

Unless you want to build a custom blog, starting a blog requires little technical knowledge. If you have access to a computer and the Internet, you'll find special blog software solutions that can be set up in minutes — usually for little to no cost. This section describes the options available.

Using a hosted blog service

Following are some of the most popular companies that provide blogging solutions on the Web:

- ✔ Blogger, www.blogger.com/
- ✔ TypePad, www.typepad.com
- ✔ LiveJournal, www.livejournal.com
- ✔ Diaryland, www.diaryland.com
- ✔ MySpace, www.myspace.com

All provide a way for you to start a blog quickly and inexpensively.

Blogger, shown in Figure 15-7, is one of the best for beginners without much technical know-how, and you can't beat the price — it's free! Setup takes fewer than five minutes and you can start posting right away. When you set up an account at Blogger, you must first enter a name for your blog and choose one of the prefab designs. Your blog is hosted on Blogger's servers, and you log into their Web site to add posts to your blog.

Blogger is a great way to get started, but if you decide you want more features and greater personalization options, consider purchasing one of the more advanced programs, such as Moveable Type, covered in the next section.

Although American Online doesn't call it *blogging*, they now offer online journals that function similar to a traditional blog. Visit hometown.aol.com to find more about AOL's online services. If you're an AOL member, search for the keyword *Journal*.

Figure 15-7:
Blogger's
free service
offers a
great way to
start a blog,
especially
for
beginners.

Doing it yourself

Serious bloggers often opt to purchase blogging software that they can install and customize on their own server. Although this option is not for the technically faint of heart, the resulting control, especially of your site's design, may be worth the investment of time and money. This solution also means that your postings are not vulnerable to the whims of a commercial company, which might change its policies or close its doors.

If you choose this option, you'll also want to register a domain name and select a Web hosting company. You find information about how to take care of both these tasks in Chapters 3 and 4, respectively. If you're setting up Web hosting to run blogging software, make sure the hosting service you choose includes the ability to install software on the server. You'll also want to be sure that any required programs or technologies needed to run blog updating software are available to you. You should be able to find any necessary software on the Web site of the company that sells the blogging software.

Two of the most robust blog software systems are

- ✔ Movable Type, `www.movabletype.org/`
- ✔ pMachine Pro, `www.pmachine.com/`

Licensing fees vary depending on what features you need, but noncommercial pricing, which is lower, is available. Both programs must be installed on your Web server and require some technical experience (although you'll find detailed instructions on their Web sites).

Part V
The Part of Tens

The 5th Wave   By Rich Tennant

"Can't I just give you riches or something?"

In this part . . .

Chapter 16 introduces you to ten great family-oriented Web sites filled with instructional resources and fun games and activities. In Chapter 17, I present ten important Web design tips, and in Chapter 18, you find suggestions for testing, updating, and promoting your Web site.

Chapter 16

Ten Great Family Web Sites

The Internet is not just a great place to showcase family photos and share stories. It's also a great place to do research, get help with homework, and enjoy a wide array of free entertainment. The sites featured in this chapter are geared toward parents and young people. If you know of other sites you want to recommend, e-mail your suggestions to me at janine@jcwarner.com and I'll add them to my family site at www.digitalfamily.com and try to include them in future editions of this book.

Earning Clams at Whyville

www.whyville.net

When members of the online community at Whyville were challenged with reporting on winter Solstice celebrations around the world, many quickly determined that the best strategy was to recruit an international team and compare notes. That wasn't so hard in a virtual world in which half the members come from outside the U.S. The real challenge came when they wanted to celebrate their success and discovered they'd first have to find how to negotiate different time zones. Most of them were only 12 or 13, with early bed times.

No one assigned the task of studying time zones, but then much of the learning that happens at Whyville isn't assigned, it's discovered. That's just one of the secrets of success in this online learning environment, which is also getting attention from adults who hope to apply some of the lessons acquired in Whyville to online communities for grownups.

Whyville.net, shown in Figure 16-1, is run by Numedeon Inc. It was started in 1999 by a small group of scientists, educators, and Internet experts who wanted to create a place where young people could find out about science through experience, not just by memorizing terms.

Whyville is a 3-D world where you can take a virtual bus around town, getting off at activity-filled places such as the Center for Disease Control, the Currency Exchange, or the House of Illusions. If you want something changed in Whyville, you can start a petition at City Hall; with enough votes, you can get your idea implemented. Members earn "clams" by solving science problems, getting published in the Whyville Times, or developing a business in Whyville's burgeoning entrepreneurial environment. The extent to which kids are acquiring business skills at Whyville is another development that's attracting attention from other sites.

Figure 16-1:
Whyville is a wondrous world of learning adventures designed to challenge kids.

Fooling Around with Yahooligans

yahooligans.yahoo.com

Run by the famous Yahoo! site, Yahooligans is a smorgasbord of stuff any kid should find interesting. The site, shown in Figure 16-2, features a directory of cool Web sites for kids, the Yahooligans TV animated series, games, music, and much more. Take a Yahooligans poll, laugh at the joke of the day, try the grab bag, and use the home page as a launching pad to many other great sites on the Web.

Figure 16-2: Yahooligans is the kid's version of the famous Yahoo! Web site.

Asking Jeeves in Kids Speak

www.ajkids.com

Designed to help kids search the Web in words they can understand, Ask Jeeves for Kids is widely considered the best search engine for children ages 7 to 17. One of the coolest features of Ask Jeeves is the ability to search for information by entering a real question, such as, "Why is the ocean full of fish?" The kid's site, shown in Figure 16-3, features a wealth of resources including a kid-friendly dictionary, thesaurus, almanac, atlas, and clip art gallery.

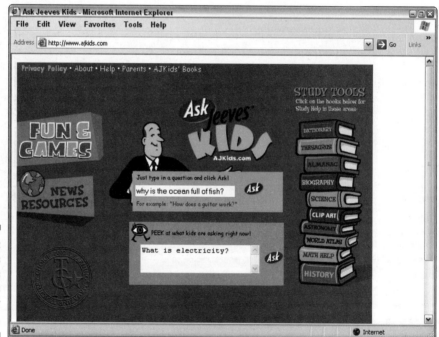

Figure 16-3: Ask Jeeves for Kids answers all your questions.

Traveling Around The World

www.nationalgeographic.com/kids

The National Geographic Web site, shown in Figure 16-4, features a special kids' section with beautifully illustrated travel stories, a news section, science reports, an online coloring book, and so much more. With the resources of the *National Geographic* magazine to draw on, the site provides a broad range of professionally produced stories, photographs, and other materials.

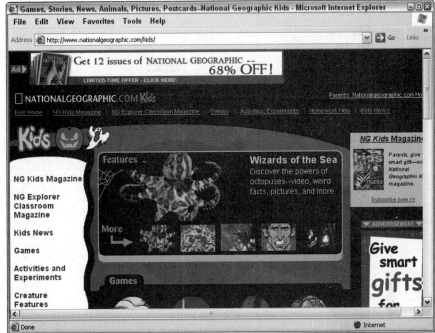

Figure 16-4: National Geographic's site for kids is a fun place to explore the world.

Sitting in the Family Corner

www.thefamilycorner.com

The *Family Corner* is an online magazine that provides informative articles, educational guides, loads of ideas for crafts, and a wide range of resources on parenting, child development stages, and how to care for pets. Updated regularly, the site, shown in Figure 16-5, features seasonal topics, such as back-to-school and holiday planning and preparation, as well as timeless sections, like the games and contest area.

Figure 16-5: The *Family Corner* magazine offers many resources for parents.

Answering Parents' Questions

`cfw.tufts.edu`

At the heart of the Tuft's University Child and Family Web Guide, you'll find a directory of hundreds of Web sites with information about child development, parenting, and other issues of interest to parents and families.

Search the site for the latest child development articles, and get expert answers to parenting questions by e-mailing the experts who manage the site. The Child and Family Web guide, shown in Figure 16-6, is designed to help parents sort through the vast amount of information on the Internet by using the site's extensive database as a filter to help eliminate unreliable information. The guide is a nonprofit resource managed by the university that features contributions by child development experts, including David Elkind, Edward Zigler, and the late Fred Rogers.

Figure 16-6:
Created
by Tuft's
University,
the Child
and Family
Web Guide
offers expert
answers to
questions
from
parents.

Finding Out at Fun Brain

www.funbrain.com

Fun Brain, shown in Figure 16-7, is an educational site full of games for kids, writing tips, a math section, and other learning areas, such as homework help and guides for teachers and parents. Fun Brain is run by Pearson Education, Inc., one of the largest publishers of textbooks and educational materials.

Figure 16-7: You'll find many educational resources at Fun Brain.

Caring for the Whole Child

www.pbs.org/wholechild/

Created as a complement to the Public Broadcasting System television series by the same name, the Whole Child is a beautiful guide to the stages of childhood development, focusing on children's emotional issues and those with special needs. Follow the links on the site, shown in Figure 16-8, to find special sections for parents and childcare providers.

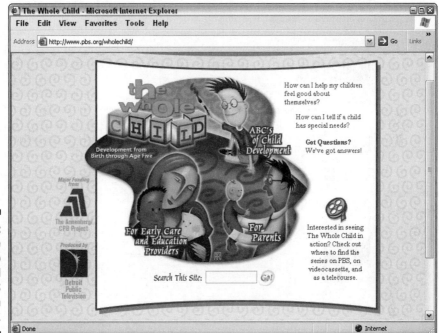

Figure 16-8: The Whole Child Web site is based on the PBS television series.

Refdesk Helps with Homework

www.refdesk.com

Dedicated to helping visitors sort through the volumes of information available on the Internet, the Refdesk, shown in Figure 16-9, is a comprehensive collection of links to government sites, news sources, phone directories, statistics, rankings, and other reference sites, including the atomic clock and a guide to time zones.

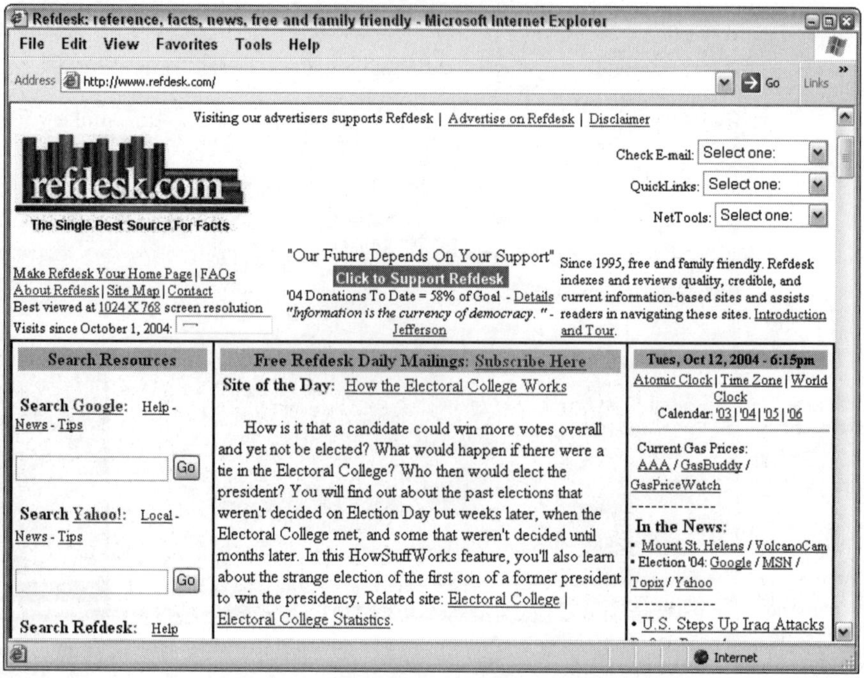

Figure 16-9: The Refdesk is a reliable reference for homework and research projects.

The Digital Family Site

www.digitalfamily.com

I created DigitalFamily.com, shown in Figure 16-10, to complement this book by providing one place where you can find links to the services, software, and other resources you need to create your own family Web site. You'll also find tips and suggestions to help you better use that technology in your home, work, and travel.

DigitalFamily.com is your one-stop site for family Web design needs. Want to register a domain name or choose a service provider? DigitalFamily.com makes it easy. Trying to decide on the best software or services for your Web site? You'll find comparisons and recommendations. DigitalFamily.com is also a great place to discover new technologies that can make your life easier and more fun, such as new multimedia options that can expand your television and movie library for free.

Figure 16-10: Digital Family provides updates and resources for your family Web design and technology needs.

Chapter 17

Ten Web Design Tips

*O*ne of the advantages of working with a team of other Web designers is that you get to compare notes and trade ideas. You may not have this luxury if you're designing a site for your family, so in this chapter I collected design tips from a variety of sources. I hope they help you create a functional and beautiful Web site for your family.

Keep It Simple

Creating a clear and intuitive navigational system is one of the most important elements in creating a Web site. Nothing is likely to frustrate your visitors more than not being able to find what they're looking for.

Make sure that visitors can easily get to all the main sections of your site from every page in the site. You can best do this by placing at the top or side of every page a set of links to each main section. This set of links is called a *navigation row* or *navigation bar*, and it's a common feature on well-designed sites. If the pages are very long, consider including a navigation bar at the bottom of the page as well. The bottom of the page is also an ideal place to include basic contact information.

Your goal is to make sure that viewers don't have to use the Back button in their browsers to move around your site.

Break Up Your Pages with White Space

One of the best design features you can add to a page is nothing at all — also known as *white space*. Understand that white space, in this case, is not always white; it's simply space that you haven't crammed full of text or images. It can be any color, but it's usually most effective if it's the color or pattern of your background.

White space gives the eye a rest — something readers need when they're staring at a computer monitor. You can use white space to separate one type of information from another and to focus the viewer's attention where you want it most. Some of the most beautiful and compelling designs on the Web use only a few well-thought-out elements against lots of white space.

Back Up Your Site

Make sure you have a system in place to back up your Web site. Even the best Internet service providers have technical problems, so you should keep a backup of your site where you have easy access to it and can get it back online quickly. Update the copy regularly to make sure you have the latest version of your site backed up.

Also keep a backup of your original source files. For example, when you develop images for the Web, you usually start in a program such as Photoshop, creating a high-resolution image that may include layers and other elements. Before the image goes on your Web site, those layers are flattened and the image is compressed or reduced and converted to a GIF or JPEG file. If you ever want to go back and alter that image, you'll want the original source file. Whether you create your own images or hire a professional designer, make sure you develop a system for saving the original text, images, and other content.

Be Consistent

Most Web sites work best, and are easiest to navigate, when they follow a consistent design. Case in point: Most readers take for granted that books don't change their design from page to page, and that newspapers don't change headline fonts and logos from day to day. Consistency is one of the primary tools used in books and newspapers to make it easy for readers to distinguish different elements and follow a story or theme.

As you lay out your Web page, keep related items close to one another and be consistent about how you design similar content elements. You want your viewers to instantly understand which pieces of information are related to each other. Distinguish different kinds of information by their

✔ Design

✔ Location

✔ Prominence

This type of organization makes following information visually much easier.

Make sure that similar elements follow the same design parameters, such as type style, banner size, and page background color. Give elements of similar importance the same weight on a page. If you use too many different elements on a page or on the same Web site, you'll confuse your viewers.

To ensure a consistent style, define a set of colors, shapes, or other elements that you use throughout the site. Choose two or three fonts for your Web site and use those consistently as well. Using too many fonts makes your pages less appealing and harder to read.

Strive for consistency in your designs — except when you're trying to be unpredictable. A little surprise here and there can keep your Web site alive.

Stay Small and Fast

Despite the promises about the arrival of unlimited bandwidth, the biggest problem on the Internet is still speed. If you make sure your pages download quickly, your viewers will be more likely to keep clicking. You may create the best design ever to grace the Web, but if it takes too long to appear on your viewer's screens, no one will wait around long enough to compliment you on your design talents.

If your page designs take a long time to download, here are a few likely reasons and suggestions for how to make them load faster. First, take a look at multimedia elements and consider reducing the size or at least offering users the option to skip large multimedia files, such as Flash animations. You don't want to make users wait too long to see the first page of your site. If you suspect that static images are the problem, consider reducing the size of the images or using optimization methods, such as compression or color reduction, which make file sizes smaller so images download faster. Optimization and other image techniques are described in Chapter 6.

Follow the Three Clicks Rule

The three clicks rule states that no important piece of information should ever be more than three clicks away from anywhere else on your Web site. The most important information should be even closer. Some information, such as contact information, should never be more than one click away.

You can make finding information easy for viewers by creating a site map (as explained in the next section) and a navigation bar (as explained in the "Keep It Simple" section).

Map It Out

As your site gets larger, providing easy access to all the information on your Web site may get harder and harder. A great solution is to provide a *site map,* which is an outline or a diagram that illustrates the hierarchy and content of your site and includes links to the most important pages in the site.

The site map can get complicated and busy if you have a lot of pages and links, so it's usually best to create a site map in outline form. Don't put lots of graphics in your site map — it should be functional above all else. A site map doesn't have to look pretty; it has to make it easy for your visitors to get to any page on the site.

Avoid Distracting Animations

A little motion brings the Web to life. Too much motion distracts viewers from what you want them to read and see.

When something is flashing in the corner of your eye, reading what's in front of you can be difficult. Animations are a great way to grab attention, but make sure you're not taking attention away from the rest of your site. Creating animations that repeat only a few times is a great compromise. Many animation programs enable you to set the number of *loops* (the number of times the animation repeats). I recommend that you let an animation run for three loops (or sequences) and then make it stop. Your visitors can always reload the page if they want to see the animation again.

Create animations that look great, attract attention, and then stop moving so your viewers can focus on the rest of the material on your pages.

Don't Cram Your Pages

Don't overwhelm your pages (and readers) with graphics, banners, frames, or other gimmicks. Likewise, avoid large graphics that can take forever to download. Give readers a few broad choices on the front page and then let them narrow their quest for the information they need as they progress through your site. Many designers recommend no more than four to eight links and no more than three images on any page.

Work as a Team

The best Web sites are created by teams of developers that include experienced programmers, designers, and editors. Remember that as you start to build your own Web site, and don't expect your site to have the flash of professional sites.

That said, why not create your own team of specialists? Do you have a teenager who studied programming in school? An aunt or an uncle who is a talented designer? Should mom or dad take on the role of project manager or should they be the ones to test everyone else's work and let an older sibling manage the development process?

If you start with the vision that everyone in your family can contribute something, you may find that building a family Web site is a great way not only to stay in touch with distant family and friends but also to bring your family together around a shared project.

Even the youngest members of your family can contribute by creating artwork that you then scan, bringing color and fun to a Web site page. (You find tips and suggestions for managing your project in Chapter 2.)

Chapter 18

Ten Tips for Testing, Updating, and Promoting Your Site

Don't think that you're finished with your site just because you've published it online. A good Web designer is never finished — you can always add more information, test your pages and links to make sure everything functions properly, and find ways to promote your Web site so friends and family will come and see your great work.

In this chapter, you find tips about adding new stories and images to your Web site, finding and correcting broken links, and using e-cards to invite people to visit your new site.

Send an E-card to Announce Your New Site

Many people send a simple e-mail message to promote their Web sites. That can work fine, but it's even more fun to send an e-card with a colorful character, animation, and music to dramatize your announcement.

`Hallmark.com` is one of my favorite e-card sites because it has lots of free cards with clever sayings, professional designs, and interactive animations. Most of the free e-cards at `Hallmark.com` even include sound. `Blue Mountain.com` is another great e-card site, but you have to pay for the pleasure of sending their professional greetings.

When choosing an e-card to announce your Web site, look for blank cards or the Friendship and Any Occasion sections, where you'll find messages that are easily personalized.

Make Your Site Easy to Find

Search engines can make it easier for friends and family to find you, but you have to be listed on them first. The good news is that registering your site with most search engines is simple and free. Google and Yahoo!, the two most important search engines, include a link on their home page for adding your URL to their database. After you add your Web address to a search engine, the address becomes available in the matches when someone searches for your Web site.

Here are a few tips to make it easier to add your Web address to the two most popular search engines:

- ✔ **Google:** By far the most popular search engine, Google is *the* place most people look when they want to find something on the Web. To make sure you're included in their search feature, point your browser to `www.google.com` and click the About Google link at the bottom of the page. Then click the Submitting Your Site link and enter the Web address of your site in the URL field. For example, to submit the site I created for this book, I entered `www.digitalfamily.com`.

- ✔ **Yahoo!:** Respected as the first search engine on the Web, Yahoo! is another important place to submit your Web site. To make sure you're included on Yahoo!, point your browser to `www.yahoo.com` and scroll down to the bottom of the page. Click the How to Suggest a Site link at the bottom left of the page. Like many search engines, Yahoo! includes free and paid submission options. Click on Submit Your Site for Free to add your URL at no cost.

Although hundreds of search services are available on the Web, Yahoo! and Google are by far the most important. If you're just trying to make your family Web site a little easier for friends and family to find if they don't already know your address, submitting your site to these two is probably all you need to do.

If you want to make sure you're listed in more places, a wide array of services are available to help you. However, most search engine submission services charge to help you get high rankings and no one can guarantee you top billing in any search engine. Why can't anyone guarantee your placement in a search engine? Because search engines intentionally make their criteria for matches secret to try to prevent sites from forcing their way to the top. Sites such as Google consider several factors when ranking Web sites and their criteria can change from week to week or month to month as they strive to provide better results.

Update Regularly

Many families have regularly scheduled phone dates, such as every Sunday evening or every Saturday morning. The routine of these calls helps family members know what to expect and when they can find each other at home.

If you want your visitors to know when to look for updates, consider making changes to your Web site on a regular basis. I like updating my family Web site every Saturday morning with new photos and stories. That way, my friends and loved ones know that they can always log in on the weekends to get the latest reports.

Wait Until New Technologies Are Widely Supported

A big mistake novice Web designers make is to try to use every new tool and technique as it becomes available. Although it may be fun to show off the latest bells and whistles of the Web, most Internet users lag behind new innovations and may not be able to see your handiwork.

With a family Web site, you're likely to be serving an audience that is not on the cutting edge of technology, so you should be careful about updating your site with the latest innovations. In general, wait to use a new technology until it's been on the Web for one to three years or until common browsers support it so users don't need a plug in. Adobe's Portable Document Format (PDF), for example, was problematic in the early days because users needed to download a special program to view a file in PDF. Today, both Netscape and Internet

Explorer browsers support PDFs and the format is commonly used for forms, brochures, and other documents that require special formatting.

If you really love a new technology and just have to use it on your site, at least try to provide an alternative. For example, if you create a section of your site that requires a special plug-in to view a 3-D virtual tour of your new house, you might also create an alternative Web page that features static 2-D photographs so that visitors who don't have the 3-D plug-in and don't want to download it can still get a glimpse of your new home.

Make Your Pages Load Quickly

No matter how beautiful your site or how many great images and stories it has, your friends and family may never see them if the pages take too long to download.

You can use a number of techniques to help ensure that your pages load quickly for your visitors, but the most important involve reducing the file size of your images and multimedia files. Text loads quickly, but pictures can take a while. Video, audio, and animation files are usually the biggest and take the longest to download.

To find out how long it will take for a page on your Web site to download, visit www.websiteoptimization.com. You can enter any URL into this free online service and get a report that shows how many seconds it will take for that page to load at a variety of connection speeds. For example, I entered www.pets.com and got the following results:

Connection Rate	Download Time
14.4K	129.21 seconds
28.8K	64.71 seconds
33.6K	55.49 seconds
56K	33.37 seconds
ISDN 128K	10.36 seconds
T1 1.44Mbps	1.08 seconds

There is no magic answer to how long your pages should take for your viewers, but faster is always better. In general, I recommend you make sure you site doesn't take more than 30 seconds on a 56K modem.

In Chapters 5 and 6 you find a number of tips for reducing the time it takes for your images to download. And in Chapter 10 you find descriptions of the best formats for multimedia on the Web and instructions for linking audio, video, and animation to your pages.

Test Your Links

It's relatively easy to create links on a Web site (especially if you use a program such as FrontPage, which is covered in Chapter 8). Unfortunately, it's also relatively easy to break links by moving files around, deleting files or images, or just typing a URL or Web address incorrectly.

As you build your Web site, it's important to check your links, but don't stop there. After you publish your pages to your Web server, you should check them again.

You can check links by simply viewing your own pages with a browser and systematically clicking each link to make sure it works. An easier way, however, is to use the Link Valet, available at

```
www.htmlhelp.com/tools/valet/
```

Just enter the URL of your Web site into the Check Site box, and Link Valet will check every link on your site to make sure that it works. The test usually takes just a few seconds. When it's finished you'll get a detailed report on the links on your site, with broken links marked in red so they're easy to find.

If you discover broken links on your Web site, you can use FrontPage to correct them. For more on setting links in FrontPage, see Chapter 8.

Ask Friends and Family to Test Your Site

Even though your Web site looks good to you, that doesn't mean it will look good to everyone else. One of the most common problems I've seen on the Web happens when designers create pages with very small type — as people get older, most of us find that it's harder to read small print.

Make sure you design your site with those with limited eyesight in mind. Better yet, ask them to review your designs. A fresh set of eyes can help you find mistakes you may have missed and point out problems that may not be apparent to you.

Make It Easy for Visitors to Contact You

Don't assume that all your visitors have your contact information. Although some families prefer not to post their street address or home phone number on their Web site (for privacy reasons), I do recommend that you at least include an e-mail address. Even if most of your visitors already have your contact information at home, your Web site can be a handy place to find it. You never know when a friend may be traveling without his or her contact list, or a loved one may lose an address book and appreciate being able to find your contact information from your easy-to-find Web site.

I also recommend that you invite feedback from your visitors. If you want to make your Web site better and more enjoyable for your visitors, ask them what they want to see on your site and how you can make it easier for them to use it.

Test for Accessibility

Making your Web site accessible means making sure anyone can access the information on your pages. Internet users who are blind or have limited vision use synthetic speech synthesizers to "read" Web sites and refreshable Braille displays that translate Web content. But if you don't design your site to be accessible to these special programs, users may not be able to understand the information on your pages.

An estimated 10 percent of the Internet audience in the United States can't view a site that does not comply with accessibility requirements, and that segment is expected to increase as more Americans over the age of 55 choose to use browsers with speech synthesizers. These programs are also used by people who can't use their hands well enough to work a keyboard or a mouse.

Designing a site that's accessible requires a little more attention to detail, but making your site inviting to everyone is mostly just about following good interface and design rules.

And the benefits go far beyond reaching people with disabilities. Accessible Web design also makes sites work better in language translation programs and can help ensure that content displays well in some of the newest browsers, such as those for PDAs and other wireless devices.

Here are a few tips for creating accessible Web sites:

✔ Use alternative text for images and multimedia. Also known as *alt text,* alternative text is an option in HTML (the language used to create Web pages) that provides a text description if the image or multimedia file can't be displayed. Alternative text is especially important when you use images as links because screen readers can't decipher text in an image.

✔ Create links that have clear descriptions about where they go, group related information together, and be consistent about where navigation links are located so they are easy to find on all your pages.

✔ Choose colors carefully. If you're distinguishing sections of your site with color coding, remember that color differences won't mean anything to someone who can't see them. Also be careful to provide enough contrast between text and background colors so that those who are visually impaired can still decipher the words. For example, light-colored text on a light background is much harder to read than dark text on a light background.

✔ If you use multimedia, provide transcripts of audio and text descriptions of video and animation files.

✔ Test your site at the Center for Applied Special Technology site. To use their free service, visit www.cast.org/bobby and enter the address of any Web site into their online testing tool, called Bobby. You get a free report listing errors or omissions that may limit accessibility.

✔ Try this simple test to see how well the content and links on your site are organized. Imagine that you're reading your Web site to someone over the phone. Start at the top of the page and read all the content from left to right. Does it make sense? How long would it take the person on the other end of the phone to find the information he or she wanted if this was the only way the person could access the information on your site?

To find more about accessible design, visit www.webable.com.

Visit Other Web Sites for Ideas

One of the best ways to acquire good habits in Web design is to visit other people's Web sites and study what works and what doesn't on their pages.

As you look at other family Web sites, ask yourself these questions: What do you like about the site, and why? Can you easily find the information you are most interested in? How do you navigate around the site? Are animations and other multimedia elements useful or distracting? Do the images load quickly? Is the text easy to read?

Sometimes the best way to discover the problems in your own site is to look for problems on someone else's Web site and then come back to your own with a fresh perspective. Chapter 1 includes a list of Web sites you can use as examples, and you'll find even more in the family section at Yahoo!

Part VI

Appendixes

The 5th Wave   By Rich Tennant

"Well, well! Guess who just lost 9 pixels?"

In this part . . .

You find many valuable resources in Appendix A, starting with a comparison of online calendar services that make it easy to keep track of appointments, special events, birthdays, and anniversaries. You also find a host of genealogy sites and software programs dedicated to helping you trace and record your family history.

The glossary in Appendix B, which contains definitions of the technical terms used in this book, is designed to take the mystery out of geek-speak. In Appendix C, you discover the valuable resources included with this book, such as predesigned Web templates, graphics, and software programs.

Appendix A

Calendar and Genealogy Resources

● ●

*O*ne of the challenges of creating a Web site is that you have so many services and software programs to choose from. To help you find two of the most popular online services — calendar and genealogy resources — I've put together this list of some of the best sites and services available.

In the following pages, you find calendar systems you can add to your Web site, genealogy services, and family tree software. For recommendations about Web design and image software, see Chapter 1. For suggestions about video editing software, see Chapter 10.

Calendar Programs

If you have trouble keeping track of all the important dates, appointments, and special events in your family, consider adding a calendar to your Web site project. Many of the online calendar services make it possible for multiple people to use the same system, so everyone with your password can view and add to each other's schedules. You can link these calendars to your family Web site or use them independently (in case you don't want everyone in the family to know your schedule):

✔ **Yahoo! Calendar (**yahoo.calendar.com**):** This free service is one of the most widely used calendar programs. You can choose from a gallery of images so that each month (or week or whatever) will have a different picture (see Figure A-1). You can choose who to share your calendar with — which is useful if you're trying to keep track of the location and time of dance recitals or soccer practices, and you want everyone else to be aware of the dates as well. Yahoo! also has a handy feature that enables you to sync their online calendar with your Palm or Outlook program. You can choose which holidays you want to have listed, and set reminders (so you will never again forget important dates, such as the South African Day of Reconciliation).

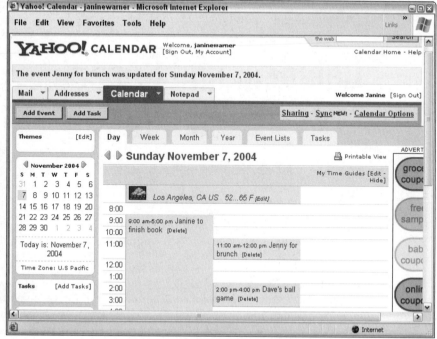

Figure A-1:
Yahoo!
makes it
easy to
create an
interactive
calendar
that you can
share with
the entire
family.

✔ **MyEvents** (www.myevents.com): This online calendar service offers a free introductory period and then charges about $4 a month. Besides all the standard calendar functions (keeping track of dates, sharing the calendar, sending reminders), MyEvents also includes contact manager and organizer features. These functions can be integrated with Palm and Outlook. The site also features limited file storage and photo album options.

✔ **Connect Daily** (www.mhsoftware.com): You can test out this service before paying for it by downloading a free version of the software. This sophisticated time-management software is designed for businesses and organizations and may be more than your family needs, but if you're trying to coordinate an entire softball team, PTA, or other group, you may appreciate the added features.

Genealogy Services and Family Tree Programs

The Internet has made it easier than ever to research family histories and trace your roots. The following services and software programs can help you with your research and with designing a family tree that you can link to from your Web site:

✓ **Ancestry.com** (www.ancestry.com): Boasting the largest collection of family history records on the Web, this popular site, shown in Figure A-2, features census records, immigration information, marriage and death records, and more — all organized in easy-to-use searchable databases. The site offers a free 14-day trial and then charges a fee for continued use of these and other services.

✓ **Genealogy.com** (www.genealogy.com): If you want to broaden your search, try the services at Genealogy.com, as shown in Figure A-3. This site also provides a free 14-day trial period.

✓ **FamilyTreeMaker.com** (www.familytreemaker.com): If you've ever tried to draw a family tree, you know how complicated it can be to create all the lines and boxes that you need to make your family history make sense. Save yourself the trouble and consider investing in FamilyTreeMaker. This program, which costs less than $30, makes it easy to organize large amounts of family history information, and it's fully integrated with Ancestry.com so you can use the two in tandem.

✓ **FamilyTreeSearcher** (www.familytreesearcher.com): Although the information on this site may not be as extensive as what you find at Ancestry.com, the price is right. This free service provides search features and lots of great advice about researching your ancestors.

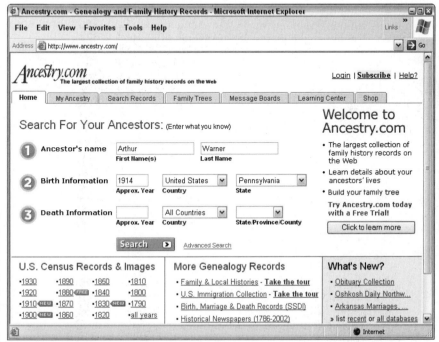

Figure A-2:
You can search for family members at *Ancestry.com*.

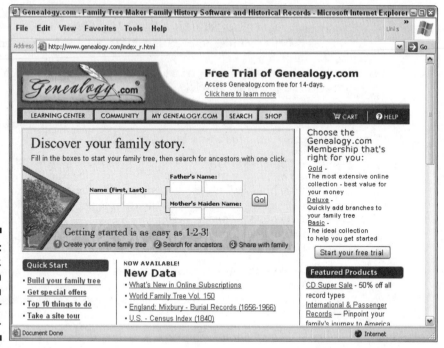

Figure A-3:
Genealogy. com can help you track your family tree.

Appendix B

Glossary

* * *

Refer to this glossary anytime you get lost in techspeak. If you can't find what you're looking for here, visit `www.webopedia.com`. To find some of the latest and most inventive terms on the Web, visit `www.Wordspy.com`. For a more comprehensive vocabulary guide, go to `www.dictionary.com`.

absolute link: Also called *absolute URL.* An HTML hyperlink that you set by using the complete URL, starting with the domain name on which the file is located. For example:

```
<A HREF="http://www.domain_name.com/directory/ filename.html>
```

See also **relative link.**

absolute positioning: An HTML feature that enables you to specify the precise location of an element in relation to the window.

Acrobat: The Adobe software suite for creating portable electronic documents called PDFs.

anchor: The destination of a hyperlink used for jump links. *See also* **absolute link** and **relative link.**

animated GIF: Part of the GIF specification that enables you to have multiple still frames in the same file to create the appearance of motion as they play in sequence. Can be created with programs such as GIF Builder and Photoshop Elements. *See also* **animation.**

animation: A series of images that, when displayed one after the other, creates the effect of movement.

antialiasing: A process that gives the illusion of smoothing the jagged edges of a graphic by intermixing pixels of adjoining colors along the edges of the graphic.

application: Any program (such as a word processor, spreadsheet, database, or desktop publishing program) that performs functions for a user.

application server: Helps the Web server to process specially marked Web pages. When the browser requests one of these pages, the Web server hands off the page to the application server, which processes it before sending the page to the browser.

attachment: An electronic file (such as text or a graphic) that's sent along with an e-mail message.

attribute: A part of the HTML specification that modifies the behavior of a tag as well as the text, graphic, or other element that the tag describes.

AVI: For *Audio Video Interleave.* A Windows-native animation format similar to QuickTime.

background: A solid color, an image, or a textured pattern that appears behind the text and graphics on a Web page.

bandwidth: The amount of data that can be sent through a communications channel. Represents the Internet's carrying capacity. Some types of information, such as graphics, take up more bandwidth than others, such as text.

batch processing: Performing the same function on many files or documents at the same time.

baud: A measure of the speed at which data transmits. Baud rate indicates the number of bits of data transmitted in one second. One baud is equal to one bit per second. Common modems today have baud rates of 33,600, or 56,000 kilobits per second (Kbps).

beta version: The last stages of development of a computer program before it's ready to be sold to the public. The beta version of the program is released to a select group of users for testing for errors, or bugs. Many companies now make beta versions of their software programs available to the public for free before releasing the final version.

bit: The smallest piece of information a computer uses. Bits are combined in various ways to represent different types of information. Eight bits form a byte.

bitmapped image: A graphic formed by an array of dots (pixels) on a screen.

bookmark: A way to save a Web site's URL for easy access later. Also known as *favorites.*

bps: For *bits per second.* A measure of how fast data transmits. *See also* **baud.**

browse: To look over a collection of information, especially in an effort to find something of interest, as in browsing through folders (directories) or browsing the Web.

browser: A program, such as Netscape Navigator or Microsoft Internet Explorer, that's used along with an Internet connection to view pages on the Web.

byte: A measurement of computer storage. One byte equals eight bits.

cache: Pronounced *cash*. A special section of RAM or disk memory that's set aside to store frequently accessed information. Cache is used also as a verb to refer to the act of storing such information. Many Web browsers cache information on your computer to help download Web pages more quickly.

CGI script: CGI stands for *Common Gateway Interface*. A program that provides greater levels of interactivity than basic HTML by passing information from browsers to servers using forms or queries. Many Web sites use CGI scripts to perform functions such as online discussion areas and shopping systems. These scripts are written in sophisticated programming languages such as Perl, C, and C++.

chat: Real-time written discussion that takes place on the Internet.

client: The Internet is a client/server arrangement. The client (usually a Web browser) is the end-user side, which usually resides on a personal computer and communicates with a Web server. *See also* **server.**

close tag: Also called *end tag*. An HTML tag that designates the end of a formatting section, usually the same as the opening tag but with a forward slash mark. For example, the close <CENTER> tag is </CENTER>. *See also* **start tag.**

compressed file: A data file modified to consume less space, often by using a program such as WinZip or StuffIt. Prior to use, a compressed file must be decompressed.

contact link: Links to the site developer's e-mail address, to an e-mail form, or to a page of e-mail addresses for key contacts. Makes contacting the people behind the Web site easy for Web site viewers.

cookie: Information stored on your hard drive by a program on a Web site that you visit. This information is used to track your preferences and activities as you use the site and if you return to it later. Cookie technology enables a Web site to greet you by name, remember your password, and provide custom information. Cookies are controversial because some people view them as an invasion of privacy. Most of the latest browsers enable you to prevent cookies from being stored on your computer.

cross-platform: Having versions for more than one operating system, such as UNIX, Macintosh, and Windows XP. Can also refer to applications, such as those created in Java, that run across multiple, incompatible computer systems with little or no modification.

CSS: For *Cascading Style Sheets*. Part of the HTML specification that enables you to define style properties (such as font, color, and spacing) and then make global formatting changes by applying those styles, similar to the way you use styles in word processing and desktop publishing programs.

cyberspace: The entire world of online information and services. Coined by William Gibson is his novel *Neuromancer*.

database: A collection of information compiled in one or more tables, with fields organized in columns and records in rows.

database program: Enables the collection of data in an organized format, permitting manipulation of the data in a variety of ways. Examples include FileMaker Pro, Access, FoxPro, and dBASE.

default: A condition set automatically in a program when no explicit selection is made. In HTML, the value assigned to an attribute when none is supplied.

desktop: In a graphical environment, a term assigned to the always open file folder that you first see when your computer finishes booting up. In Windows, the physical path to the desktop is `c:\windows\desktop`. Desktops are traditionally decorated with background images and can include shortcuts to programs, files, and folders.

desktop publishing program: An application used to typeset publications such as newsletters and magazines. Two examples or this type of program are PageMaker and QuarkXPress.

DHTML: For *dynamic HTML*. A part of the HTML specification that adds the capability to change style or positioning properties with a scripting language. DHTML includes Cascading Style Sheets, layers, timelines, and behaviors. *See also* **scripting language.**

dialog box: An on-screen message area that conveys or requests information.

digital format: The form of something, such as an image or a sound, when it's stored as computer data.

dingbats: Ornamental characters such as bullets, stars, and flowers used to decorate a page.

Director movie: An animation, a presentation, or an interactive title created in Macromedia Director, the most widely used program for creating multimedia.

directory: A list of computer files on a disk, a CD, or a drive. May be nested into subdirectories to further organize data. A *folder* is another name for a directory. *See also* **nested.**

dithering: A method used to simulate natural shading in an image with a limited color range. Shades are represented with combinations of colored dots (pixels) on-screen in various patterns. Often used to give the appearance of smoother transitions between shades.

document source: The HTML code behind a page displayed on the Web. You can view this information for almost every Web page.

domain name: A unique identifier that assigns a name to a specific IP address. IP addresses are long, hard-to-remember numbers. A computer on the Internet is perfectly happy to take you to the Web site of 204.71.200.67 if you ask for it by IP address, but www.yahoo.com is much easier for you to remember.

DOS: For *disk operating system.* The underlying control system for many personal computers. Usually refers to MS-DOS, the original operating system for IBM-compatible computers. Today, most people use the Windows operating system rather than DOS.

download: To move information from a remote computer to your computer. For example, when you download images from a Web site, you copy them from the server to your computer to display or save them. *See also* **upload.**

dpi: For *dots per inch.* A measure of image resolution that counts the dots in a linear inch. The higher the dpi, the better the resolution (and the larger the file size). A 600-dpi printer gives you more detailed printouts than a 300-dpi printer. Most images created for the Web are 72 dpi because that's the resolution of computer monitors.

DSL: For *digital subscriber line.* A high-speed Internet access option that works over standard copper telephone wires like the ones already installed in most homes. With DSL, data can be delivered at a rate of 1.5 Mbps (around 30 times faster than through a 56 Kbps modem).

dynamic: Marked by continuous activity or change.

element: A component of a hierarchical structure (for example, a Web site). Also, any shape individually manipulated in a graphic. In this usage, the term *element* is synonymous with *object.*

e-mail: For *electronic mail.* A system that enables one computer user to send messages to other users over a network.

e-mail address: A domain-based address used for sending e-mail messages to a specified destination. Within company systems and commercial service providers such as America Online, the e-mail address is often just the name the person has chosen as an address. On the Internet, e-mail addresses must include the @ symbol and an extension, such as .com or .org. An example is editor@JCWarner.com.

embed: To place a command directly in a program. Also, an HTML tag used to link objects and elements that require plug-ins for viewing.

encrypt: To convert data into a format that can't be read without a key or a password. Encryption is the most commonly system used to transfer information over the Internet privately.

end tag: *See* **close tag.**

end user: A person who uses a computer program or device to perform a function, such as word processing.

environment: The hardware or operating system (or both) for applications, for example, Macintosh or Windows.

Ethernet: One of the most widely used standards on a LAN (local area network). Ethernet was cooperatively developed by Xerox Corporation, DEC, and Intel in the 1970s and enables relatively fast data transfer rates — up to 1000 Mbps. If you connect your computer to the network at your office, you likely use an Ethernet card to do so.

event: A user-initiated happening, such as an icon that changes at a mouse click. You can design elements on Web sites to respond to events.

extension: (1) Tags or attributes introduced by a browser company, such as Netscape or Microsoft, but not part of the current HTML specifications. (2) Filename extension. The latter portion of a filename, such as .doc for Microsoft Word documents and .gif for Graphics Interchange Format. Macintosh filenames don't require extensions. However, all files displayed by a browser must include extensions.

FAQ: For *frequently asked questions.* A list of questions and answers with basic information about a Web site or other resource. The FAQ concept originated as a method for Internet users to find answers to common questions online.

favorites: A way to save a Web site's URL for easy access later. Also known as *bookmarks.*

Fetch: The most popular FTP program on the Macintosh for transferring files between client and server.

filename: The name of a document (or file) on a computer, such as a word-processing document or a graphics file.

Flash: One of the most popular animation programs on the Web. Macromedia Flash uses vector-based technology to create fast-loading animations that can incorporate sound, video, and still images.

folder: A container of files held on a disk or a drive. Computer files are often stored in folders, which can be nested (in subfolders) to facilitate the organization of data. Called *directories* on DOS or UNIX systems and on early versions of Microsoft Windows. *See also* **directory** and **nested.**

font: A complete collection of letters, punctuation marks, numbers, and special characters with a consistent and identifiable typeface, weight, and size. Sometimes used to refer to typefaces or font families.

font family: A set of fonts in several sizes and weights that share the same typeface.

frames: A Netscape HTML extension, now supported by Microsoft Internet Explorer, that enables more than one HTML document to display on a Web page. Creates distinct sections of a page that can be scrolled and that can contain links that alter the contents of other sections, or frames, on the same Web page.

FTP: For *File Transfer Protocol.* A system for copying files to and from servers elsewhere on a network, such as the Internet.

GIF: For *Graphics Interchange Format.* A bitmapped image format that uses compression to reduce file sizes. CompuServe pioneered the format for storing and transmitting graphics over remote networks. It's currently the most universally accepted graphics file format on the Web.

graphic: A representation of an image on a two-dimensional surface.

graphical environment: An environment that includes the use of graphics in addition to text.

GUI: For *graphical user interface.* An interface that uses graphical icons to represent a computer program or operating system. Graphical interfaces, such as the ones used under Windows and on Macintosh computers, are considered more intuitive than text-based operating systems, such as DOS.

home page: The first page that appears when you access a Web site. Also called the *title page* or *front page.* On a small site (for example, a personal site), the home page may be the only page.

host: A computer that enables users to communicate by using application programs such as e-mail, Telnet, and FTP. Any computer capable of connecting to others on the Internet is a host. This term generally refers to Web servers.

HTML: For *HyperText Markup Language.* The programming language used to create Web pages and other files for distribution over the Internet. HTML is a subset of SGML (Standard Generalized Markup Language). *See also* **hypertext.**

HTML editor: A program you use to alter or create HTML pages. HTML editors can be text or WYSIWYG (what-you-see-is-what-you-get) editors such as Dreamweaver or HTML text editors such as BBEdit.

HTTP: For *Hypertext Transfer Protocol.* The protocol that makes the transfer of information between a Web browser and a Web server possible.

hyperlink: Also called *link.* A programmed connection between locations in the same file (Web site) or two different files. *See also* **hypertext.**

hypertext: A word or series of words linked to another location by HTML programming. You click these words to skip from one document to the next or from one area of a document to another area of the same document. *See also* **HTML.**

icon: A small image meant to convey a message graphically. Common icons, such as a the scissors icon representing the Cut command in the Microsoft Word toolbar, are often more universally understood than words.

image map: A set of coordinates to designate distinct areas of a GIF or JPEG image by using square, circular, or polygonal shapes. These areas can be linked to any URL so that a user reaches different destinations by selecting different sections of the image.

inline image: An image that can be given a specific location on a Web page in context with text and other multimedia elements. Inline images can be viewed by a Web browser and don't require a plug-in or a separate window for viewing.

interface: The point of communication or interaction between a computer and a human operator or any device. The layout and design of the graphic controls for a computer or program. *See also* **GUI.**

interlacing: A process that enables an image to load in several stages. Creates the illusion that graphics (and therefore whole pages) load more quickly and gives the reader a chance to see a fuzzy but recognizable image quickly enough to know whether to wait or move on.

Internet: Note the capital *I.* An *internet* is a network; the *Internet* is an international collection of interconnected networks. The Internet is the largest internet in the world.

intranet: A private Web site set up and maintained within a corporation or an organization. Unlike Internet sites, intranet sites are restricted to a particular audience, usually the employees of the company.

IP: For *Internet Protocol.* Enables information to pass from one network (set of computers) to another by using a unique string of numbers (as an address) for each network.

ISP: For *Internet service provider.* A national or local company that sells access to the Internet. Well-known examples in the United States include America Online and AT&T WorldNet.

Java: A programming language invented by Sun Microsystems that can be used on any computer platform. This versatility makes Java especially popular on the Internet because it enables programmers to create one program that works on many different computers, such as Macintosh or Windows. Programs written in other languages, such as C or C++, require different versions for each platform.

JavaScript: A scripting language that enables interactive features on Web sites. JavaScript can interact with code written in HTML and shares some of the features of Java.

JPEG: For *Joint Photographic Experts Group.* A file format commonly used on the Web for full-color, continuous-tone images (such as photographs).

jump link: A hyperlink that connects to an anchor in a specific part of a page. Use jump links to link text from one part of a page to another or from one page to a particular place on another page. *See also* **anchor.**

kilobits per second (Kbps): A measurement of communication speed of modems and other devices.

kilobyte (K): 1024 bytes of data. *See also* **byte.**

link: *See* **hyperlink.**

load: To transfer program instructions or data from a disk or a drive to a computer's random-access memory (RAM).

loop: A set of program instructions that execute repeatedly until a condition is satisfied. Animations are often designed to loop so that the images that make up the animation repeat.

lossy compression: So-called because not all detail is preserved when a file is compressed (some loss occurs).

macro: A stored list of commands to perform tedious and often-repeated tasks. Macros are often used in Microsoft Word to automate common tasks.

markup language: Special characters embedded in a text file to instruct a program how to handle or display the file's contents. HTML is a markup language.

megabyte (MB): 1024 kilobytes or 1,048,576 bytes. *See also* **byte.**

menu: A list of options that a program or a Web site presents to a user.

menu bar: In graphical programs (and many desktop applications), menus representing the program's most common functions are often positioned for easy access in a horizontal bar across the top of the window. On a Web site, the menu bar is often a collection of graphic or text links that provide access to all the main pages of the site.

metacharacter: A character in a text file that signals the need for special handling. In HTML, metacharacters are angle brackets (< >), the ampersand (&), the pound sign (#), and the semicolon (;).

Microsoft Internet Explorer: One of the two most widely used graphical Web browsers. (Netscape Navigator is the other.) *See also* **browser.**

modem: A device that converts electrical pulses from a computer to signals suitable for transmission over a telephone line.

multimedia: The presentation of information on a computer using video sequences, animation, sound (either as background or synchronized to a video or animation), and vector illustrations.

nanosecond: One-billionth of a second.

netiquette: Internet etiquette. The written and unwritten rules for behavior on the Net. Many guides to netiquette are available on the Internet; two of the most popular are at www.albion.com/netiquette/ and www.fau.edu/netiquette/net/.

nested: One structure occurring within another. HTML tags often are nested by placing one formatting tag inside another. Subfolders are also nested within folders.

Netscape Navigator: One of the two most widely used graphical Web browsers. Microsoft Internet Explorer is the other. *See also* **browser.**

node: An individual connection point in a network.

PDF: For *portable document format.* A file format that carries all font and layout specifications with it, regardless of the platform on which it's viewed. PDF is considered by many to be the best format for putting documents on the Web when they must be as close as possible to their print counterparts. Requires the Adobe Acrobat viewer, which is now built into most browsers.

PERL: For *Practical Extraction and Reporting Language.* A language developed for UNIX systems that's frequently used for writing scripts for the Web.

pixel: Stands for picture element. The smallest dot that a computer can display on-screen. Images created for the Web and spacing attributes in HTML tags are commonly measured in pixels.

plain text: A text format that doesn't include formatting codes designating the layout and appearance of text.

platform: A computer hardware and software standard, such as Windows, IBM PC-compatible, and Macintosh personal computer.

plug-in: An accessory or a utility program that extends the capabilities of an application, such as Real Audio Player.

program: *See* **application.**

properties: Characteristics of an object that define its state, appearance, or value.

protocol: A set of rules for how programs on a network interact. These rules generally include requirements for formatting data and error checking.

query: A method by which data is requested from a server. You enter a query to search a database.

RAM: For *random access memory.* Computer memory that stores the ongoing work of an operating system and applications running at the moment. Think of a computer's RAM as short-term memory and its hard drive as long-term memory.

raster image: The horizontal pattern of lines, made up of pixels, that forms an image on a computer screen. *See also* **bitmapped image.**

raw code: The HTML programming behind a Web page.

relative link: Also called *relative URL.* A link set by using a path within a Web site directory structure that doesn't include the domain name. For example:

```
<a HREF=/resources/file_name.html>
```

See also **absolute link.**

render: To convert an outline of an image into a detailed version. Used when working with three-dimensional images.

resolution: The number of picture elements per unit in an image. Resolution on a printer is described in dots per inch (dpi). Resolution on a monitor is described in pixels horizontally and lines vertically.

ROM: For *read-only memory.* Storage capacity that is read but not deleted or altered. For example, you can't save data to or delete information from a standard CD-ROM; you can only read it or copy information from it.

sans serif: A typeface category in which the individual characters have no cross-stroke at the end of the main stroke.

scripting language: A computer language, such as JavaScript or VBScript, that can run in a Web browser and makes adding interactive features to a Web site possible.

scrolling: Moving a window horizontally or vertically to make the information that extends beyond the viewing area visible.

search engine: 1. A Web site that contains searchable databases or search programs capable of retrieving other Web pages based on user queries. 2. A program created to search the contents of a Web site for information related to a specific topic or keyword that a user supplies.

serif: A typeface category in which the individual characters have a cross-stroke at the end of the main stroke.

server: Also called a *Web server.* A computer connected to the Internet that "serves" files by sending them to another computer. The Internet is a client/server arrangement. The server is on a remote computer and responds to requests from the client. *See also* **client.**

shareware: Copyrighted software that is freely shared with others provided that certain distribution restrictions, as specified by the author, are followed. These restrictions often involve paying a fee to the author for continued use after a free trial period.

Shockwave: A Macromedia product for viewing Director files, Flash movies, and FreeHand files. Shockwave plug-ins exist for both Macintosh and Windows systems.

special characters: Typed characters, such as ~ and &, and foreign characters, such as letters with accents. On Web pages, these characters must be created as HTML entities or by using special character tags. With the exception of the underline (or underscore) character, you should not include these characters in file names for pages that appear on the Web.

splash screen: An opening screen that appears when you start a program or first access some Web sites. Many splash screens on the Web are created in Macromedia Flash.

start tag: In HTML programming, identifies the start of an HTML element. Can include attributes. *See also* **close tag.**

streaming: A technology that enables sound, video, or other data to begin playing as soon as enough material is downloaded so that the file can play as the rest downloads.

string: A series of related text or formatting characters.

subdirectory: Also called a *subfolder.* A directory (also known as a folder) that resides inside another directory. *See also* **directory.**

surfing: The act of moving from one place to another on the Web with no apparent plan or pattern — following any "wave" (or link) that looks good.

synchronize: To arrange events so that they happen simultaneously. FrontPage features a synchronize option that enables you to make sure that the files on your Web server are the same as the files in your Web site folder on your hard drive.

syntax: Rules that govern the use of code in programming languages.

system administrator: The person or group responsible for configuring and maintaining a network or Web server. Also called a *network administrator.*

T1 line: A high-speed, dedicated connection to the Internet. Transmits a digital signal at 1.544 Mbps.

T3 line: A very high-speed, dedicated connection to the Internet. Transmits a digital signal at 44.746 Mbps.

tag: The formal name for an element of HTML, usually enclosed in angle brackets (< and >).

TCP/IP: For *Transmission Control Protocol/Internet Protocol.* A suite of protocols and services used to manage network communications and applications over the Internet.

third party: An accessory, such as a plug-in or programming code, manufactured by a separate vendor and designed to work with a given brand of computer equipment or application.

tool: 1. An icon or palette item in a graphical program that performs specific functions when selected. 2. A useful software program.

typeface: The distinctive design of a set of type. Grouped into two categories: serif and sans serif.

UNIX: Pronounced *you-nicks.* An operating system written in the C programming language for a variety of computers, from PCs to mainframes. Many Web servers use the UNIX operating system.

upload: To move information from your computer to a remote computer, as in uploading Web site files to a server.

URL: For *Uniform Resource Locator.* Pronounced *U-R-L* or *earl.* An Internet address that consists of the server and any additional path information required to locates a Web page or other file on the Internet. For example:

```
http://www.domain_name.com
```

utility software: Software used to maintain and improve a computer system's efficiency.

vector graphics: Images whose shapes are described by geometric formulas. Vector files are resolution independent, meaning they're always drawn at the best possible resolution of the device generating them. Because even a fairly complex geometric shape can be described in a few lines of text as a formula, vector graphics tend to be much smaller than typical bitmap images, which have to be described by using several bits of data for each pixel in the image.

viewer: 1. A special program launched by a browser to display elements, such as sound files or video, that the browser can't display. 2. A person who visits a Web site.

viewing window: A defined area of the computer screen through which portions of text or other information can be seen. *See also* **window.**

Web designer: Also called a *Web developer.* A professional or hobbyist who creates Web pages.

Web page: One file in a collection of files that make up a Web site. Usually used to describe the first page that appears on a Web site. *See also* **home page.**

Web server: *See* **server.**

Web site: A specific location on the Internet, housed on a Web server and accessible through a URL. Consists of one or more Web pages.

Webmaster: One of many titles used to describe people who design Web sites. (I've always preferred Electronic Goddess.)

window: A frame on a computer screen that displays information, such as a document or an application.

Windows: The Microsoft operating system (most commonly available in versions 2000, ME, NT, XP Home, XP Professional, and XP Media Center).

wizard: A special miniprogram within a software product that leads you step by step through a task.

World Wide Web Consortium (W3C): An industry group that seeks to promote standards for the evolution of the Web and interoperability among Web products by producing specifications and reference software.

WYSIWYG: For *what-you-see-is-what-you-get.* Pronounced *wizzy-wig.* Describes HTML authoring tools and other programs that attempt to show on-screen what the final document will look like.

zip: A compression method used on Windows and DOS computers. Uses the .zip file extension.

zipped archive: A file that consists of compressed files.

zoom: To enlarge a document view so that it fills the screen, or to make it smaller so that more of the document can be seen.

Appendix C

About the CD

System Requirements

Make sure that your computer meets the minimum system requirements shown in the following list. If your computer doesn't match up to most of these requirements, you may have problems using the software and files on the CD. For the latest and greatest information, please refer to the ReadMe file located at the root of the CD-ROM.

- A PC with a 300 MHz Pentium or faster processor; or a Mac OS computer with a 68040 or faster processor
- Microsoft Windows 98 or later; or Mac OS system software 7.6.1 or later
- At least 128MB of total RAM installed on your computer; for best performance, we recommend at least 256MB
- A CD-ROM drive
- A sound card for PCs; Mac OS computers have built-in sound support
- A monitor capable of displaying at least 256 colors or grayscale, but millions of colors is recommended
- A modem with a speed of at least 56K

If you need more information on the basics, check out these books published by Wiley Publishing, Inc.: *PCs For Dummies,* by Dan Gookin; *Macs For Dummies,* by David Pogue; *iMac For Dummies* by David Pogue; *Windows XP For Dummies* by Andy Rathbone; and *Windows 2000 Professional For Dummies* by Andy Rathbone.

Using the CD

To install the items from the CD to your hard drive, follow these steps.

1. **Insert the CD into your computer's CD-ROM drive. The license agreement appears.**

   Note to Windows users: The interface won't launch if autorun is disabled. In that case, choose Start⇨Run. In the dialog box that appears, type **D:\start.exe**. (Replace D with the proper letter if your CD-ROM drive uses a different letter. If you don't know the letter, see how your CD-ROM drive is listed under My Computer.) Click OK.

   Note for Mac users: The CD icon will appear on your desktop. Double-click the icon to open the CD and then double-click the Start icon.

2. **Read through the license agreement, and then click the Accept button if you want to use the CD.**

   The CD interface appears. The interface allows you to install the programs and run the demos with just a click of a button (or two).

What You'll Find on the CD

The following sections are arranged by category and provide a summary of the software and other goodies you'll find on the CD. If you need help with installing the items provided on the CD, refer to the installation instructions in the preceding section.

Shareware programs are fully functional, free, trial versions of copyrighted programs. If you like particular programs, register with their authors for a nominal fee and receive licenses, enhanced versions, and technical support.

Freeware programs are free, copyrighted games, applications, and utilities. You can copy them to as many PCs as you like — for free — but they offer no technical support.

GNU software is governed by its own license, which is included inside the folder of the GNU software. There are no restrictions on distribution of GNU software. See the GNU license at the root of the CD for more details.

Trial, demo, or *evaluation* versions of software are usually limited by either time or functionality (such as not letting you save a project after you create it).

Software programs on the CD

Family Tree Maker 9

Commercial version. For Windows.

Now in its ninth version, Family Tree Maker is a robust program with features that will help you to build, research, and share your family tree. For more information and updates, visit the My Family Web site at www.myfamily.com/.

Fetch

Shareware version. For Mac.

Fetch is a program for transferring files from one computer to another by using the File Transfer Protocol (FTP). This program is commonly used for publishing a Web site to a commercial service provider from a Macintosh computer. For more information and updates, visit the Fetch Softworks Web site at www.fetchsoftworks.com/.

Macromedia Dreamweaver MX 2004

Trial version. For Mac and Windows.

Dreamweaver MX 2004 is the latest version of Macromedia's award-winning Web design program. The tryout version is fully functional and will work for 30 days after installation. For more information, visit www.macromedia.com.

Macromedia Contribute 3

Trial version. For Windows.

Contribute works with Dreamweaver to make it easy for even the most novice Web designers to contribute to an existing Web site. This program is ideal for collaborative projects in which an experienced Web designer creates the site and templates and less experienced designers add updates and additional contents. The tryout version is fully functional and will work for 30 days after installation. For more information, visit www.macromedia.com.

WS_FTP Pro from Ipswitch

Evaluation version. For Windows.

WS_FTP is a program for transferring files from one computer to another by using the File Transfer Protocol (FTP). This program is commonly used for publishing a Web site to a commercial service provider from a Windows computer. For more information and updates, visit the Ipswitch Web site at www.ipswitch.com/.

Author-created material

In the `Author Files` section of the CD, you'll find a number of files that I've created to go with this book. First, you find a collection of multimedia files in a variety of formats, such as MPEG, Windows Media, and QuickTime. I included these files so that you'd have what you need to follow the exercises in Chapter 10 and to help you appreciate the levels of quality you can expect from different multimedia formats and compression settings.

The rest of what you'll find on the CD is a collection of Web site templates and graphics that you can use to create your own custom Web sites. Chapters 11 through 14 are designed to help you create a specific kind of Web site, such as a baby site or a wedding site. In each of the corresponding folders on the CD, you'll find everything you need — templates, graphics, and even a completed sample site.

When you copy images from a CD to your hard drive, you may find that the files are locked, meaning you can't save changes to them. To correct this on a PC, right-click the folder name and choose Properties. In the Attributes area of the Properties dialog box, deselect the Read Only option. Click Apply, and then click OK. If you're using a Mac, ⌘-click the folder name, choose Get Info, and deselect the Locked option.

Ch 10 Multimedia

For Windows and Mac.

In the `Ch10 Multimedia` folder, you'll find multimedia files in a variety of formats to help you appreciate the many format options you can choose for video. The files were provided also so that you'd have an audio file and a Flash file to use in the exercises in Chapter 10.

Here's what you'll find in the `Ch10 Multimedia` folder:

- `logo-animation.swf`: This is an animated version of the logo I use on my own Web site. I include this on the CD only to ensure that you have a Flash file you can use if you don't have your own and want to follow the instructions in Chapter 10 for inserting a Flash file into a Web page. This file is provided for your use in the exercises in this book and may not be used on any Web site published on the Internet or for any other purposes.

- `jungle-animals.wav`: Again this file is included only to ensure that you have a sound file you can use as you follow the exercise in Chapter 10 for embedding a background sound or for adding a sound file to a Web page. This file is provided only for your use in following the exercises in this book and may not be used on any Web site published on the Internet or for any other purposes.

✔ video-clips: This folder contains one video clip in a variety of formats to help you appreciate the differences in video quality and compression options. You may use these files to follow along with the exercises in Chapter 10, but these files may not be used on any Web site published on the Internet or for any other purposes.

Ch11 Baby Site

For Windows and Mac

The Ch11 Baby Site folder contains all the template pages and images you need to create the design for the baby Web site featured in Chapter 11. Inside this folder are three subfolders:

✔ sample-baby-site: This folder contains a completed Web site that you can use as a model. The images and other content in this folder are provided for your use in following the exercises in this book and may not be used on any Web site published on the Internet or for any other purposes.

✔ template-baby-site: This folder contains the pages you should work with as you create your own site.

✔ photoshop-files: This folder contains all the graphics for the site in their original .psd format, which makes them easy to edit in Photoshop Elements 3.

Ch12 Wedding Site

For Windows and Mac

The Ch12 Wedding Site folder contains all the template pages and images you need to create the design for the wedding Web site featured in Chapter 12. Inside this folder are three subfolders:

✔ sample-wedding-site: This folder contains a completed Web site you can use as a model. The images and other content in this folder are provided only for your use in following the exercises in this book and may not be used on any Web site published on the Internet or for any other purposes.

✔ template-wedding-site: This folder contains the pages and graphics you should use as you build your site.

✔ photoshop-files: This folder contains the graphics in a format that makes them easy to edit.

Ch13 Travel Site

For Windows and Mac

The `Ch13 Travel Site` folder contains all the template pages and images you need to create the design for the travel Web site featured in Chapter 13. Inside this folder are three subfolders:

- ✔ `sample-travel-site`: This folder contains a completed Web site that you can use as a model. The images and other content in this folder are provided for your use in following the exercises in this book and may not be used on any Web site published on the Internet or for any other purposes.

- ✔ `template-travel-site`: This folder contains the pages you should work with as you create your own site.

- ✔ `photoshop-files`: This folder contains all the graphics for the site in their original `.psd` format, which makes them easy to edit in Photoshop Elements.

Ch14 Sports Site

For Windows and Mac

The `Ch14 Sports Site` folder contains all the template pages and images you need to create the design for the sports or hobby Web site featured in Chapter 14. Inside this folder are three subfolders:

- ✔ `sample-karate-site`: This folder contains a completed Web site that you can use as a model. The images and other content in this folder are provided for your use in following the exercises in this book and may not be used on any Web site published on the Internet or for any other purposes.

- ✔ `template-sports-site`: This folder contains the template pages and graphics you should use as the basis for your site.

- ✔ `photoshop-files`: This folder contains the graphics in a format that makes them easy to edit.

Troubleshooting

I tried my best to compile programs that work on most computers with the minimum system requirements. Alas, your computer may differ, and some programs may not work properly for some reason.

The two likeliest problems are that your system doesn't have enough memory (RAM) for the programs you want to use, or you have other programs running that are affecting the installation or running of a program. If you get an error message such as Not enough memory or Setup cannot continue, try one or more of the following suggestions and then try using the software again:

- ✔ **Turn off any antivirus software running on your computer.** Installation programs sometimes mimic virus activity and may make your computer incorrectly believe that a virus is infecting it.

- ✔ **Close all running programs.** The more programs you have running, the less memory is available to other programs. Installation programs typically update files and programs; so if you keep other programs running, installation may not work properly.

- ✔ **Have your local computer store add more RAM to your computer.** This is, admittedly, a drastic and somewhat expensive step. However, adding more memory can really help the speed of your computer and allow more programs to run at the same time.

If you have trouble with the CD-ROM, please call the Wiley Product Technical Support phone number at 800-762-2974. Outside the United States, call 1-317-572-3994. You can also contact Wiley Product Technical Support at www.wiley.com/techsupport. John Wiley & Sons will provide technical support only for installation and other general quality control items. For technical support on the applications themselves, consult the program's vendor or author.

To place additional orders or to request information about other Wiley products, please call 877-762-2974.

Index

• G •

Wiley Publishing, Inc., End-User License Agreement

READ THIS. You should carefully read these terms and conditions before opening the software packet(s) included with this book "Book". This is a license agreement "Agreement" between you and Wiley Publishing, Inc. "WPI". By opening the accompanying software packet(s), you acknowledge that you have read and accept the following terms and conditions. If you do not agree and do not want to be bound by such terms and conditions, promptly return the Book and the unopened software packet(s) to the place you obtained them for a full refund.

1. **License Grant.** WPI grants to you (either an individual or entity) a nonexclusive license to use one copy of the enclosed software program(s) (collectively, the "Software") solely for your own personal or business purposes on a single computer (whether a standard computer or a workstation component of a multi-user network). The Software is in use on a computer when it is loaded into temporary memory (RAM) or installed into permanent memory (hard disk, CD-ROM, or other storage device). WPI reserves all rights not expressly granted herein.

2. **Ownership.** WPI is the owner of all right, title, and interest, including copyright, in and to the compilation of the Software recorded on the disk(s) or CD-ROM "Software Media". Copyright to the individual programs recorded on the Software Media is owned by the author or other authorized copyright owner of each program. Ownership of the Software and all proprietary rights relating thereto remain with WPI and its licensers.

3. **Restrictions on Use and Transfer.**

   (a) You may only (i) make one copy of the Software for backup or archival purposes, or (ii) transfer the Software to a single hard disk, provided that you keep the original for backup or archival purposes. You may not (i) rent or lease the Software, (ii) copy or reproduce the Software through a LAN or other network system or through any computer subscriber system or bulletin-board system, or (iii) modify, adapt, or create derivative works based on the Software.

   (b) You may not reverse engineer, decompile, or disassemble the Software. You may transfer the Software and user documentation on a permanent basis, provided that the transferee agrees to accept the terms and conditions of this Agreement and you retain no copies. If the Software is an update or has been updated, any transfer must include the most recent update and all prior versions.

4. **Restrictions on Use of Individual Programs.** You must follow the individual requirements and restrictions detailed for each individual program in the About the CD-ROM appendix of this Book. These limitations are also contained in the individual license agreements recorded on the Software Media. These limitations may include a requirement that after using the program for a specified period of time, the user must pay a registration fee or discontinue use. By opening the Software packet(s), you will be agreeing to abide by the licenses and restrictions for these individual programs that are detailed in the About the CD-ROM appendix and on the Software Media. None of the material on this Software Media or listed in this Book may ever be redistributed, in original or modified form, for commercial purposes.

5. **Limited Warranty.**

   (a) WPI warrants that the Software and Software Media are free from defects in materials and workmanship under normal use for a period of sixty (60) days from the date of purchase of this Book. If WPI receives notification within the warranty period of defects in materials or workmanship, WPI will replace the defective Software Media.

   (b) **WPI AND THE AUTHOR(S) OF THE BOOK DISCLAIM ALL OTHER WARRANTIES, EXPRESS OR IMPLIED, INCLUDING WITHOUT LIMITATION IMPLIED WARRANTIES OF MERCHANTABILITY AND FITNESS FOR A PARTICULAR PURPOSE, WITH RESPECT TO THE SOFTWARE, THE PROGRAMS, THE SOURCE CODE CONTAINED THEREIN, AND/OR THE TECHNIQUES DESCRIBED IN THIS BOOK. WPI DOES NOT WARRANT THAT THE FUNCTIONS CONTAINED IN THE SOFTWARE WILL MEET YOUR REQUIREMENTS OR THAT THE OPERATION OF THE SOFTWARE WILL BE ERROR FREE.**

   (c) This limited warranty gives you specific legal rights, and you may have other rights that vary from jurisdiction to jurisdiction.

6. **Remedies.**

   (a) WPI's entire liability and your exclusive remedy for defects in materials and workmanship shall be limited to replacement of the Software Media, which may be returned to WPI with a copy of your receipt at the following address: Software Media Fulfillment Department, Attn.: *Creating Family Web Sites For Dummies,* Wiley Publishing, Inc., 10475 Crosspoint Blvd., Indianapolis, IN 46256, or call 1-800-762-2974. Please allow four to six weeks for delivery. This Limited Warranty is void if failure of the Software Media has resulted from accident, abuse, or misapplication. Any replacement Software Media will be warranted for the remainder of the original warranty period or thirty (30) days, whichever is longer.

   (b) In no event shall WPI or the author be liable for any damages whatsoever (including without limitation damages for loss of business profits, business interruption, loss of business information, or any other pecuniary loss) arising from the use of or inability to use the Book or the Software, even if WPI has been advised of the possibility of such damages.

   (c) Because some jurisdictions do not allow the exclusion or limitation of liability for consequential or incidental damages, the above limitation or exclusion may not apply to you.

7. **U.S. Government Restricted Rights.** Use, duplication, or disclosure of the Software for or on behalf of the United States of America, its agencies and/or instrumentalities "U.S. Government" is subject to restrictions as stated in paragraph (c)(1)(ii) of the Rights in Technical Data and Computer Software clause of DFARS 252.227-7013, or subparagraphs (c) (1) and (2) of the Commercial Computer Software - Restricted Rights clause at FAR 52.227-19, and in similar clauses in the NASA FAR supplement, as applicable.

8. **General.** This Agreement constitutes the entire understanding of the parties and revokes and supersedes all prior agreements, oral or written, between them and may not be modified or amended except in a writing signed by both parties hereto that specifically refers to this Agreement. This Agreement shall take precedence over any other documents that may be in conflict herewith. If any one or more provisions contained in this Agreement are held by any court or tribunal to be invalid, illegal, or otherwise unenforceable, each and every other provision shall remain in full force and effect.

USINESS, CAREERS & PERSONAL FINANCE

Grant Writing For Dummies
0-7645-5307-0

Home Buying For Dummies
0-7645-5331-3 *†

Also available:
- Accounting For Dummies †
  0-7645-5314-3
- Business Plans Kit For Dummies †
  0-7645-5365-8
- Cover Letters For Dummies
  0-7645-5224-4
- Frugal Living For Dummies
  0-7645-5403-4
- Leadership For Dummies
  0-7645-5176-0
- Managing For Dummies
  0-7645-1771-6

- Marketing For Dummies
  0-7645-5600-2
- Personal Finance For Dummies *
  0-7645-2590-5
- Project Management For Dummies
  0-7645-5283-X
- Resumes For Dummies †
  0-7645-5471-9
- Selling For Dummies
  0-7645-5363-1
- Small Business Kit For Dummies *†
  0-7645-5093-4

OME & BUSINESS COMPUTER BASICS

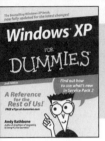

Windows XP For Dummies
0-7645-4074-2

Excel 2003 For Dummies
0-7645-3758-X

Also available:
- ACT! 6 For Dummies
  0-7645-2645-6
- iLife '04 All-in-One Desk Reference
  For Dummies
  0-7645-7347-0
- iPAQ For Dummies
  0-7645-6769-1
- Mac OS X Panther Timesaving
  Techniques For Dummies
  0-7645-5812-9
- Macs For Dummies
  0-7645-5656-8

- Microsoft Money 2004 For Dummies
  0-7645-4195-1
- Office 2003 All-in-One Desk Reference
  For Dummies
  0-7645-3883-7
- Outlook 2003 For Dummies
  0-7645-3759-8
- PCs For Dummies
  0-7645-4074-2
- TiVo For Dummies
  0-7645-6923-6
- Upgrading and Fixing PCs For Dummies
  0-7645-1665-5
- Windows XP Timesaving Techniques
  For Dummies
  0-7645-3748-2

OOD, HOME, GARDEN, HOBBIES, MUSIC & PETS

Feng Shui For Dummies
0-7645-5295-3

Poker For Dummies
0-7645-5232-5

Also available:
- Bass Guitar For Dummies
  0-7645-2487-9
- Diabetes Cookbook For Dummies
  0-7645-5230-9
- Gardening For Dummies *
  0-7645-5130-2
- Guitar For Dummies
  0-7645-5106-X
- Holiday Decorating For Dummies
  0-7645-2570-0
- Home Improvement All-in-One
  For Dummies
  0-7645-5680-0

- Knitting For Dummies
  0-7645-5395-X
- Piano For Dummies
  0-7645-5105-1
- Puppies For Dummies
  0-7645-5255-4
- Scrapbooking For Dummies
  0-7645-7208-3
- Senior Dogs For Dummies
  0-7645-5818-8
- Singing For Dummies
  0-7645-2475-5
- 30-Minute Meals For Dummies
  0-7645-2589-1

NTERNET & DIGITAL MEDIA

Digital Photography For Dummies
0-7645-1664-7

Starting an eBay Business For Dummies
0-7645-6924-4

Also available:
- 2005 Online Shopping Directory
  For Dummies
  0-7645-7495-7
- CD & DVD Recording For Dummies
  0-7645-5956-7
- eBay For Dummies
  0-7645-5654-1
- Fighting Spam For Dummies
  0-7645-5965-6
- Genealogy Online For Dummies
  0-7645-5964-8
- Google For Dummies
  0-7645-4420-9

- Home Recording For Musicians
  For Dummies
  0-7645-1634-5
- The Internet For Dummies
  0-7645-4173-0
- iPod & iTunes For Dummies
  0-7645-7772-7
- Preventing Identity Theft For Dummies
  0-7645-7336-5
- Pro Tools All-in-One Desk Reference
  For Dummies
  0-7645-5714-9
- Roxio Easy Media Creator For Dummies
  0-7645-7131-1

Separate Canadian edition also available
Separate U.K. edition also available

vailable wherever books are sold. For more information or to order direct: U.S. customers visit www.dummies.com or call 1-877-762-2974.
K. customers visit www.wileyeurope.com or call 0800 243407. Canadian customers visit www.wiley.ca or call 1-800-567-4797.

SPORTS, FITNESS, PARENTING, RELIGION & SPIRITUALITY

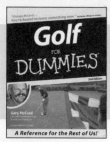

0-7645-5146-9

0-7645-5418-2

Also available:

- Adoption For Dummies
  0-7645-5488-3
- Basketball For Dummies
  0-7645-5248-1
- The Bible For Dummies
  0-7645-5296-1
- Buddhism For Dummies
  0-7645-5359-3
- Catholicism For Dummies
  0-7645-5391-7
- Hockey For Dummies
  0-7645-5228-7

- Judaism For Dummies
  0-7645-5299-6
- Martial Arts For Dummies
  0-7645-5358-5
- Pilates For Dummies
  0-7645-5397-6
- Religion For Dummies
  0-7645-5264-3
- Teaching Kids to Read For Dummies
  0-7645-4043-2
- Weight Training For Dummies
  0-7645-5168-X
- Yoga For Dummies
  0-7645-5117-5

TRAVEL

0-7645-5438-7

0-7645-5453-0

Also available:

- Alaska For Dummies
  0-7645-1761-9
- Arizona For Dummies
  0-7645-6938-4
- Cancún and the Yucatán For Dummies
  0-7645-2437-2
- Cruise Vacations For Dummies
  0-7645-6941-4
- Europe For Dummies
  0-7645-5456-5
- Ireland For Dummies
  0-7645-5455-7

- Las Vegas For Dummies
  0-7645-5448-4
- London For Dummies
  0-7645-4277-X
- New York City For Dummies
  0-7645-6945-7
- Paris For Dummies
  0-7645-5494-8
- RV Vacations For Dummies
  0-7645-5443-3
- Walt Disney World & Orlando For Dummies
  0-7645-6943-0

GRAPHICS, DESIGN & WEB DEVELOPMENT

0-7645-4345-8

0-7645-5589-8

Also available:

- Adobe Acrobat 6 PDF For Dummies
  0-7645-3760-1
- Building a Web Site For Dummies
  0-7645-7144-3
- Dreamweaver MX 2004 For Dummies
  0-7645-4342-3
- FrontPage 2003 For Dummies
  0-7645-3882-9
- HTML 4 For Dummies
  0-7645-1995-6
- Illustrator CS For Dummies
  0-7645-4084-X

- Macromedia Flash MX 2004 For Dummies
  0-7645-4358-X
- Photoshop 7 All-in-One Desk Reference For Dummies
  0-7645-1667-1
- Photoshop CS Timesaving Techniques For Dummies
  0-7645-6782-9
- PHP 5 For Dummies
  0-7645-4166-8
- PowerPoint 2003 For Dummies
  0-7645-3908-6
- QuarkXPress 6 For Dummies
  0-7645-2593-X

NETWORKING, SECURITY, PROGRAMMING & DATABASES

0-7645-6852-3

0-7645-5784-X

Also available:

- A+ Certification For Dummies
  0-7645-4187-0
- Access 2003 All-in-One Desk Reference For Dummies
  0-7645-3988-4
- Beginning Programming For Dummies
  0-7645-4997-9
- C For Dummies
  0-7645-7068-4
- Firewalls For Dummies
  0-7645-4048-3
- Home Networking For Dummies
  0-7645-42796

- Network Security For Dummies
  0-7645-1679-5
- Networking For Dummies
  0-7645-1677-9
- TCP/IP For Dummies
  0-7645-1760-0
- VBA For Dummies
  0-7645-3989-2
- Wireless All In-One Desk Reference For Dummies
  0-7645-7496-5
- Wireless Home Networking For Dummies
  0-7645-3910-8

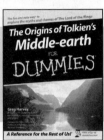

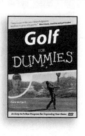